The Fairground Organ

THE FAIRGROUND ORGAN

Its Music, Mechanism and History

ERIC V. COCKAYNE

WITH AN APPENDIX BY RONALD LEACH, ARIBA, M Inst RA

DAVID & CHARLES

NEWTON ABBOT LONDON VANCOUVER

To

Francis J. Buckley

and

Charles Henry Hart

0 7153 4985 6

First published 1970
Reprinted 1974

Printed in Great Britain by
W J Holman Limited Dawlish
for David & Charles (Holdings) Limited
South Devon House Newton Abbot Devon

Published in Canada by
Douglas David & Charles Limited
3645 McKechnie Drive West Vancouver BC

Contents

Illustrations

PLATES

IN THE TEXT

Figures | *Page*

Foreword

SOME years ago I visited a traction engine rally and heard some fair organs playing, the first I had heard for many years. I visited my local library to find out something about them—and found nothing! Further research revealed that no book had ever been published on the subject, in English at any rate. Since then I have gathered material on the subject from various sources. These have included the Patent Office and back numbers of *The World's Fair*. I have studied many photographs, both old and new. Much of the information has been obtained, literally, in the field, where organ owners have allowed me to examine their instruments and measure, photograph and sketch various parts. Much has been obtained by word of mouth from showmen and others with memories of fairgrounds, and by correspondence. Some has been obtained from the few references to organs in books dealing with various aspects of the fairground. Another source of information has been a number of reprinted catalogues which are obtainable in the USA. Books dealing with both church and theatre organs have also helped to piece the story together.

Some of the material in this book appeared in the pamphlet I wrote for the Fair Organ Preservation Society entitled *The Fair Organ—How it Works* and in the Society's journal *The Key Frame*. This material has mostly been rewritten and a number of the diagrams have been redrawn. An effort has been made in this book to cover all aspects of the subject as far as possible—the music, the mechanism and pipework, maintenance, and the history of the organ. This, it is hoped, will provide a general introduction to the subject and perhaps inspire others to produce more detailed works on particular aspects.

The layout of the book has given me cause for thought. The

obvious approach would have been to deal with the subject in strict historical order. It has, however, not been possible to adopt this approach, due mainly to the difficulty of dating the many changes which fair organs have undergone. The famous fair organ builders kept their trade secrets very well! I decided, therefore, to deal first with the music, then with the way in which the organ works, describing as many typical mechanisms as possible, and finally to add a historical chapter. The appendices supplement the main part of the book. As far as possible the parts of the organ have been described in a logical sequence and no particular specialised knowledge on the part of the reader has been assumed.

Terminology has caused some difficulty. Traditionally, certain terms are used by showmen. These, sometimes, have different meanings from those used by the builders of church and theatre organs. Some parts of fairground organs have no names at all and these have had to be invented. In general I have elected to use expressions in general use rather than technical terms, the meanings of which may not be immediately obvious.

Although this book deals mainly with the fairground organ I have not hesitated to include references to mechanical continental street and dance organs. Quite a few of these were exported and many of them were built by firms which also made fair organs. The instruments have, therefore, much in common. For a similar reason I have, from time to time, referred to church or theatre organs.

As far as possible I have selected photographs of parts of organs and ancillary equipment rather than general views, as a reasonable number of these have already appeared in books and pamphlets dealing with the fairground.

Comments will be welcomed. Also, I will be pleased to receive information of any sort about mechanical organs.

St Albans, 1970 EVC

1 Music

On mechanical musical instruments the performer is replaced by a medium on which the music has been recorded or scored, and a sensing device which 'reads' it and which causes the instrument to play. Music has been scored on discs, strips, and cylinders (made of wood, paper, cardboard, or metal) by means of perforations, raised tags, or metal pins and staples. Of these, perforated paper rolls and cardboard strips and pinned and stapled barrels have all been used to operate fairground organs.

It is impossible to discuss the music of mechanical organs without mentioning the music sensing devices and very brief references will be made to them in each of the sections which follow. The various systems used will be discussed in greater detail in Chapter 3.

Organ builders have devised various methods of making organs play for as long as possible without attention. Obviously, the ideal situation on the fairground is one where the organ plays a prearranged programme of the length required and then repeats it automatically as many times as required. Some of the ways in which this is done will be considered in this chapter.

In the heyday of the fairground organ, all the organ manufacturers had special sections of their works devoted to the production of music. The music was marked out by an experienced musician who was familiar with the peculiarities of the instruments for which he was working.

In addition to making the organ's pipes play, the music marker must arrange for the playing of percussion effects and for the operation of a number of other auxiliary mechanisms. The marker works either from a piano copy, an orchestral score, or his own arrangement of the music concerned. In the early days music publishers were only too pleased to have their tunes popularised on the fairgrounds without regard to performing rights and would send copies of the sheet music to firms producing organ music. Performing rights began to be exercised (as far as fairgrounds were concerned, at any rate) in the early 1920s.

What music did these organs play? We must remember that, before the invention of the gramophone and radio, people were dependent for their music on the parlour and public-house pianos and the town band. Only the large towns had their own orchestras or were visited by touring ones. The fair organ provided music which was otherwise lacking and people would visit the fairs to hear it. Some organs were, of course, no more than noise makers but the more responsible showmen saw that their instruments were kept in good shape and that they had a wide and extensive repertoire. Marches, waltzes, operatic overtures and selections, light orchestral pieces, and popular songs and ballads were all heard on the fairgrounds. Sunday charity concerts, featuring the organs, were a popular event and these occasionally included performances by vocalists. The programme of one such concert is reproduced in Figures 1a–d. The following lists, which have been compiled from advertisements in *The World's Fair*, give, in contrast, some idea of the more popular music which was played at the peak of the fair organ's popularity and in the years before its decline. The style (and errors) of the advertisements have been preserved.

In 1906 Arthur Righini (as agent for Ch. Marenghi) was able to supply the following music books:

I hear the pipes calling, Jenny mine
I love a lassie (song)
Molly, the jolly little lady (song)
Joconde (galop)
Marengo (march)
Robert Bruce (Scotch reel)
Victorious soldiers (march).

In 1908, as agent now for Limonaire Frères he was offering the following:

Put me amongst the girls
She's a lassie from Lancashire
If those lips could only speak
Has anyone seen a German band?
The new colonial march
Abide with me.

Later in the same year the list included:

The Merry Widow waltz
A Waltz Dream
Love me and the world is mine
When the sunset turned the ocean's blue to gold
Abide with me
Lead kindly light.

In 1920 the Bristol Showmen's Stores were advertising the following Marenghi music:

Maxina
Wyoming
N'everything
Give me the moonlight, give me the girl.

THE BARREL

Geometrically, it would be more accurate to describe the barrel as a 'cylinder' but the former expression will be used as it is in general use. Barrels are built on two solid ends, about two inches thick, and octagonal in shape. Eight planks are stretched on the edges of these, each plank being the full length of the barrel. The barrel is constructed by a skilled joiner who glues the ten pieces together into a hollow, but rigid shaft. Steel trunnions are fitted axially to each end. The completed assembly is suspended from these in a lathe and turned externally. The trunnions are housed in plain bearings in the ends of the organ casing. Attached to one end of the barrel is a wormwheel, with a driving worm.

The tunes on a barrel organ are changed either by hand or automatically. These features will be described later but they are mentioned now as the method of tune changing affects the way in which the wormwheel is mounted. In hand-changed organs the worm is mounted on the crankshaft which pumps the bellows. If automatic change has been added the worm is mounted on a new countershaft at the end remote from the crankshaft. The organ casing has an opening at this end, which is fitted with a removable cover. This enables the barrel to be inserted or removed by means of a cradle which, in the old days, the makers brought to the site for this purpose.

The diameter of the barrel was standardised at twelve or fourteen inches (30·5 or 35·5cm), the latter size being the nominal maximum diameter which fair organs in Great Britain could accommodate, though larger sizes were made for continental dance halls and cafes. Smaller sizes, down to seven inches in diameter, were used on small organs.

Each barrel organ had its own characteristics and tunes were not interchangeable. They were scored onto the barrel by means of pins or staples, according to the length of note required. The tunes on the barrel are read by pivoted fingers, or keys, which are mounted on a frame. As the barrel rotates, the staples and pins on it lift the keys. The opposite ends of the keys move push-rods, or stickers, which in turn operate the organ's mechanism or 'action'. This is entirely mechanical and is known as a 'tracker' action.

The keys of the barrel organ are spaced equidistantly along the full available space inside the length of the organ casing, and this length, to a certain extent, determines the number of tunes that can be accommodated on the barrel. The keys are located as closely as possible to line up with the pipes they control. For example, in a small organ, the bass notes would probably be limited to C, D, and G. C might be at one end of the key frame (the assembly holding the keys), D at the other, and G in the middle.

Barrel organs had a repertoire of nine or ten tunes, mostly dependent upon the space available, and it will be helpful if some particulars are cited from parts of a barrel organ in the author's possession, which played nine tunes. The width of the keys is a shade under 2mm ($\frac{3}{32}$in), to give the necessary clearance for the peggings (ie, the pins and staples) which are 2mm thick and pitched longitudinally on the barrel at 2mm. The keys are

Page 17: *(right)* Continental music marker's cylinder (from the Organ Museum, St Albans, Herts); *(below)* Continental music punching machine

Page 18: *(above)* Generator on a showman's road locomotive; *(below)* portable electric light engine (from an old Savages catalogue). (A similar model can be seen on page 108, lower)

Knutsford "Royal" May Day Festival, 1925.

Grand

Organ · Recital

— ON —

THE HEATH, KNUTSFORD,

— ON —

Sunday Evening, May 3rd,

at 8 o'clock,

By kind permission of Messrs. John Collins and Sons, of Liverpool,

Under the direction of F. J. Buckley, Esq, of Ashton-under-Lyne.

PROGRAMME, SIXPENCE.

Proceeds to Knutsford and District War Memorial Cottage Hospital Fund.

Fig 1a. Programme of a fair organ recital given for charity

PROGRAMME.

1. GRAND MARCH..."Tannhauser"........................*Wagner*

The stillness of the magnificent hall in which is to be tried the Tournament of Song, the victor claiming the hand of the fair Elizabeth, is rent by the blare of trumpets heralding the approach of the Landgrave, succeeded by the murmur of courtiers gathering to welcome their Royal Arbiter: the brasses again proclaim their announcement and the concourse greet their Sovereign in loyal song.

2. OVERTURE .... "Masaniello"...........................*Auber*

The overture opens *sforzando* and works through effectively "paused" passages to the main number of the opera, which forms the principal theme.

3. SACRED CHORUS..."Hallelujah" ("Messiah")...... *Handel*

Hallelujah: for the LORD GOD OMNIPOTENT reigneth. The kingdom of this world is become the kingdom of our Lord, and of His Christ; and He shall reign for ever and ever. KING OF KINGS AND LORD OF LORDS. HALLELUJAH!

4. SUITE....... "Ballet Egyptien" (Four parts) ....*Luigini*

Part I commences with a unison melody in quick *tempo*, developing into a second melody in common time played *staccato*. The second part is in slow valse time: the third consists of a solemn theme embellished with a lighter development in Arabic strain, and the final number opens with a plaintive passage alto, with tremulous violin accompaniment reverting to the second melody of Part I, now orchestrated with heavy bass.

5. OVERTURE .... "Oberon" .... *Weber*

The story of the opera is concerned with the affairs of Elf-Land. The leading themes are horn solo, reminiscent of fairy visions, a portion of the fairies' chorus, military work (court scene), and Puck's invocation to the spirits.

6. TWO PIECES ... (*a*) Introduction to "La Traviata"... *Verdi*

The short prelude to this opera is a pretty *andante* piece of pathetic conception, chiefly given over to the violins, and repeated with flute added.

(*b*) Intermezzo from "Cavalleria Rusticana"......... *Mascagni*

Who is not familiar with the beautiful melody, set to harp-like accompaniment, which might be the invocation of the deserted Santuzza for her wayward swain Triddu, the ill-fated duellist of "Rustic Chivalry"?

Fig 1b. Programme (*continued*)

7. PRELUDE......... Act III, "Lohengrin" .... *Wagner*

A legend founded on the Celtic Legends of King Arthur, and the search for the Holy Grail. "Lohengrin" was written about the middle of last century. The introduction to Act 3 contains a brilliant bass melody, of universal renown.

8. ANTHEM .... "Land of Hope and Glory" .... *Elgar*

Sung by Mr. Frank Osmond.

LAND of Hope and Glory;
Mother of the free;
How shall we extol Thee,
Who were born of Thee.
Wider still and wider,
Shall Thy bounds be set;
God who made Thee mighty,
Make Thee mightier yet.

9. FANTASIA ...... "Les Cloches de Cornville"......... *Planchette*

This Opera had a great vogue in this country and the Continent, and depicts the story of the missing Marquis of Corneville whose reappearance, the legend trolls, will be signified by the supernatural pealing of bells. The heir's return has the additional effect of dislodging a notorious local miser whose hoards were in the Chateau, and who frightened away interference by parading armoured figures before the windows.

10. GRAND OVERTURE....."William Tell"............... *Rossini*

This is undoubtedly Rossini's *chef d'œuvre*, and is more in the form of a Symphony in four movements than an overture. The first movement, "Morning" *(andante)*, is ushered in with a short *cadenza* on the horns. All is peaceful until the signs of gathering tempest, a roll on the drums, herald the approaching "Storm," which constitutes the second movement, starting with a wailing shake in the violins, and a trembling of the tree-tops. (*agitato*, woodwind), finally bursting out in all its fury, then subsiding gradually in a sobbing wail. The sun reappears, and the delicate "Pastorale" of Movement Three is given out on the organ in the violins, with echo in the flutes, merging into a clever violin-flute *obligato*. Suddenly the woods resound to the stirring call of trumpets, the mounted guards of a grand army march by and the Finale, military in its every note, brilliantly concludes the work.

11. CHORAL MARCH ... Entrance of the Peers ("Iolanthe") ... *Sullivan*

Those of us who have seen this famous one of the "All British" Operas will never forget the majestic entry of Lords in Act I, and Gilbert's paradoxical spectacle of robed and coronetted nobles autocratically adjuring "ye lower middle classes" to do homage to them, and with equal stern solemnity chanting the repeated phrase "Tzing Boom, Tantara"! Sullivan's music, as humourous as the librettist's situation is the acme of droll pomposity. The repetition of the development "We are peers of highest station," is set to a spirited counter-melody in the woodwinds.

Fig 1c. Programme (*continued*)

12. TONE POEM ...."1812"..................... *Tschaikowsky*

Written to commemorate Napoleon's retreat from Moscow in September, 1812, this overture is probably the best-known descriptive musical picture in existence. The opening is a Russian hymn of supplication for protection against the French Victor, whose leviathan army is around the city. A rapid movement breaks away from the slow theme, the triumphant "Marseillaise" is rasped out in the brass, and with the shrill cries of surprised peasantry, the enemy is at hand. Farther afield, a false feeling of immunity exists: folk song (with a setting of *canon*) and castinet dance are in progress when the invader appears. In Moscow, the inhabitants have decided to lay waste their city by fire, and succeeding a losing battle of defence, a passage of descending quatrains in unison, the initial hymn now is given out triumphantly, the Great Strategist has been out-manœuvred, and to the accompaniment of guns booming, victorious chimes and leaping flames (a wonderful piece of musical depiction) the "Marseillaise" gives place to the Russian National Anthem, now thundered forth, whilst the broken besiegers flee into the intense horrors of the Slav snows, and the Corsican has received the forerunner of Waterloo.

GOD SAVE THE KING.

The Organ, made by the famous firm, Gavioli et Cie, Paris, is the largest size made. It is chromatic from contra-basses to piccolo, has 110 keys and self-actuated registration, and is blown by three double-acting feeders and spring-loaded reservoir.

Programme subject to alteration without Notice.

F. ALCOCK, PRINTER, CAXTON HOUSE, KNUTSFORD.

Fig 1d. Programme (*continued*)

pitched at 18mm (about $\frac{11}{16}$in), there being a circumferential track of peggings under each key, and eight such tracks between any two consecutive keys. The organ has 45 keys and there are accordingly 405 tracks on the barrel which is just under 2ft 8½in (82·5cm) long, and about 10in (25·4cm) in diameter. It can be moved laterally (in addition to its rotary motion) in nine steps, by hand or automatically.

Figure 2 represents a view of the barrel seen from the rear of the organ, facing the hook or sensing end of the keys, which are mounted above the barrel and upon its vertical centre line. The

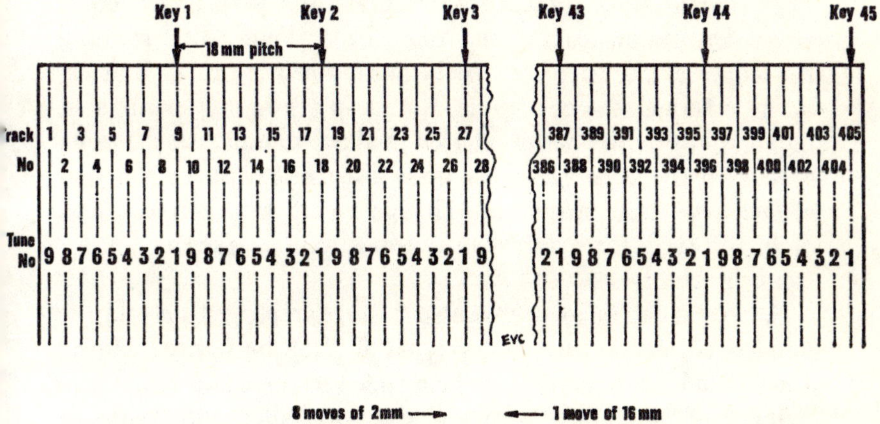

Fig 2. Method of laying out nine tunes on the barrel of a 45 key organ

barrel is at its extreme position to the left and is set for playing the first tune. If the tune change is manual, any tune in any order may be selected and the organ will continue to repeat this tune until another change is made. If the changing is automatic the organ plays the tunes in a fixed order, usually repeating each tune twice, then changing to the tune numerically next on the barrel. At the end of the repertoire it reverts to the first tune and repeats the cycle. For the present the organ is assumed to be self-changing.

As set in the diagram, key 1 registers with track 9, key 2 with track 18 . . . key 45 with track 405. The change from the first to the second tune moves the barrel 2mm to the right and brings key 1 to register with track 8, key 2 with track 17 . . . key 45 with track 404, and so on. After the ninth tune has been played three times the barrel is moved back to its position on the extreme left.

When the barrel organ was in general use most owners had a spare barrel at their music marker's workshop. When new, this would have been covered with paper and fitted into the organ so that the exact key frame spacing could be established—a most critical measurement. This was done by tapping each key lightly with a small hammer to make a small indentation in the paper covering, actually the method of marking out tunes. These indentations provided an accurate and permanent record of the key frame spacing and were made along a line running the length of the barrel, at the beginning of the tunes. A mock-up key frame was set up in the shop using the permanent indentations on the barrel referred to above to establish the exact spacing of the keys. The mock-up was marked with the function of each key—note, drum, tune-change, etc. If the organ was new, or in the shop for overhaul, the tunes were marked out direct from the key frame.

When an organ owner wanted a barrel repegged he told the builders either the titles or the types of tunes he wanted. Unless a completely new barrel was being set up, the spare barrel was stripped of pins and staples and the holes filled with putty or similar compound. If necessary, the barrel was trued up on a lathe. Barrels could be re-turned once or twice as the key frame mechanism, within limits, adjusted itself automatically to the diameter of the barrel.

The blank barrel was covered with paper and positioned beneath the keys. The music marker indicated where the pins were to go by tapping the appropriate key, the point of which made a small indentation in the paper. The position of staples was indicated by two marks, one at the beginning and one at the end of the note concerned. These marks were linked by a pencil line to indicate that a staple was required and not two separate pins. The barrel was then ready for pinning. A special hand punch was used to ensure that the exposed parts of all pins and staples were the right distance above the surface of the barrel.

A foot-operated punch which was used to insert pins and staples, and which automatically regulated their distance above the surface, is preserved in the USA.

As can be appreciated, barrel marking was a very skilled job. It was complicated by the fact that the music scored on the barrel could not be read at sight, unlike music scored on paper or cardboard strips. This was due to two factors. First, it is impossible, merely by inspection, to sort out one tune from another (remember, there are several tunes on each barrel). Second, the arrangement of the keys is not in the same sequence as the notes of the musical scale.

Some excellent and ingenious arrangements have been made for barrel organs and an example, together with some explanatory notes, is given in Appendix II.

Frequently, when business was bad (due to trade slumps and so on) organ owners would have what was known as a 'part strip' carried out. That is, only two or three tunes were replaced. Needless to say, it was the 'pop' tunes which were scrapped; the marches, waltzes, etc would be retained. This was not popular with the builders, as replacing tunes in this way took about twice as long as stripping the full barrel. They took it philosophically, however, as at least it kept their staff employed in bad times.

Originally, the method of tune changing was quite primitive and followed the same routine as could be seen on the tiny monkey-and-stick organs. Two controls were necessary. The first was a lever to lift the tips of the keys clear of the barrel. The second was a pivoted sprung lever, or knife, which engaged in one of a number of grooves turned in one of the barrel's trunnions. The grooves were equal in number to the tunes on the barrel and the distance between their centres was equal to the distance between the centres of each row of pins. Tune changing was accomplished, first, by raising the keys clear of the barrel. The knife was then raised clear of the groove in which it had been located and the barrel was either pulled out or pushed in by tapping it with the palm of the hand. It was then locked in its new position by lowering the spring-loaded knife into whichever groove was now located beneath it. Finally, the keys were lowered into position. The wormwheel, which had straight teeth like an ordinary spur wheel, was made wide enough to remain in mesh with the worm when the barrel was shifted axially. Street barrel pianos had a tune-change handle, one complete turn of which lifted the keys, moved the barrel, dropped the keys, and indicated the number of the tune now in position on a dial by means of a moving finger.

Self-changing mechanisms had been perfected for musical boxes many years before they became general in fairgrounds. It was not until 1906 that Wright & Holmes Bros produced an adaptation of this for the first book organ which was converted to barrel operation. The musical box changer was entirely mechanical but the adaptation, of course, took advantage of pneumatic developments and very soon most of the old barrel organs in rides were fitted with it.

One type is illustrated in Figure 3. As basic pneumatics are not dealt with until Chapter 2, the description of this auto-change mechanism concentrates, as far as possible, on the mechanical action. The way in which the pneumatics work will be apparent later.

The assembly consists of a change unit, for changing the tune, and a counter unit, for counting the number of repeats. In this case the organ plays each tune three times before moving on to the next.

The change unit consists of a snail (*a*)—a larger version of the helical unit in an alarm clock, whereby the time of alarm is selected—combined with a nine-toothed ratchet, a snail motor (*b*), a catch spring (*c*), a snail lever (*d*), and a barrel lever (*e*). The fulcrum of the barrel lever is at its lower end and is on a small shaft (*f*), on which is wound a strong spring (*g*). The snail moves the top end of the barrel lever against the pressure of this spring. Below the snail is the barrel trunnion (*h*). The movement of the barrel lever is transmitted to one of the barrel's trunnions by a boss which projects from the barrel lever, and which fits into a groove or rebate turned in the barrel trunnion. The circumference of the barrel is indicated by a broken line.

The counter unit consists of the counter cam and ratchet assembly (*i*). This comprises a cam, a little thicker than the snail

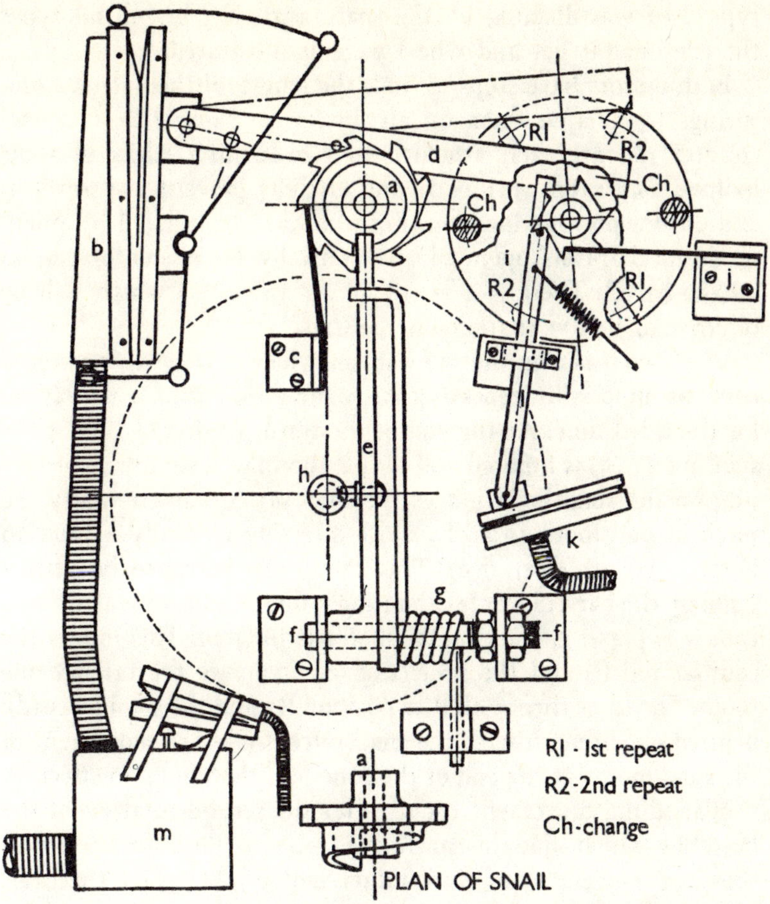

Fig 3. Automatic tune-changing and repeating mechanism as used on barrel organs

lever, with two flats diametrically opposite on its periphery. Two discs are attached to the cam, one on each side, and the snail lever is positioned between them so that its end rests on the cam. A six-toothed ratchet is mounted on the front face of the assembly. There is also a catch spring (*j*), the counter motor (*k*), and the counter rod (*l*). A large counter unit has been illustrated for the sake of clarity. The two discs of the spool have round cams, which are shown cross-hatched and in full outline. The usual counter unit was smaller and an oval cam was incorporated. The type used was dictated by the space available, but in all types the counter ratchet and wheel were as illustrated.

Both motors have stops to limit the length of their stroke, and springs to collapse them on air discharge. The snail lever and counter rod are each attached to the opening edges of their motors. The catch springs to the ratchets prevent any reversal and ensure positive location. Both motors are inflated by pneumatic mechanisms operated automatically by means of staples on the barrel. There is a ventil, or air valve (*m*) which will be referred to in the chapter on registers.

The sketch shows the mechanism when it is set to change a tune, as opposed to repeating it. Assume that tune 4 is playing for the third time. At the end of the third playing of tune 4 the snail motor (*b*) is inflated and moves the snail lever (*d*). A projection on the snail lever moves the snail (*a*) circumferentially the pitch of one tooth in a clockwise direction (actually a fraction more to ensure clearance). This causes the barrel to be shifted 2mm by the barrel lever (*e*) and tune 5 then begins to play. While tune 5 is playing, the counter motor is inflated. This moves the counter rod (*l*) and the projection on it moves the ratchet one tooth. The cams turn with it to position R1 and the snail lever (*d*), is lifted out of mesh with the snail ratchet (*a*). The movement of the snail motor at the end of the tune has, therefore, no effect. A similar idling movement occurs after the second rotation of the barrel by which time the cams have turned to position R2. When the third movement of the counter motor takes place the cams move to the change (Ch) position and the snail lever drops and is once again in mesh with the snail ratchet for a change to tune 6.

On self-changing barrels a small gap of about ¾in or 2cm (about two bars in waltz time) was left between the beginning and end of each tune. This enabled the barrel to be shifted sideways when the tune was changed without damage to the keys, or to the pins and staples. All barrel organs, with or without a self-changer, had a key frame lifting lever, a manually operated lever, which lifted all the keys at once. This was used when the organ had finished playing for the day or when a barrel was to be changed.

Organs using cardboard books and paper rolls are generally

regarded as being superior in many ways to barrel organs, chiefly because the mechanics of the instrument do not dictate the length of the tune. To the showman, however, the barrel organ had many real advantages and, for the record, these are listed below:

(i) The simple direct tracker action is much more trouble-free than tubular pneumatic action.

(ii) The pins and staples are very sturdy, long-lived, and far less liable to damage than cardboard books or paper rolls.

(iii) The barrel organ can prolong a note indefinitely. There were many cases of the dominant (soh) being sustained through a dozen bars of medium 2/4 time with unbroken effect. This is impracticable with the keyed book organ.

(iv) The wages of an attendant, and the difficulty of obtaining a suitable one are saved.

THE CARDBOARD BOOK

Organs operated by cardboard music books were, and still are, known to showmen as 'paper' organs. In this book, however, organs operated by cardboard books will be referred to as 'book' organs. This is to distinguish them from those operated by paper rolls, which will be referred to as 'paper roll' organs.

A cardboard music book consists of a long strip of folding cardboard on which music is scored either by punched-out rectangular slots of varying lengths, or by circular holes. The strip is made from two layers of cardboard, each layer consisting of a row of cardboard rectangles which have been creased down their centres. The two layers are glued together so that two adjacent edges of rectangles in the top layer lie over the central creases of the rectangles in the bottom layer. As the rectangles are creased, the strip can be folded quite easily, first one way and then the other in a zig-zag fashion, to form a compact block, or book as it is called. The folds are sometimes reinforced with linen tape and the edges of the book are planed or smoothed to make sure it runs smoothly and accurately. All music markers had their own personal labels which they glued to the outside covers of their books. Some of these have been reproduced in the pages which follow. Arthur Prinsen is one of the few music markers still practising today and his monogram is shown in Figure 4.

Music is transported through the sensing device, or key frame, by means of a pair of rubber rollers. One type of key frame is fitted with pivoted keys which read the music. These are under spring pressure and their tips press against the underside of the cardboard. When a slot in the music appears above a key its tip rises and this movement causes a valve system to be actuated which, in turn, operates the organ. This type of music is always

ORGELBOEKEN en ROLLEN **ORGAN BOOKS** **CARTONS d'ORGUES**

ARTHUR PRINSEN

NOTEUR – COMPOSITEUR

Ploegsebaan 15, BRASSCHAAT BELGIUM

Tel. (03)63.08.73 Postcheck 1219 28 H.R.A. 42.498

Fig 4. Arthur Prinsen's monogram

punched with rectangular slots of varying lengths. Varnish is often applied round the slots to protect them from wear caused by the action of the keys. This type of frame will be referred to as a 'keyed frame'.

In the other type of frame the music passes over a row of holes drilled in a metal plate, which is known as a mouthpiece or tracker bar. As a perforation passes over a hole, air *escapes* from the pneumatic system. The resulting *drop* in pressure operates the organ's mechanism. This type of frame will be referred to as a 'keyless frame'. Music used on keyless organs can either be perforated with circular holes or rectangular slots. If rectangular slots are used for keyless music they are slightly narrower than those used for the music of keyed organs (3mm as opposed to 4mm).

The term 'key frame' will be used when both types of frame are under discussion.

The music marker uses either a cylinder or a plank to help him score the music. A cylinder is illustrated on page 17 (right). The music the marker works from rests on a stand at the top. Beneath this is a cylinder, turning axially on trunnions. The cylinder is as wide as the widest music the marker prepares. A wheel is fixed to one of the trunnions and around its rim is fixed a brass timing strip which carries several rows of perforations. A section of a timing strip is shown in Figure 5. An assortment of these strips is available and the distances between the perforations in any one row indicate the lengths of notes—quavers, crotchets, minims, and so on. The distance between the two notches on the right-hand side of the example illustrated is 16cm (6⅜in). A pointer engages in the holes of any selected row and the distance the cylinder turns can be regulated accordingly. Paper strips about one metre long can be fixed round the cylinder and these are usually marked off in bars, and further subdivided into beats, according to the time signature of the music.

The problem facing the marker is to score the paper so that it corresponds with the musical arrangement he has in mind. The function of each key on the organ is shown on a card which can be fixed in a holder above the cylinder. A pointer is free to slide laterally on a rod beneath the card and can be locked in any position by

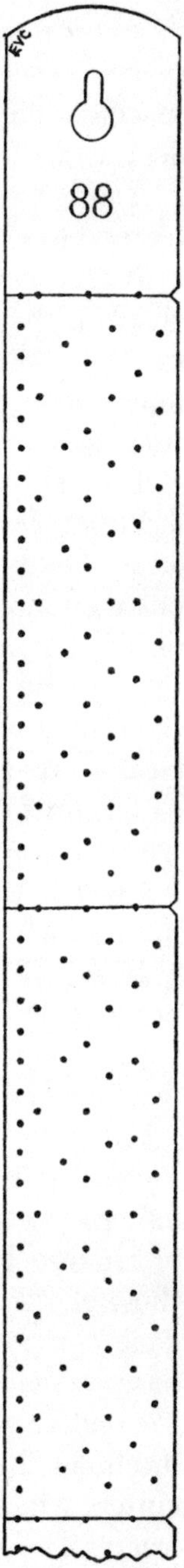

Fig 5. Timing strip from a music marker's cylinder. This can be seen in position on the wheel on the left-hand side of the apparatus on page 17 (right)

means of a catch which engages in a racked strip, or comb. The spacing of the teeth on this corresponds to the key. frame spacing. There is a plunger on the pointer which, when depressed, indents the paper which is fixed to the cylinder.

Another type of machine had a full set of keys mounted at correct key frame spacing, with the tips just clear of the cylinder's periphery. The marker could select at once the particular key required and would tap it with a small narrow-headed hammer. With either system the beginnings and ends of all notes were indented on the paper covering the cylinder, which was faced with rubber or a similar reasonably plastic material.

The method by which a marker works when using a plank is described by R. de Waard in his book *From Music Boxes to Street Organs*. In essence, the device consists of a plank about one metre long on which the drafting paper rests. A raised ledge on the far side of the plank from the marker can be fitted with timing strips which give similar information to that supplied by the timing wheel on the cylinder described above. The ledge also ensures that the paper can be accurately aligned. A sliding gauge, resembling a T-square, notched on one edge in accordance with the key frame spacing and bearing the scale of the organ for which the music is being prepared, enables the marker to indicate where the music is to be perforated.

When the music has been marked out the paper strips are perforated by means of a treadle-operated punch, as shown on page 17, lower, which looks like a cross between a large sewing machine and a jig-saw cutter. This is known on the continent as a kapmachine or kaptafel. The paper passes through a guide and under a cutting head, which makes the necessary perforations, either rectangular slots of standard width and of various lengths, or circular holes. If slots are punched it is usual to punch all those of the same length at the same time. To enable this to be done cutters of the required length can be fixed in the cutting head, which can be moved across the music. The female part of the cutter is adjustable and lies beneath the music. Some machines have a multiple head, incorporating various-sized cutters which can be brought into use as required by a series of levers. The paper patterns thus prepared are used as stencils

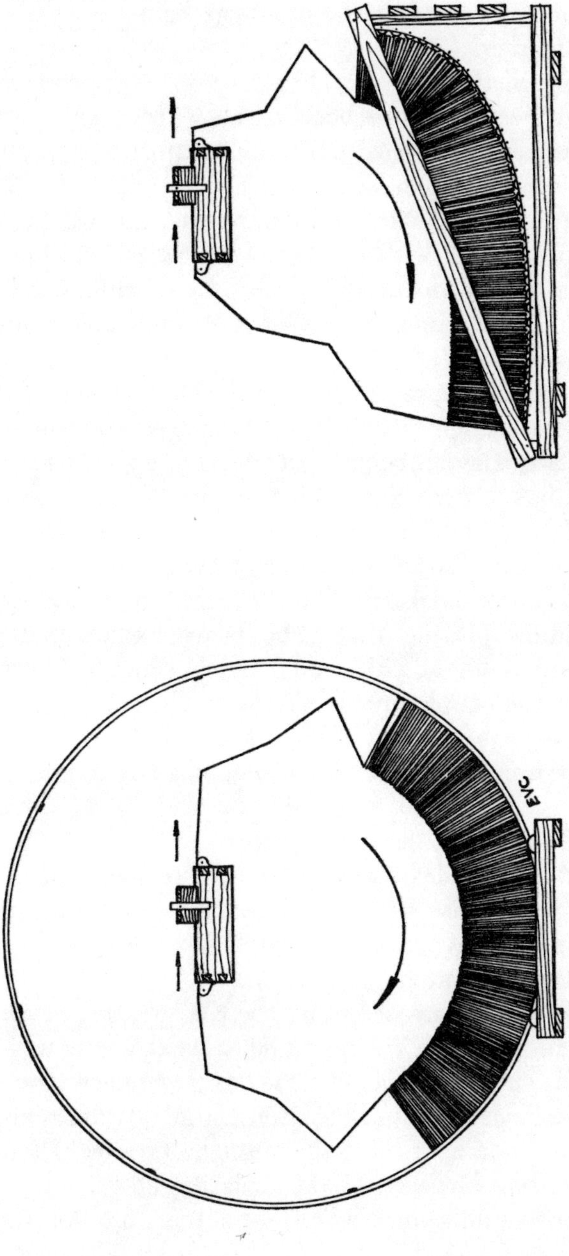

Fig 6. Two methods of obtaining a continuous performance from a book organ: (left) a music wheel; (right) a music hopper

from which the blank music books are marked out. If only one copy is required a blank music book may be marked directly by the music marker.

Two main methods of providing a continuous programme of music have been used on book organs—the hopper and the wheel. These are illustrated in Figure 6. In each, a continuous loop of music is employed, perhaps long enough to play for three-quarters of an hour. In both systems the weight of the played music is used, either to rotate the wheel which rests on the four castors of an inverted trolley, or to cause the bulk of the music to slide round the hopper, over small rollers provided for this purpose.

At one time a feature of the fairground was the box for holding music patented by Gaviolis in 1895 (specification number 11044).* Early Gavioli book organs were supplied with two of these. The boxes were about thirty inches (76cm) high and of suitable cross-sectional dimensions to receive the music books, which were made up of a number of tunes glued together to form a continuous book about thirty inches thick, and of about thirty minutes playing time. The boxes, which had lifting handles, had a lid at either end which could be opened as required or padlocked shut if necessary. They had clips which fitted into slots at each end of the organ case. Music was drawn from one box and passed along a trough, via the key frame, into a similar but empty box at the off-take end on the other side. Here a cam-oscillated flapper imparted a shake to the pages to ensure that they folded correctly into the receiving box. When the whole of the music had been played the empty supply box at the on-take end was replaced by a full box and the full box at the off-take end by an empty one. The lid of the box which had just been filled was fastened shut. The box was turned over and was ready for replaying when the lid at what was now the top, was opened. The advantages of these boxes were reasonably long playing time, relative ease of handling large quantities of music and the protection afforded to the music by the box. The system had a short life, however, as the replacing of old numbers by later hits proved difficult in practice. Another objection was that

* All patent specification numbers are British.

Page 35: *(left)* Steam organ engine, or 'model' (by Walkers); *(right)* centrifugal blower mounted inside truck of an 89 key organ. This has replaced the original crankshaft-operated feeders

Page 36: (right) 89 key frame (Gavioli). The cover plate, lower transport roller and driving wheel have been removed. The guide pulleys for the driving belt are still in position. Some of the keys have been raised; *(below)* 84 key frame (Mortier). This is of similar construction to the frame shown above, except that the music is driven by gearing from the rear of the frame

it was possible to use the boxes only for Gaviolis' music. This was the narrowest of any make and fitted the boxes exactly. Gaviolis may have done this deliberately to push their own sales. The sight of a man loading a full music box onto the platform of a roundabout from the off-take end of the organ and riding round to the on-take end to unload it was a sure indication of the instrument's make.

THE PAPER ROLL

Music can consist of perforated paper rolls which are wound from a supply to a take-up spool. The quality of the paper used for the rolls is much more critical than that of the cardboard used for the music of book organs. A good paper must have many qualities. These are thinness (about 0·003in (0·076mm)), a fair degree of stiffness, resistance to abrasion, good dimensional stability under humid conditions, an ability to perforate easily and cleanly and, last but not least, good ageing properties.

Paper roll music is read as it passes over a tracker bar. In this case, unlike the book organ with a keyless frame, air *enters* the holes in the tracker bar, as the air inside is at a reduced pressure. The resulting *increase* in pressure operates the organ.

The manufacturer of paper rolls has to face a difficulty which his opposite number supplying cardboard books is spared. It is this. The take-up spool on an organ using paper rolls is rotated at a constant number of revolutions per minute and it will, therefore, wind on more paper per revolution as it gets fuller. This has to be allowed for when the rolls are cut, otherwise the tempo of the music would increase very noticeably towards the end of a long roll. (At one time up to ten tunes were scored on one roll, which may have been up to three hundred feet (about 90 metres) long, playing for twenty-five minutes.) This problem does not arise, for example, on tape recorders, where the tape is given a positive drive across the soundheads by means of a capstan. Here the take-up spool merely winds on the tape which is fed to it, as on a cinematograph projector. Another complication which present-day music suppliers have to allow for is that the paper they use may be of a different thickness from that used on the original rolls. The allowances made for acceleration of winding speed, therefore, may have to be changed, which is difficult, especially if old rolls are being copied.

The method by which the marker of paper rolls approached his job is similar to that used by the marker of cardboard books. The medium, however, lends itself much more easily to mass production methods once a master copy has been prepared.

As a general rule the playing time of a paper roll is longer than for an equivalent bulk of cardboard music. The main disadvantage of paper roll music, apart from its liability to tear, is the fact that it has to be rewound. Even though a roll can be rewound in a much shorter time than it takes to play it there is a limit to the speed at which rewinding can take place without damage to the music. It is general practice for the rewind process to be triggered-off automatically by special perforations at the end of the roll, but showmen have never liked the silence which prevails while rewinding takes place. An ingenious idea aimed at partially overcoming this objection was patented by F. C. Hands in 1932 (specification 379,956). His mechanism was so arranged that a short musical phrase or rhythm solo was repeated as many times as required while rewinding was taking place. Hands's trade plate is reproduced in Figure 7.

A much more satisfactory but more complicated arrangement is to duplicate the tracker bar and its associated mechanisms.

Fig 7. F. C. Hands's trade plate

Thus, at the end of one music roll, the other music roll begins to play automatically while the first rewinds. The first roll can either be left in place to play again or be replaced by another. F. C. Hands patented a twin tracker bar device to do this, as did Wurlitzer in the USA and a number of German firms. Technically, there is no great difficulty in arranging for automatic rewind—an inspection of a player piano will suggest several ideas. Complications, however, arise when twin tracker bars are used. These complications are caused by the fact that one tracker bar has to be switched, pneumatically, out of operation and the other brought in. This means that if a tracker bar has, say, seventy air inlets, each of these has to be disconnected from the rest of the organ's action and the corresponding inlets on the other tracker bar connected in their place. This involves using a bank of seventy pneumatic motors with corresponding tubing complications. One method of doing this is referred to in the chapter on registers and their control.

2 The Pneumatic System

THE BASIS OF A PNEUMATIC SYSTEM

THE mechanism, or action, of a fairground organ, like some church organs and player pianos, is nearly always operated by a tubular pneumatic system. The basis of any such system is the use of air which is either at a higher or a lower pressure than that of the atmosphere. That is, the system works either by compressed air or by means of a partial vacuum.

An organ, whether mechanically or manually played, also needs a supply of air to sound the pipes. This is not necessary on the player piano, as the musical sound is produced by the physical impact of the hammers on the strings. Organs, then, need a supply of wind for two purposes—to operate the action and to sound the pipes.

Usually, a high-pressure system is used both to work the action and to sound the pipes. This type of system is found on most of the fair organs in Britain. Sometimes, both a high- and a low-pressure system is used on an organ. This can necessitate two separate pumping systems, as in the Wurlitzer band organs. (The term 'band organ' is the US equivalent of the English expression 'fair organ'.) Occasionally a combined pumping system is used to create both high- and low-pressure air supplies simultaneously. This system is found on some European orchestrions. The choice of systems is governed, among other things, by the type of music the instrument is designed to play from. The three main forms of music—barrel, cardboard book, and paper roll—were examined in the first chapter.

If we admit compressed air into pneumatic devices called 'motors' we can obtain a certain amount of movement which can be used to operate valves, relays, and other mechanisms. The pneumatic motors found on fair organs are, in general, of two types and of very simple construction. The simplest is known as a 'puff' and is made by drilling a shallow cylindrical cavity in a block of wood. A small hole is drilled either in the bottom or side of the cavity and this is connected to a pneumatic tube. The open side of the cavity is covered with thin leather, the centre of which is reinforced with a disc of thicker leather, cardboard, or similar material. One piece of wood usually contains a number of puffs. When a puff is filled with compressed air the leather-covered side is forced outwards.

The other type of motor is slightly more complicated. The shape varies but in one form it consists of two oblong pieces of wood joined at one of the shorter ends with a leather hinge. A piece of thinner leather is glued round the other three sides and over the hinge when the two pieces of wood are slightly open (at about twenty degrees). A hollow wedge-shaped box is thus formed, sometimes known as a 'purse'. One of the wooden sides is drilled with a hole through which air can enter and escape and this side is fastened to the framework of the organ. An alternative design is made from two wooden discs, joined with thin leather and looking rather like a large collapsible pill-box. One of the discs has a hole drilled in it and is fastened to the organ framework. In either case one side of the motor is free to move.

A pneumatic motor expands when it is filled with compressed air. Unlike a child's rubber balloon, however, it does not collapse automatically when the air is allowed to escape, since the leather has little elasticity and is not stretched. We find, therefore, that arrangements have to be made to assist the moving part of the motor to return to its original position when the air is exhausted. There are two ways of doing this.

The first, and most common, is to use either a return spring or gravity, that is, the weight of the moving part of the motor or some other weight. This means that when compressed air enters the motor it must exert a greater pressure than that of the returning device. It means also that the motor must be charged with compressed air for the whole of the time it is expanded.

The second method of returning a motor to its original position is to use another motor. This may be done quite simply by letting one motor operate in one direction and the other in the opposite direction. Alternatively, pneumatic locks may be used. In this arrangement the motor latches itself onto a catch when it opens. When the return motion is required a second motor releases the catch and the first motor returns to its original position, due to spring or other pressure. If a pneumatic lock is used only a short puff of compressed air is needed to open the first motor. It will then stay open until another puff of air enters the second motor and releases the catch. This method has certain advantages and is used in connection with register changing (see Chapter 4).

Motors which are operated by the entry of compressed air are usually lined with cardboard or similar material. If this were not done the leather would blow outwards when the motor was filled with air. This would delay the action and weaken the structure.

Full credit for the pneumatic motor must be given to Charles Spackman Barker (1806–79). Barker was an organ builder who (according to *Grove's Dictionary of Music and Musicians*) 'invented the pneumatic lever' which he patented in 1839 and passed on for exploitation to Bryceson of London, who made barrel organs for churches. This 'lever' was, of course, the now familiar pneumatic motor. It was originally designed, as organs increased in size and wind pressure, to replace the excessive manual effort required to draw the slider in the wind-chest. Its usage very quickly spread to the key and pedal boards.

The air supply to the motors and pipes is controlled by valves. These can either be in the form of discs, or strips of wood, hinged with leather, called pallets. Simple leather flaps are sometimes used. Valves are often coupled together in pairs so that air can enter the mechanism by one route and escape by another.

Many sorts of springs are used in connection with valves and motors and these are made either from wire (piano wire for the small ones) or flat metal. A selection of motors, springs, and valves is illustrated in Figure 8.

Air is conveyed from one part of the mechanism to another by ducts, or trunks, or by tubing. Large trunks are often made

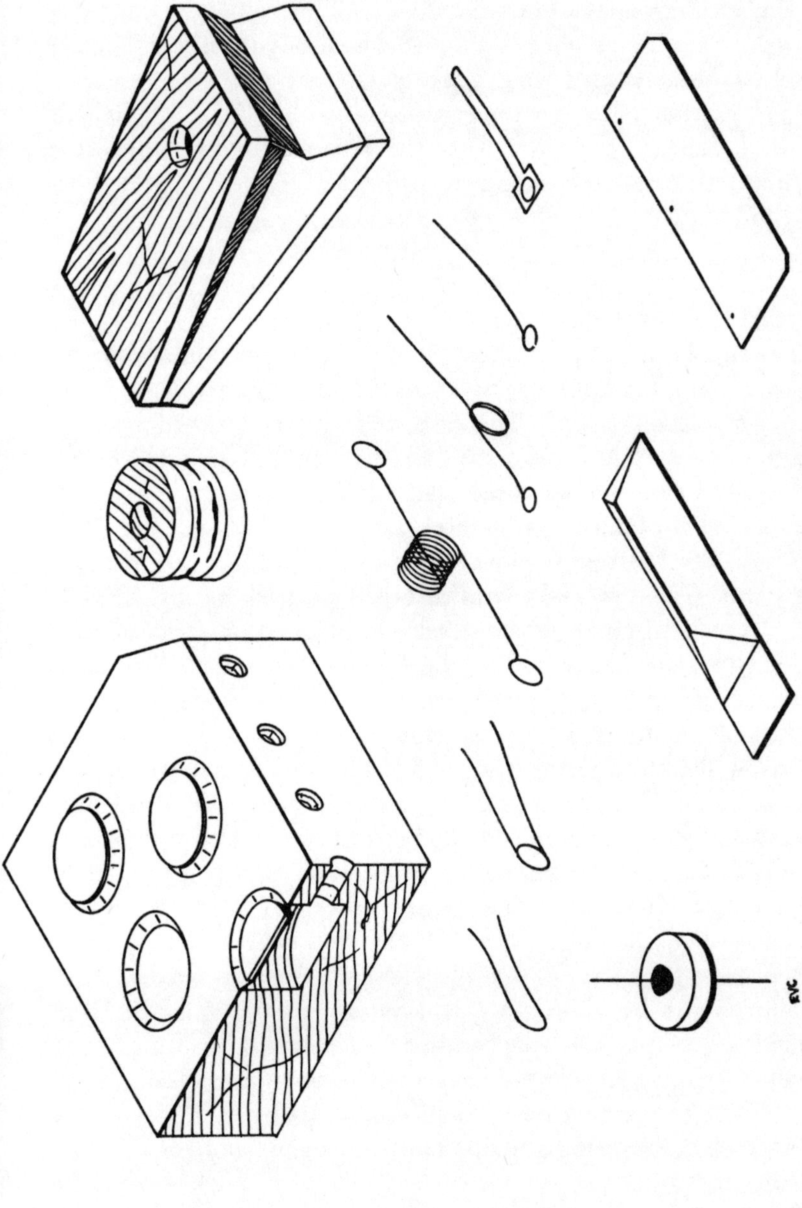

Fig 8. Selection of pneumatic motors, springs, and valves

of wood and are of rectangular cross-section. Reinforced rubber tubing, rather like that found on vacuum cleaners, is also used. The smaller tubes were originally made of rubber or varnished paper. Nowadays plastics tubing, which is virtually indestructible, is usually used when replacements are made.

It is from these basic mechanisms, which consist mainly of wood, leather, and wire, that the organ action is built. How they are assembled and used will be explained as and when appropriate.

MOTIVE POWER

The supply of compressed air for working the action and sounding the pipes of a fair organ is built up in the reservoir by means of a pumping system. The early organs were turned by hand and some Dutch street organs are, in fact, still operated in this way. Later, steam was used and, finally, electricity. Steam was probably introduced as far back as the mid 1860s, when S. G. Soame (of Marsham) pioneered the first vertical steam organ engines. These were known as 'organ models', or just 'models' for short. An organ model developed between one and one-and-a-half brake-horse-power at the organ's crankshaft. On three-abreast gallopers the model was mounted on the smokebox of the centre engine, where the chimney would normally be, and driven by steam from the engine's boiler. Sometimes it was mounted on the smokebox bracket of a showman's road locomotive if this was of the traction centre type. These disappeared in about 1914. Within fairly wide limits the model could be fixed anywhere near the centre truck and was sometimes mounted on the organ itself. A two-step cone pulley took the belt drive to the organ driving wheel. In the early models speed control was by a heavy Watt-type governor, which in later models gave place to a Pickering or other type leaf-spring governor. Organ engines were advertised from time to time in the showmen's weekly paper *The World's Fair* by William Oakley (of Walsall) as being suitable both for organs and for shooting galleries. Other makers included Walker (of Tewkesbury) and Tidman (of Norwich), the latter firm also making several horizontal models. A Savage organ engine is shown in Figure 9 and one by Walkers on page 35 (left).

This association with steam power was probably the reason for many people calling a fair organ a 'steam organ' which, of course, it is not—it is pneumatically operated. The steam organ

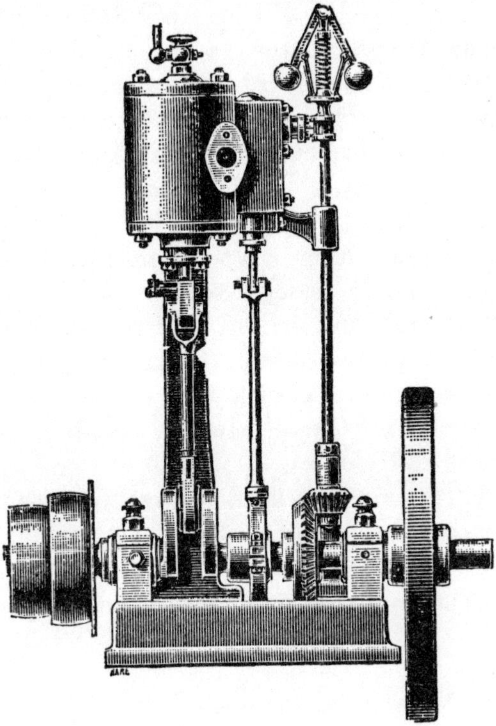

Fig 9. Steam organ engine (or 'model') made by Savages

proper uses steam to blow the pipes and is known as a 'calliope'. These instruments were popular in the USA in fairs and circuses and on river boats but, so far as the writer knows, there are none in Great Britain.

As the two-pole dynamo became more reliable and electricity became more common on the fairground the steam-driven organ engine was replaced by an electric motor mounted on or in the organ case. This motor was driven by electricity from a portable electric light engine, or a dynamo on a showman's road locomotive.

The portable electric light engine, which was introduced in about 1875, was mounted in an enclosed truck, the side and end shutters of which could be removed when it was in use. The firebox was located at one end of the truck, with the main crankshaft above it giving as long a belt drive as practicable to the dynamo at the far end. It was a very useful tool, particularly in the days before 1902, when traction engine speeds were limited to 4mph in the country and 2mph in the town. For big jumps, from Nottingham Goose Fair to Hull, for example, it had particular value as it was designed as a standard railway-carriage truck-load. The output varied but the larger ones could cope with the illumination of a well-presented show or roundabout of the period, and cases have been recorded of 'portables' dealing with the ride and lighting load of a small machine like the short-lived Joywheel of 1911. Makers included Tidman, Savage, and Robey. Some electric light engines were still working in the late 1920s. One of Savage's electric light engines is shown on page 18 (below).

The alternative source of electricity was the dynamo mounted on the smokebox bracket of a showman's road locomotive as illustrated on page 18 (above). The very early locomotives had no dynamos but in due course they became a standard fitting.

THE WIND SUPPLY

The air pressure in the reservoir may range from approximately eight inches of water gauge (manometer) on a large organ to over twelve inches on a small organ, ie, 0·288 to 0·432lb per square inch (21·1 to 31·6 g/sq cm). This pressure may be built up in one of two ways, either by feeders or a centrifugal blower. The feeders and reservoir from a Gavioli organ are illustrated in Figures 10a–c.

The driving wheel of the organ (*a*) is attached to a crankshaft (*c*) which, by means of connecting rods (*d*), turns the rotary motion into a reciprocating one. Oil holes (*e*) are provided so that the bearings may be lubricated. Some bearings were made

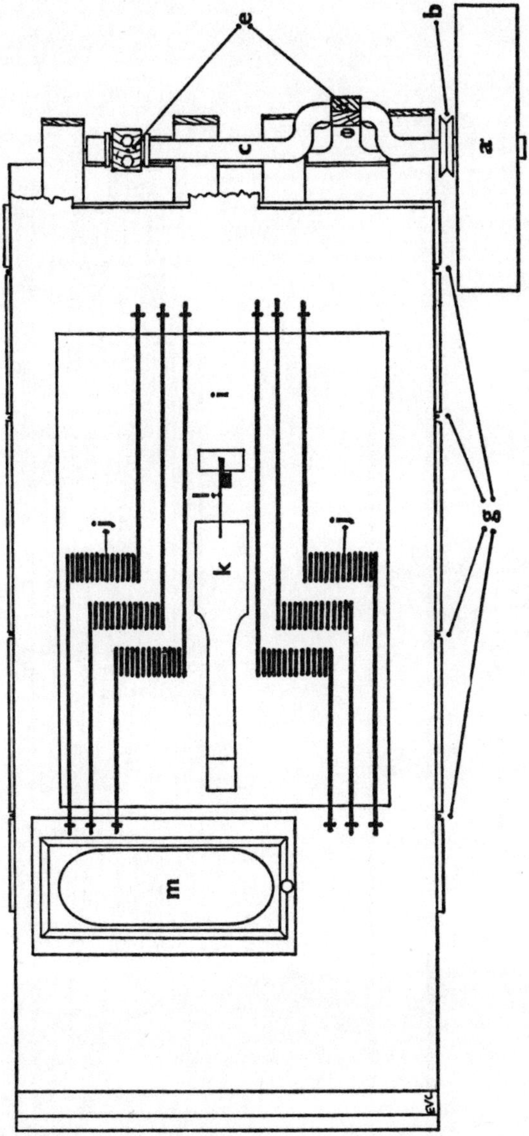

Fig 10a. Bellows from an 89 key Gavioli organ—plan

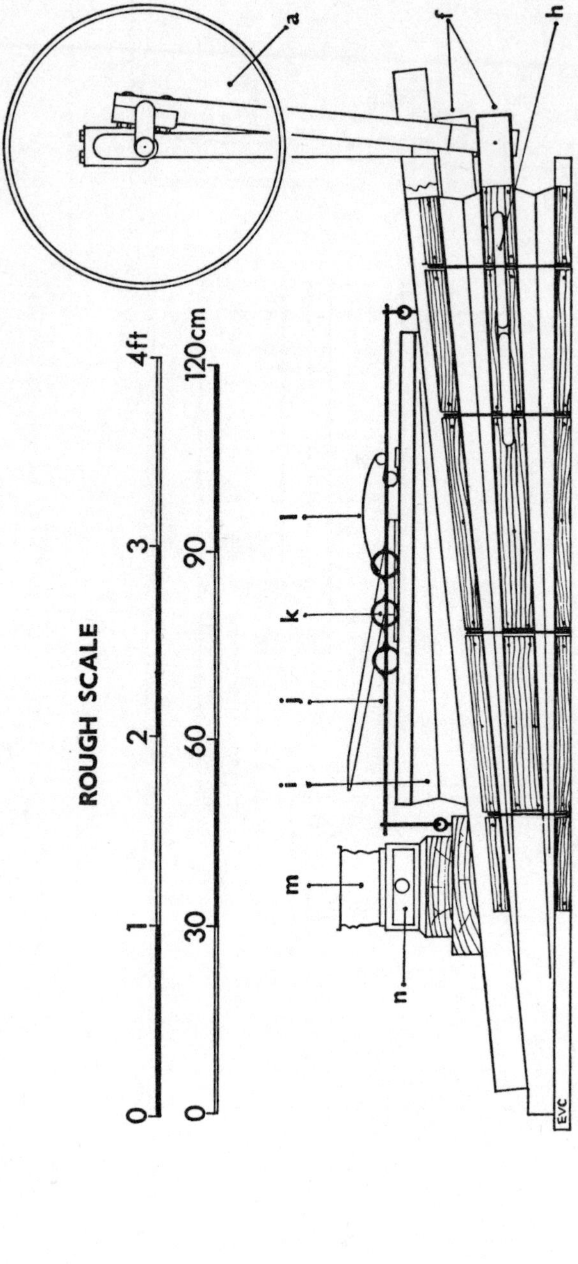

Fig 10b. Bellows—side elevation

of lignum vitae, which needed no lubrication. The reciprocating motion is used to work the feeders (*f*) up and down. Depending on the size of the organ there may be two or three of these and they are situated at the bottom of the organ case. Unlike domestic bellows they are double acting. The rectangular outer boards are fixed at an acute angle and securely fastened to the organ case. Stay rods (*g*) also help to give rigidity. A third movable

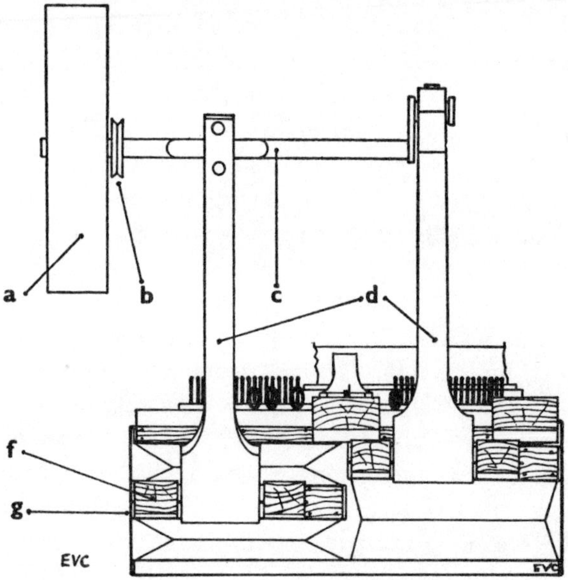

Fig 10c. Bellows—end elevation

board pivoted in the angle formed by the other two, pumps air to the reservoir on both upward and downward strokes. Air is drawn in through grooves (*h*) cut in the sides of the movable centre board. The feeders are fitted with one-way flap valves of leather and air is drawn in through these and forced out again through channels cut in the wood, to the reservoir or reservoirs (*i*) which lie immediately above. Also connected to the crankshaft is either gearing and shafting, or a pulley (*b*) and belting, which transport the music through the key frame.

Many organs, however, have had the feeders replaced by a centrifugal blower, which is rather like a large electric fan. This is also used in church and theatre organs. Nowadays it is generally regarded as a superior method of building up the supply of compressed air in the reservoir. The blower is normally turned by an electric motor although, with suitable gearing, it could be done by a steam organ engine. Organs with centrifugal blowers usually have a separate electric motor to transport the music. In these circumstances the organ driving wheel, crankshaft, and connecting rods, together with the feeders, may be removed. The blowers of theatre and church organs have to run as silently as possible. The blowers of fair organs, however, need not be so silent in operation as there is much more background noise in the open air. This enables smaller, high-speed units to be built. These can be accommodated more easily in the often limited space available inside a fair organ. Sometimes blowers are mounted outside the organ case proper, behind one of the side wings, as shown on page 35 (right).

Whether the air pressure is built up by a feeder system or by a centrifugal blower, the air must be fed into and stored in a reservoir (*i*), or reservoirs—some organs have more than one. In the fair organ this is usually made of two oblong boards hinged at the narrow ends and joined round the other three edges with reinforced leather, the assembly looking rather like an outsize pneumatic motor. The lower board may be an integral part of the feeder system. The upper board lifts at its hingeless end and is under pressure from a number of strong springs (*j*). These help to keep the air inside the reservoir at a constant pressure.

The reservoir has a safety valve to prevent overinflation. In its simplest form the valve consists of a leather flap on the inside of the top board. This flap is normally pressed against an escape hole by the pressure of the air inside the reservoir, and is linked by a cord to the lower part of the case. If the reservoir is overfilled the cord pulls the flap away from the hole and allows air to escape until the top board collapses enough to slacken the cord and allow the flap to seal the escape hole again.

Another type of safety-valve (*k*) is illustrated in the sketches. It is fixed to the top board of the reservoir, outside, and consists of a spade-shaped piece of wood pivoted on a leather hinge at the point where the 'blade' joins the 'handle'. The blade covers the escape hole. If the reservoir gets too full the handle part of the device comes into contact with a stop, which presses it down. This lifts the blade and uncovers the hole, allowing air to escape. A spring (*l*) closes the valve when the pressure falls.

The air passes from the main distribution outlet (*m*) via a filter tray (*n*) to other parts of the organ including the windchests.

The bellows just described have never been dismantled and it is, therefore, not possible to state with certainty how the internal channels are arranged. The writer has, however, been able to obtain details of those on a Hooghuys organ, the bellows of which are built to a similar design. A cross-section, not to scale, is shown in Figure 11.

Air is drawn in through the valves (*a*) which are tensioned with springs and set into the surface of the reciprocating centre

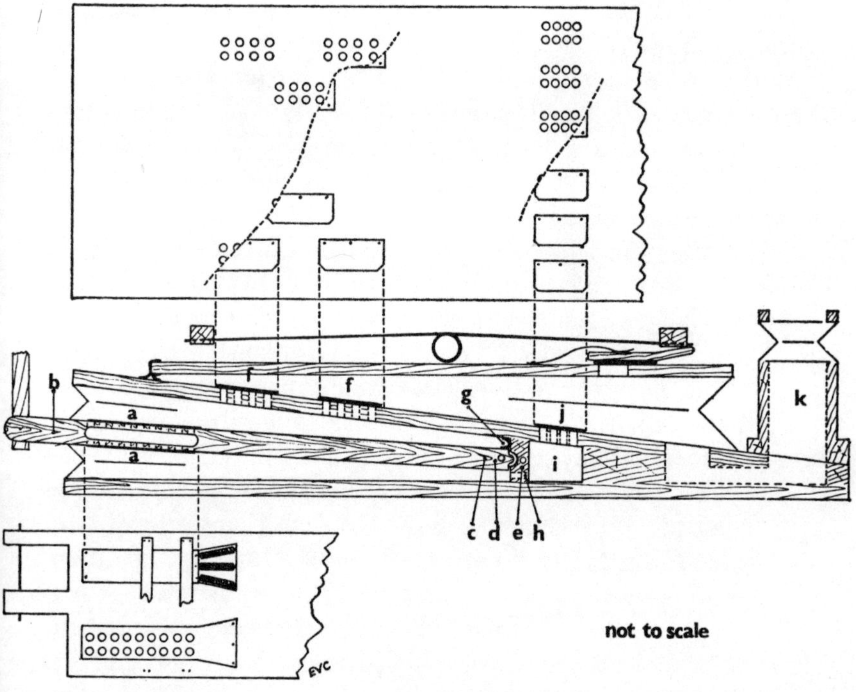

Fig 11. Bellows from a 70 key Hooghuys organ—cross-section showing wind channels and valves

board (*b*). The hinged end of this board (*c*) fits into a wooden bearing. Holes (*d* and *e*) are drilled in the centre board and the main assembly. Two lengths of rope keep the centre board in place. The ends of the rope are inserted into the holes and secured by pegs. Air from the top compartment passes into the reservoir above it via simple flap valves (*f*) which are pinned along their longer edges. The area adjacent to the hinge is sealed with a leather strip (*g*). Air from the lower compartment passes through a series of channels (*h*) into an adjoining compartment (*i*), and from there to the reservoir via valves (*j*), which are similar to valves (*f*). A channel leads from the reservoir to the outlet duct (*k*) which is connected to the main wind-chest and auxiliary mechanisms.

WIND-CHESTS

The main wind-chest occupies a central position inside the organ and usually extends the whole width of the case. Its main purpose is to supply wind to the pipes as and when required, although it also provides and controls the wind supply to a number of auxiliary devices. Constructional details vary, the one to be described being from the same Gavioli organ as the bellows illustrated in Figures 10a–c.

Basically, this type of chest, which is illustrated in Figures 12a–b, consist of a long narrow airtight box, divided horizontally into an upper and a lower section by means of a partition.

The lower section (*a*) is connected via the opening (*b*) to the main wind supply from the bellows and is kept charged with air while the organ is in play. A number of hinged oblong valves, or pallets (*c*), are fitted to the underside of the partition. When these are pushed down air can escape into the upper section of the chest (*d*), via rectangular ports (*e*). Each pallet is fitted with a return spring (*f*) which normally keeps it in the closed position.

The upper section of the chest differs from the lower as it is divided crossways into compartments, there being one compartment above each pallet. Each compartment is airtight and has a specific function. It may be connected to pipes sounding certain notes, or to other effects.

Page 53: *(above)* 61 key frame (Verbeeck). The cover plate has been removed. This photograph was taken prior to restoration; *(left)* 70 key frame (Hooghuys). The top covers have been removed. The pneumatic motor for operating the muting system can be seen on the right; it is connected by means of a rod to an operating lever to the left of the driving pulley

Page 54: Register relay boxes: *(above)* A cross-section of the top box is depicted in Figure 26. This appears to have been cut down, at some time, to a four-way from what was formerly an eight-way box; *(below)* this box was originally installed in a 112 key Gavioli. The original marking has been preserved and reads as follows (from left to right): Violins, Clarinettes, Saxophone, Declanchement, Violoncelle, Trompette, Cymbale (on the main box); Forte, Declanchement (on the small box)

The pipes may be mounted directly on top of the compartments; if this is the case the feet of the pipes fit into holes drilled in the top of the chest (*g*). They may, however, be mounted on a valveless chest (*h*). This is a simple box which is screwed to the main wind-chest. Inlets in the bottom of it correspond to outlets on the main chest. The interior of the valveless chest is partitioned so that air is channelled to the pipes which are mounted

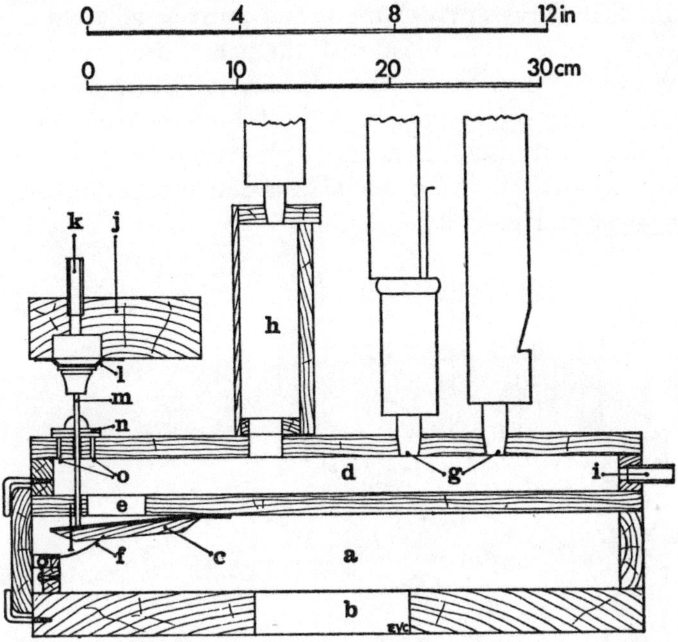

Fig 12a. Main wind-chest from an 89 key Gavioli organ—cross-section

on the top of it. The purpose of such a box is twofold. First, it raises the pipes above the main chest. Second, it enables the pipes to be arranged in a more regular fashion than they would be if mounted directly on the main chest. Small outlet holes (*i*) may also be drilled in the front or top of the main wind-chest, through which air passes to work remotely situated pipes or other devices, either directly or by means of relay valves.

A puff-board (*j*) is fitted above the chest, extending the whole of its width. Each puff is connected via a tube (*k*) to the key frame. The diaphragm (*l*) of each puff bears on a mushroom-headed push-rod (*m*). This push-rod goes through a hole drilled in the wind-chest and bears on the top of a pallet. A disc valve (*n*) is fixed to each push-rod. It is positioned so that when the push-rod is forced down by the diaphragm of the puff it seals exhaust holes (*o*) which are drilled round the push-rod hole.

In order to save space the puffs are often staggered. This means that the position of the pallets must be adjusted accordingly. In the example illustrated, the pallets are staggered in a corresponding manner to the puffs, every other pallet being about two inches (5cm) in front of or behind those on either side of it. For clarity this has not been shown on the cross section, though the general layout should be apparent from the isometric view given in Figure 12b.

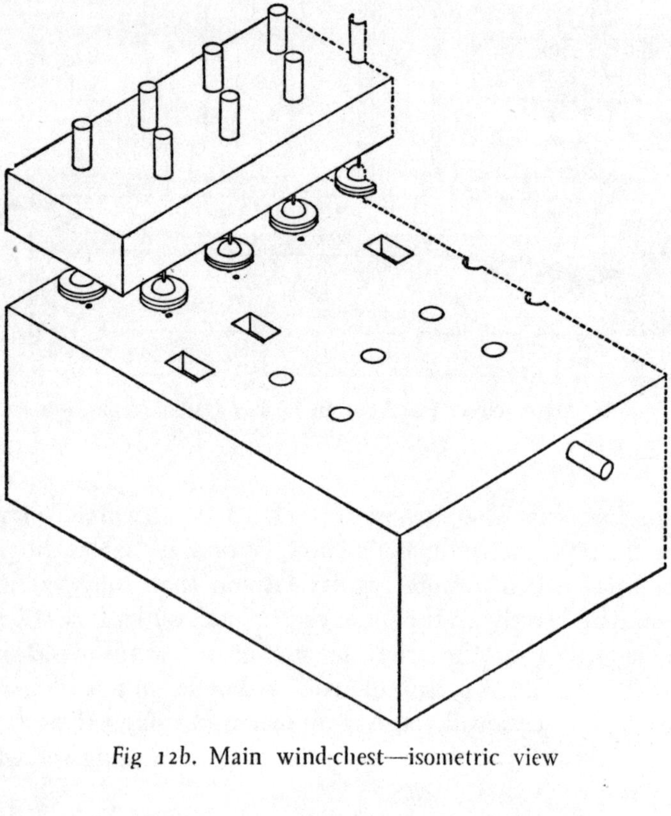

Fig 12b. Main wind-chest—isometric view

Notes are sounded on receipt of air signals from the key frame. The air, which is above atmospheric pressure, travels along tubes and, on reaching any particular puff, inflates it and moves the diaphragm downwards. In turn, the diaphragm forces the push-rod down. This action opens the pallet and compressed air flows from the lower part of the chest into the compartment above the pallet. At the same time the disc valve fitted to the push-rod closes the exhaust ports. The compressed air now flowing into the upper section either sounds pipes, which may be mounted above it, or travels via an outlet hole to operate other pipes or mechanisms. When the key frame cuts off the supply of air, the air pressure in the puff falls to that of the atmosphere and the pallet spring is able to return the pallet to the closed position. As the push-rod is forced up the exhaust valve lifts with it, unsealing the exhaust ports. This allows the air pressure to drop quickly.

It is often convenient to have certain pipes and effects installed in parts of the organ remote from the main wind-chest. This may be because they form a separate register or because it is better to have them at the front of the organ for acoustical reasons or for ease of access. In these circumstances the pipes are mounted on what is known as an 'off-note' chest as illustrated in Figure 13. Tubing is taken from the appropriate compartments on the main wind-chest (via the outlet holes already mentioned) to corresponding puffs on the off-note chest, which contains its own set of pallets. The off-note chest is supplied with air from the main reservoir.

As with the main chest the layout of the puffs may be staggered to save space. This is so in the example illustrated. Instead of the pallets being staggered as well, as in the main wind-chest, every other pallet is reversed and hinged at the opposite end to those on either side of it.

A different type of off-note chest, which is used to work a xylophone, is shown in plan in Figure 14a. Cross-sections along the lines XX and YY appear in Figures 14b and 28 respectively. Cross-section YY embraces the ventil or air valve and this will be discussed in Chapter 4. Cross-section XX shows the way in which the off-note chest operates.

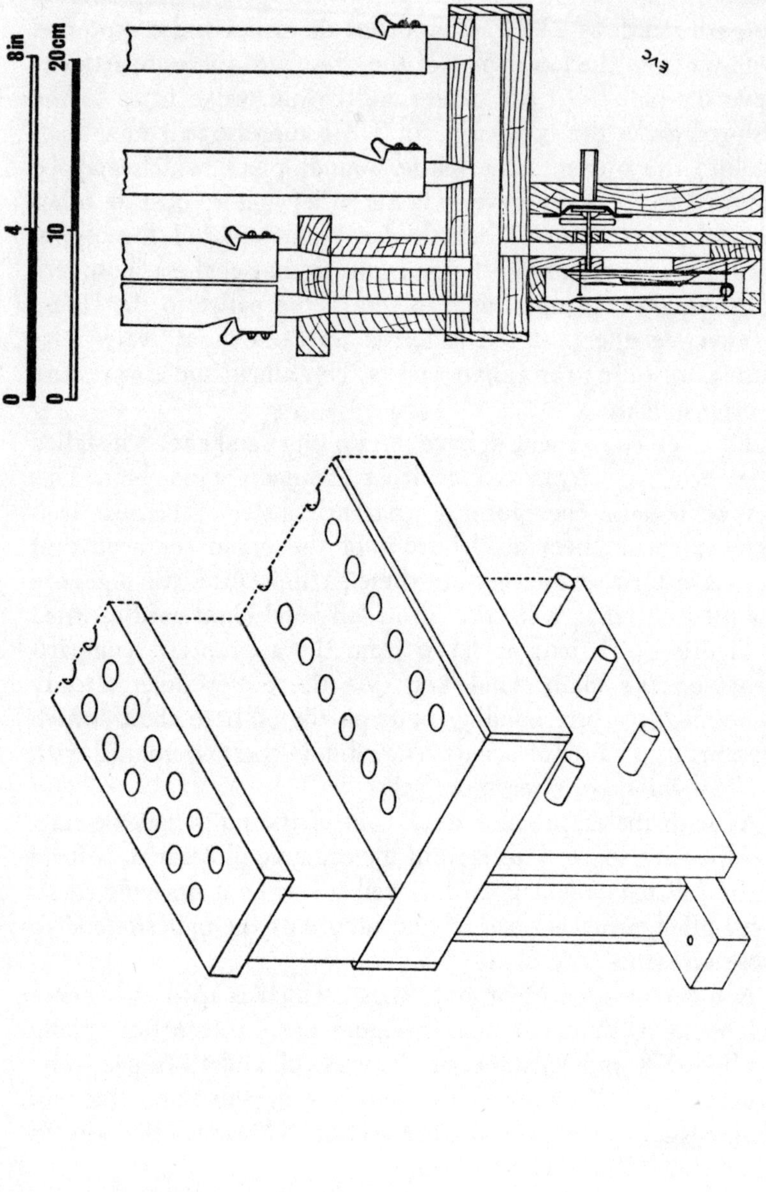

Fig 13. Off-note chest: (left) isometric view; (right) cross-section

The puff-board is of the usual design and consists of a strip of wood (*a*) drilled with a number of cylindrical cavities (*b*). These are covered with thin leather (*c*). Channels (*d*) connect the puffs, via tubing, to the corresponding outlets on the main wind-chest. A puff is inflated whenever a valve opens on the main chest. Each diaphragm is fitted with a cardboard disc on which is glued a wooden button (*e*). The puff-board is mounted beneath the xylophone's wind-chest.

This wind-chest consists of a long narrow airtight box (*f*) with a pair of valves for each note on the xylophone. One valve (*g*) is inside and the other (*h*) is outside. The inside valve, which is conical in shape, is attached to a fibre bar with forked ends. These fit round two vertical metal pins and keep the assembly in position. The valve is unsprung but a small lead weight (*i*) mounted above it ensures that it closes smartly when required. The lower valve is of the hinged pallet type. The two valves are connected by a metal push-rod (*j*). When the outside valves are open they just make contact with the wooden buttons on the puffs when the latter are deflated. The lower board of the wind-chest is drilled with channels (*k*) so that, depending on the position of the valves, the next part of the mechanism (the hammer motor) is either connected to the wind-chest or to the atmosphere.

The hammer striking mechanism consists of a large puff-board (*l*) with elongated cavities (*m*). Wooden blocks (*n*) are glued to the outside of the leather which covers the cavities. One end of the block is hinged. Fixed to the other end is a short length of flexible cane (*o*) on the end of which is a hardwood ball which acts as a striker. A flat metal spring (*p*) ensures that the striker is lifted clear of the bar when the motor is not inflated.

When the xylophone is working the wind-chest (*f*) is charged with air at a higher pressure than that of the atmosphere. The appropriate puff (*b*) is inflated, when required, by air from the main wind-chest. The wooden button (*e*) closes the outside valve (*h*) and seals the outlet hole from the channel (*k*); at the same time the push-rod (*j*) causes the inner valve (*g*) to open. Air passes from the inside of the chest to the hammer motor (*m*) which it inflates. This causes the end of the hammer to move

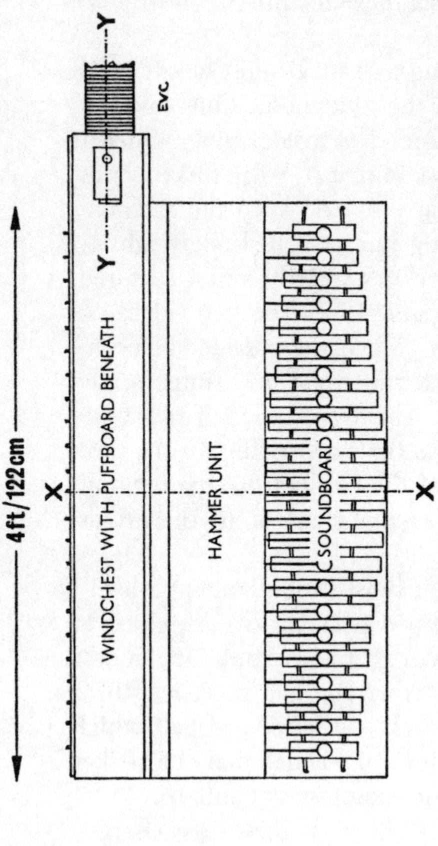

Fig 14a. Xylophone unit from a large dance organ—plan

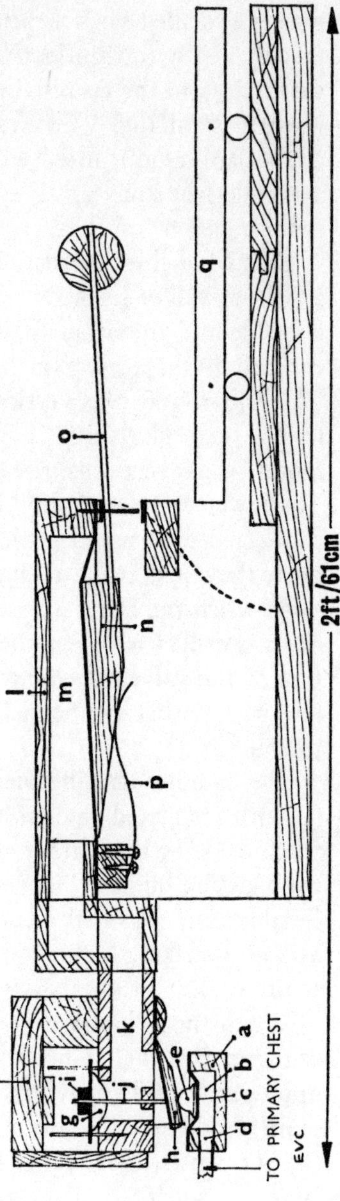

Fig 14b. Xylophone unit—cross-section along XX

down. The flexibility of the cane causes the hammer-head to overtravel slightly, to strike the bar (*q*) and come to rest a small distance above it. If the hammer were adjusted so that it remained resting on a note while the motor was inflated the sound of the impact would be deadened. As soon as the wind supply to the puff (*b*) is cut off it deflates, and the force of gravity, acting on the lead weight (*i*) closes the inside valve (*g*) and opens the outside valve (*h*). The air in the hammer motor is now able to escape into the atmosphere via the outlet hole and is assisted in this by the pressure of the hammer-motor spring (*p*). The striker is lifted well clear of the bar, ready for the next cycle of operations.

This type of mechanism is of the single-stroke variety. Quite often, for tuned percussion effects, a reiterating mechanism is used.

3 Key Frames and Tracker Bars

MANY varied and ingenious devices have been used on mechanical musical instruments to read the music. The devices used on mechanical organs work either by mechanical, pneumatic, or electrical means, or by various combinations of these. Electrical methods are outside the scope of this book. Music reading devices will be divided into key frames, as used on barrel and book organs, and tracker bars, as used on paper roll organs.

THE BARREL ORGAN KEY FRAME

As mentioned in Chapter 1 the music-reading device on a barrel organ is in the form of a key frame. The general construction of the barrel organ is of a very simple and trouble-free nature and underwent no major changes during the many years it was in general use.

The early barrel organs were operated entirely by mechanical means although in later years pneumatic motors were incorporated to work percussion effects, change registers, and operate the figures on the organ's proscenium. The self-changing mechanism, which was described in Chapter 1, was also, of course, pneumatically operated. We are concerned here, however, only with the key frame. A cross-section of one type is illustrated in Figure 15. This frame is simply constructed from several lengths of well-seasoned wood, which are screwed together as indicated. Slots are cut in two of the members. The distance between centres of these slots determines the number and general layout of the tunes on the barrel. The keys are pivoted on a length of wire which runs the length of the frame. This is bent into a loop at each end and held in place by screws. Wooden fillets are glued in the channel in which the wire rests and these help to secure it.

The key frame is positioned above the barrel so that the tip of each key can be moved by the action of the pins and staples

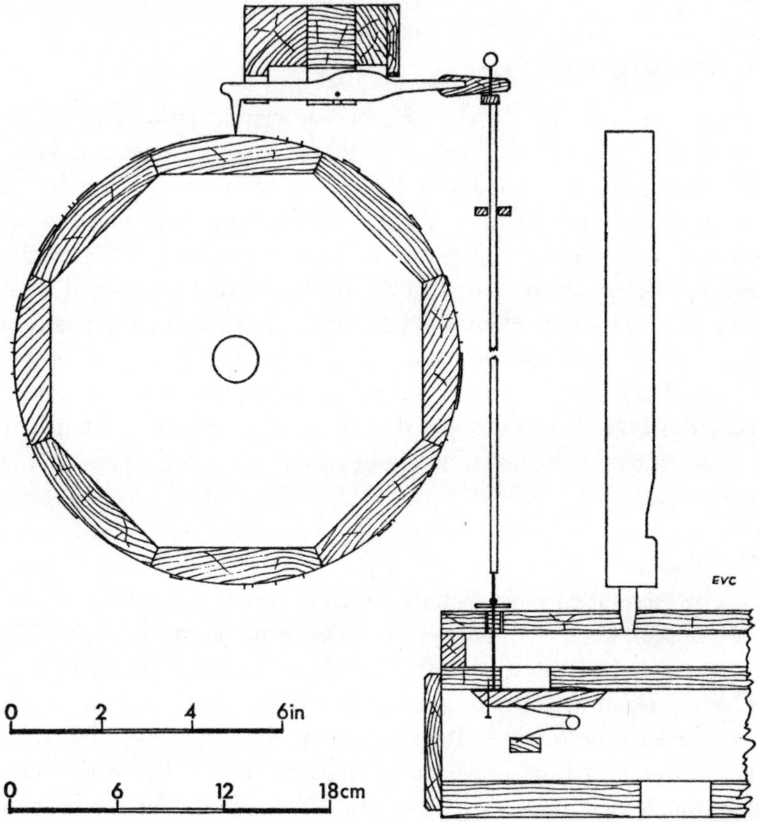

Fig 15. Key frame and action from a 45 key barrel organ—cross-section

on the barrel as it revolves. The key frame is also pivoted so that the keys can be lifted clear of the barrel.

The end of the key not in contact with the barrel carries a wooden button on a screwed rod. This can be adjusted to give the required amount of movement to the push-rod or sticker with which it makes contact. The wind-chest is fitted beneath the barrel and the lower end of each push-rod enters the wind-chest by means of a small hole drilled in the top of the chest above the appropriate pallet. From this point onwards the operation of the organ is similar to those operated by cardboard books or paper rolls.

THE BOOK ORGAN KEY FRAME

There are two types of key frame—it can be either 'keyed' or 'keyless'. On a keyed frame a number of metal levers, or keys, are arranged across the frame parallel to each other. These levers are concealed except for the ends, which are visible as a row of curved teeth projecting above the bed of the frame. When the music is in position all the keys are depressed by the cardboard and can rise only when slots in the music move into position above them. On a keyless frame the teeth are replaced by a row of small holes drilled in a metal plate. When the music is in position the holes are sealed by the cardboard. When a slot in the music moves into position above them they are open to the atmosphere.

The Frame

The general construction of a frame, which is similar for both keyed and keyless organs, is evident from Figures 16a-b. The frame on which these drawings are based comes from an 89 key Gavioli organ and has had a number of minor alterations made to it from time to time. Its position on the organ has obviously been altered at least once, possibly twice. The writer has, therefore, made one or two adjustments and omissions for the sake of clarity.

The main frame (*a*) is made from oak. In the example illustrated two corners were box-jointed while the other two were simply screwed together and strengthened with blocks of wood. There is no reason why all corners should not be dovetailed as suggested in the diagram. A metal plate (*b*) acts as a music guide on the far side of the frame. This is in two parts. A wooden fillet (*c*) is fitted on the near side. Grooves (*d*) are cut in the sides

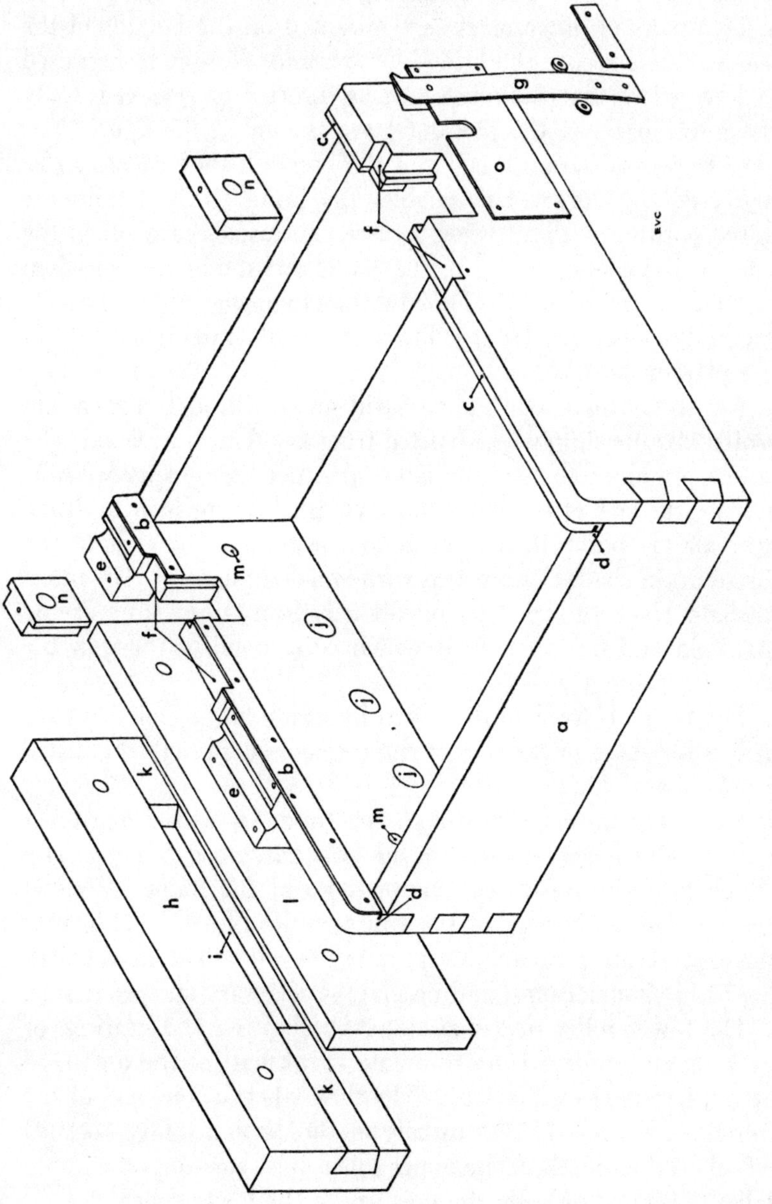

Fig 16a. Key frame (lower part) from an 89 key Gavioli organ—exploded view

of the frame below both the metal guide and the wooden fillet. These grooves receive the metal edges of a sliding cover plate.

Two pairs of hinge blocks are mounted on the far side of the frame. These secure the bridge, or lid, and allow it to be raised or lowered so that the music can be inserted or removed. Only the lower parts of the blocks (*e*) are shown in the figure. The blocks are made from beech and the pressure they exert can be regulated by screws. This enables the bridge to be left in the raised position without using a catch. Recesses (*f*) are cut in the sides of the frame so that the bridge is accurately located when lowered. A metal catch (*g*) on the frame engages with a boss on the bridge when the latter is lowered, thus locking it securely in the playing position.

Air enters the frame's pneumatic system through a manifold which is quite simply constructed from two blocks of wood. The outermost block (*h*) has the main air inlet hole on its far side. The nearer face of the block has a channel (*i*) cut in it to distribute air via ports (*j*) in the side of the frame. The ends of the distribution channel are sealed with wooden plugs (*k*). The intermediate block of wood (*l*) makes a self-contained unit of the manifold and has ports in it which correspond to those in the side of the frame.

The frame is fixed to the organ by coach bolts. Holes (*m*) are drilled for these in the side of the frame and through the distribution manifold.

Music is transported through the frame by a pair of rubber rollers. The lower roller runs in two hardwood bearings (*n*), which fit into recesses cut in the sides of the frame. A metal keeper plate (*o*) screws to the front of the frame. This secures the outer bearing of the lower transport roller. The inside bearing has a shoulder on it and no plate is necessary on the far side.

The lower roller is driven either by shafting and gearing, or by belts and pulleys from the main crankshaft of the organ, or by a separate electric motor. A toothed wheel at one end of the spindle of the lower roller usually meshes with a similar toothed wheel on the spindle of the upper roller, but sometimes the upper roller is rotated only by the pressure of the lower roller.

An exploded view of the bridge is shown in Figure 16b.

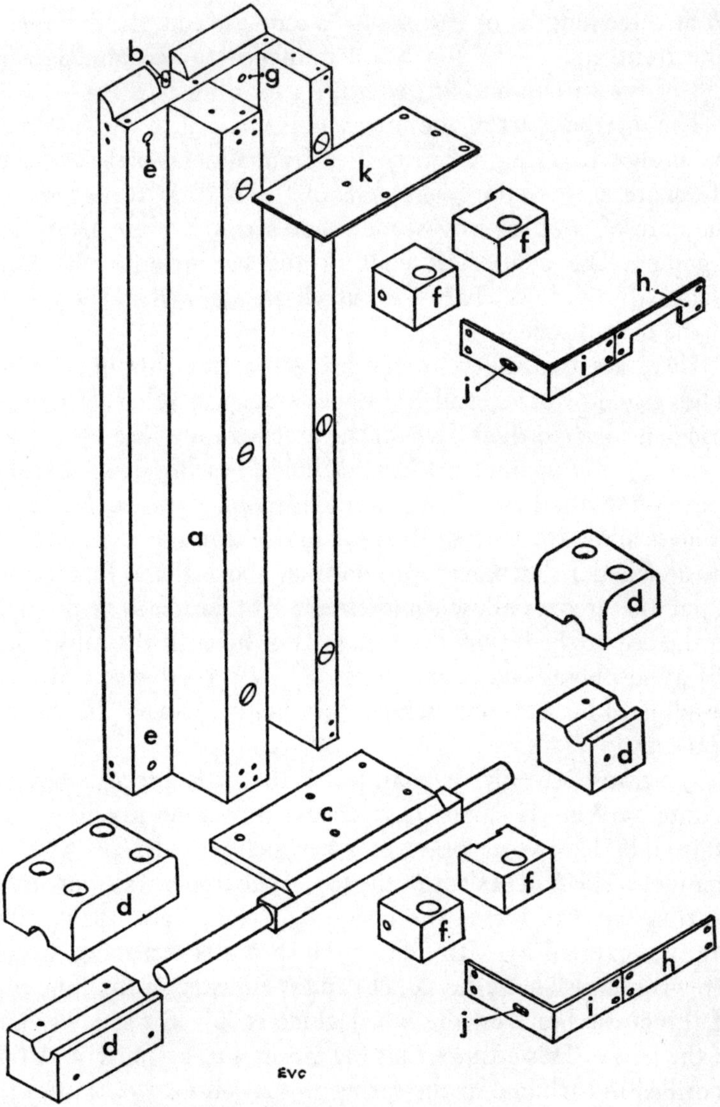

Fig 16*b*. Key frame (bridge)—exploded view

Reference to page 36 (right) will also help to make the method of construction clear. The main part of the bridge (*a*) is made from three lengths of oak securely screwed and glued together. The front end of the top board is shaped to accommodate the end of the catch and is fitted with a locating boss (*b*).

The internal part of the hinge (*c*) is screwed to the far end of the bridge. It is simply constructed from a metal plate and a bar of square cross-section. The ends of the bar are turned so that they are of circular cross-section, and bar and plate are welded together. The cylindrical ends of the bar fit into the hinge blocks (*d*), the lower halves of which are screwed to the far side of the main frame.

There are two rollers in the bridge—a free running grooved roller made of brass, and the upper transport roller. When the bridge is lowered the ridges on the grooved roller keep the music pressed firmly against the keys or holes, bearing down between them—not on them. Thus, when used on a keyed frame the grooves allow the ends of the keys to rise through and above the music when a slot moves into position above them. In a keyless frame the grooves allow compressed air to escape from the holes in the bed of the frame, through slots or holes in the music, into the atmosphere. The pressure exerted by the grooved roller can be adjusted by set-screws which fit in holes (*e*) above the wooden bearings.

The transport roller is mounted so that it is directly above its counterpart in the main part of the frame. Both rollers have adjustable hardwood bearings (*f*) which are drilled with oil channels. The notches cut in the top of the upper transport roller bearing serve to locate the ends of a semi-elliptic spring. The pressure exerted by each end of the spring is controlled by set-screws (not visible in the sketch) and is adjusted so that one edge of the music bears on the metal guide strips on the lower part of the frame. This ensures that the music runs accurately. A hole is drilled in each end of the spring so that oil may pass from the oil hole (*g*) above it, through the spring and bearing to the spindle.

All bearings are held in place by flat (*h*) or angled (*i*) keeper plates which are screwed to the wooden framework of the bridge. The angled keeper plates which help to secure the grooved roller have oil holes (*j*) in them which coincide with the oil channels in the bearings. Part of the keeper plate for the outside end of the upper transport roller is cut away to give clearance for the gear wheel mentioned above. A flat brass keeper plate (*k*) screws to the front or rising end of the bridge and serves to secure the bearings at that end. The flat metal part of the hinge plate at the opposite end serves a similar purpose.

The internal fittings are held in position by various blocks and strips of wood which are fixed to the inside of the frame. These have not been shown but their positions will be obvious when the remainder of the mechanism is described.

Two different pneumatic systems are used in the key frames of book organs, the 'pressure' system and the 'exhaust' system. In the pressure system compressed air passes from the key frame to work the next part of the action. In the exhaust system, air (at a higher pressure than that of the atmosphere) escapes from the key frame and the resulting drop in pressure operates the mechanism. Keyed organs can use either system, the pressure system being the more common. Keyless organs use only the exhaust system. The system used by paper roll organs is described later in this chapter.

Keyed Systems—Pressure Operated

Two examples of the pressure pneumatic system are illustrated in Figures 17 and 18. The touch-boxes (*a*) are fitted with a pair of coupled valves (*b*) and (*c*) for each key (*d*). Unlike the touch-box found on manually played organs, however, the touch-box on mechanical organs is divided into two or three sections, which are mounted either one above the other or side by side (or a combination of both), according to the particular system employed. This is done because it is obviously desirable for the music to be as narrow as possible, both for economic reasons and for ease of handling. The touch-boxes are therefore arranged so that the valve gear can be packed into the narrowest possible space (about 3·5mm is allocated to each key). The arrangement varies in the examples illustrated. In both cases, however, the effect of allowing a key to rise is the same. The outside valve (*c*) shuts

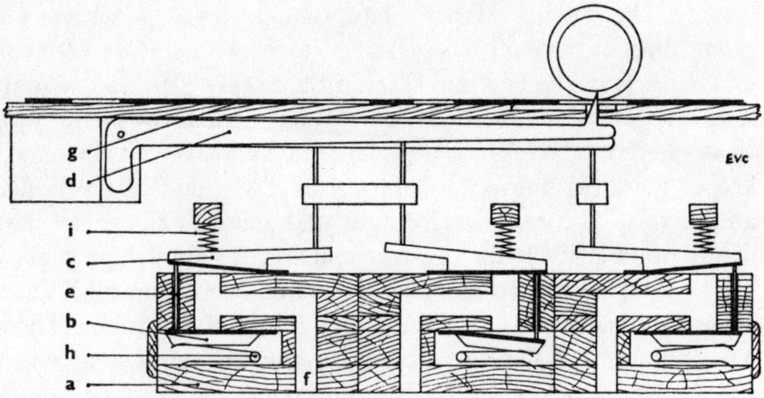

Fig 17. Keyed frame, pressure system with three touch-boxes, as patented by Anselme André Marie Gavioli (specification 11044 of 1895)

while that on the inside (*b*) is opened, the two valves being connected by a short rod (*e*). Compressed air from inside the touch-box can therefore flow via the port (*f*) to a pneumatic device which it operates. This is not shown in the diagrams. As soon as the key is forced down by the cardboard of the music (*g*) the inside valve (*b*) closes, cutting off the supply of compressed air to the pneumatic device referred to above. At the same time the

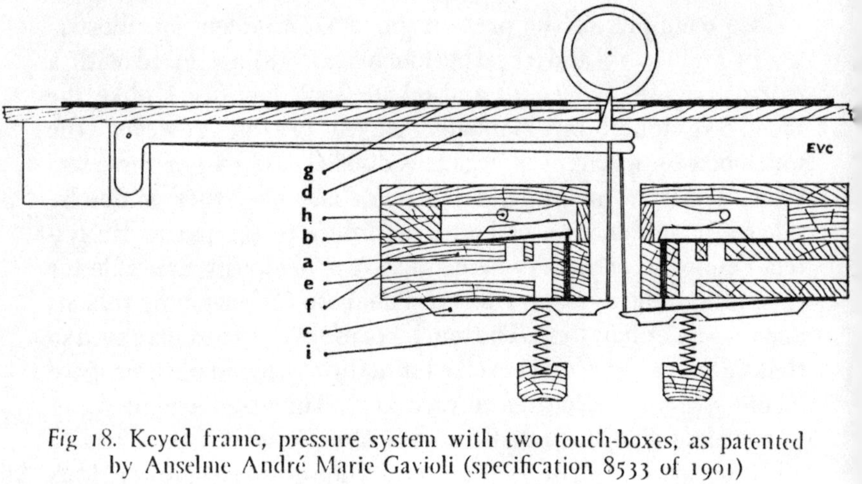

Fig 18. Keyed frame, pressure system with two touch-boxes, as patented by Anselme André Marie Gavioli (specification 8533 of 1901)

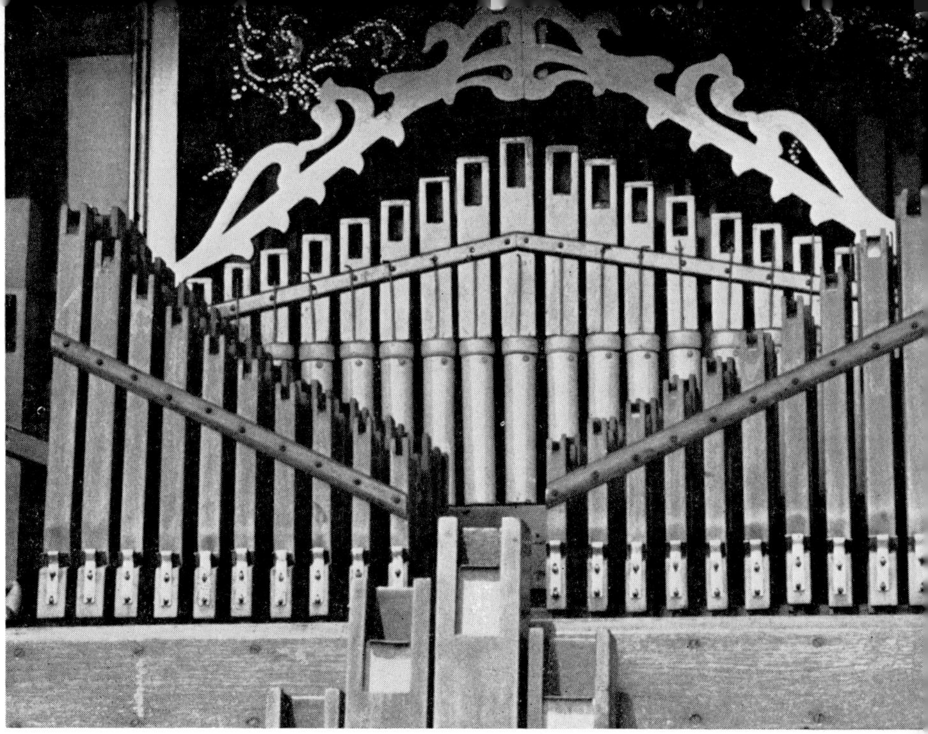

Page 71: *(above)* At the back, the front rank of the clarinet mixture. In front of the clarinets, four ranks of violins. In the foreground, part of the baritone register is visible (from an 89 key Marenghi which can be seen on page 125, above); *(below)* in the foreground, piccolos with stopped flutes as helpers. Behind, fourteen brass trumpets. Above the trumpets, two brass trombone resonators are visible; the third trombone is missing, as evidenced by the cut-away portion in the middle of the canopy (from a barrel organ)

Page 72: *(above)* Part of a clarinet mixture; notice the variety of pipes used (originally from a 112 key Gavioli); *(below)* a baritone register—reeds in front and flues at the back. These pipes are mounted low down, in front of the organ (from an 89 key Marenghi)

outside valve (*c*) opens, allowing the compressed air to escape into the atmosphere via the exhaust port (*f*). This causes the pressure to drop and the pneumatic device returns to its original position. Both methods employ two springs per key—one (*h*) to shut the inside valve and the other (*i*) to lift the key (*d*) when a slot comes into position above it. These springs are necessary to ensure prompt action. Notice that the valves of the touch-box are not coupled to each other, the small connecting rod (*e*) being completely free. The distance the various levers travel is regulated by adjusting screws. As one can imagine, the regulation of a keyed frame is a tricky job and not to be undertaken lightly.

Figures 17 and 18 are based on drawings which accompanied patents filed by the Gavioli family (specification 11044 of 1895 and 8533 of 1901). The shape of the keys is as on the original drawings. In general, however, keys are shaped as shown in Figure 19.

The variations in air pressure, caused by the actions of the keys, inflate or deflate pneumatic motors which open or close the pallets in the wind-chests. Sometimes a relay system is incorporated. Views of Mortier and Verbeeck keyed frames are shown on pages 36 (below) and 53 (above).

Keyed Systems—Exhaust Operated

One example of the keyed frame using the exhaust pneumatic system is illustrated in Figure 19. Here the keys (*a*) are pivoted roughly halfway along, although this is obviously not essential. Two rows of valves (*b*) are arranged one above the other. The end of each key is connected to its exhaust valve by a vertical rod (*c*), which is pivoted to the key at the top and threaded at the lower end, which passes through a hole in the end of the exhaust valve (*d*). A leather nut (*e*) allows the amount of vertical movement to be regulated. The lower end of the rod fits loosely into the hole in the end of the exhaust valve. The method of operation is quite straightforward. When a slot in the music (*f*) moves into position above a key, the key rises due to pressure from its spring (*g*). The other end depresses the vertical push-rod and opens the valve, allowing the compressed air in this part of the

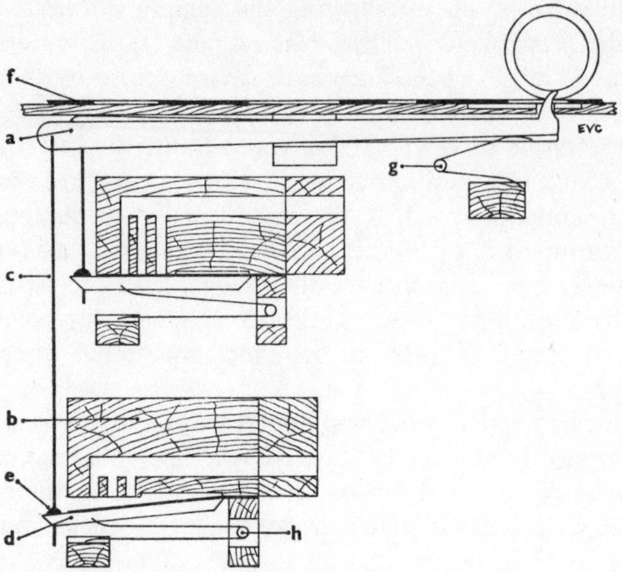

Fig 19. Keyed frame, exhaust system with two touch-boxes, probably Bursens

system to escape into the atmosphere. The resulting drop in pressure operates the action. As soon as the key is pressed down by the cardboard of the music the valve is able to shut, aided by the pressure of the spring (*h*) beneath it and air pressure builds up again immediately.

The keys are connected alternately to the upper and lower valve chests, the inlets to which are staggered, one up and one down. Smaller escape channels, of about $\frac{3}{32}$in (2mm) diameter, are drilled downwards to the lower face of the box, three for each inlet. The reason for this is that it would not be possible to have holes of the same diameter as the inlet holes all in a line (remember, the inlets are staggered). Note the slight channel cut in the lower face, which allows the valves to bed more efficiently on the exhaust outlets.

Maintenance is simplified, as it is possible to unscrew the blocks to which the tubes are connected, thus leaving the mechanism free.

Another type of exhaust pneumatic system, as used on

Hooghuys organs, is illustrated in Figure 20 and on page 53 (left). The steel keys (*a*) are pivoted on a common rod (*b*). The exposed tips (*c*) at the other end are kept in position by the teeth of a brass comb (*d*). A length of spring wire (*e*) is secured to the key by a metal loop (*f*). The compression of the wire causes the key to rise when a slot in the music appears above it. Connected to the rising end of the key is a wire (*g*), with a U-bend at its lower end. The shorter side of the U is threaded to receive a leather button (*h*), the position of which can be adjusted by turning it on the threaded end of the wire. The exposed end of the wire passes through a small wooden shoulder which is mortised into the outer face of a small pallet valve (*i*). This is hinged on leather in the usual way and moves between two guide pins. A flat metal spring (*j*) normally keeps it in the closed position. There are four rows of these pallet valves, the one illustrated being in the bottom row. Keys 1, 5, 9, etc are connected to the top row; keys 2, 6, 10, etc to the second row, and so on.

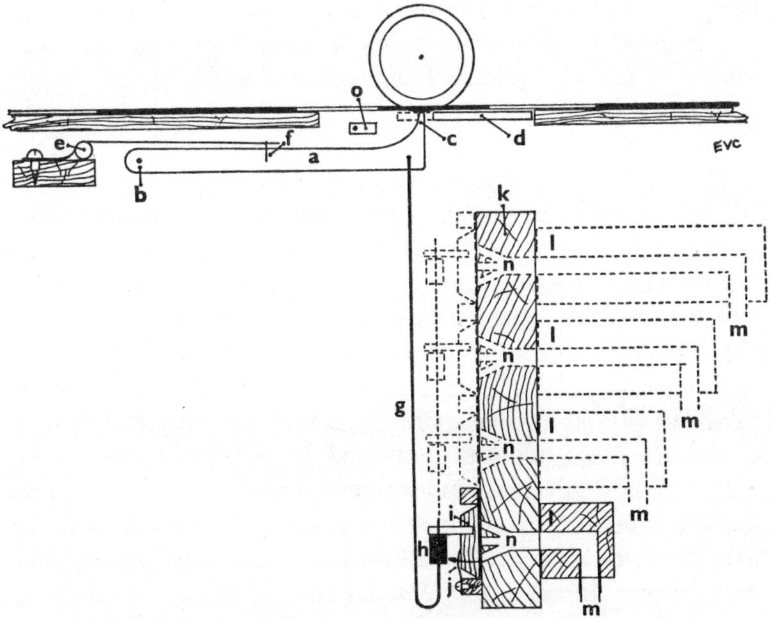

Fig 20. Keyed frame, exhaust system with four touch-boxes, Hooghuys

The channel board (*k*) has four inlet manifolds (*l*) connected to it. The widths of these are such that the supply pipes (*m*) from the primary mechanism can be neatly and easily connected. Each connecting channel in the board (*n*) divides into three smaller escape channels in a similar manner to the other exhaust pneumatic mechanism just described.

The method of operation should be clear from the diagram. When a key rises under spring pressure the leather button (*h*) on the connecting rod (*g*) presses against the shoulder on the pallet (*i*) and opens it, as indicated by the arrow. The escape of air causes a drop in pressure which operates the next part of the mechanism. This particular frame is well thought out and beautifully made. It can easily be disconnected from the organ and all parts are accessible for maintenance and repair. The scale of the organ to which this key frame is fitted is discussed in Chapter 6.

The pneumatic system found on organs with an exhaust pneumatic key frame has to incorporate a relay system, as the escape of air from the key frame is not sufficient to operate the action directly. This also applies to keyless organs. One such system is described in the following section.

Keyless Systems

The keyless frame can work only on the exhaust pneumatic system. A cut-away sketch of one version of the sensing device is shown in Figure 21. The keys found on a keyed frame are replaced by a row of outlet holes drilled in a metal plate (*a*), which forms the top of a wooden box. The interior of the box is divided into airtight compartments, one beneath each hole, by thin metal plates (*b*), let into the sides (*c*) of the box. Each compartment (*d*) has an inlet hole into which a short metal tube (*e*) is securely fixed. This is connected by a flexible tube to the corresponding part of the pneumatic action. To avoid overcrowding the tubes and to make construction and connection easier, half the inlet holes are drilled on one side of the box and half on the other. In addition, the holes on each side are arranged in two rows, holes being alternately in the upper and lower rows. This further simplifies connection. The bottom (*f*) of the box can be removed. A pad of felt (*g*) covered with thin leather (*h*) renders the connection airtight.

When the organ is playing each compartment of the box is filled with compressed air. The compressed air can get out only through the holes in the top of the box. These are, however,

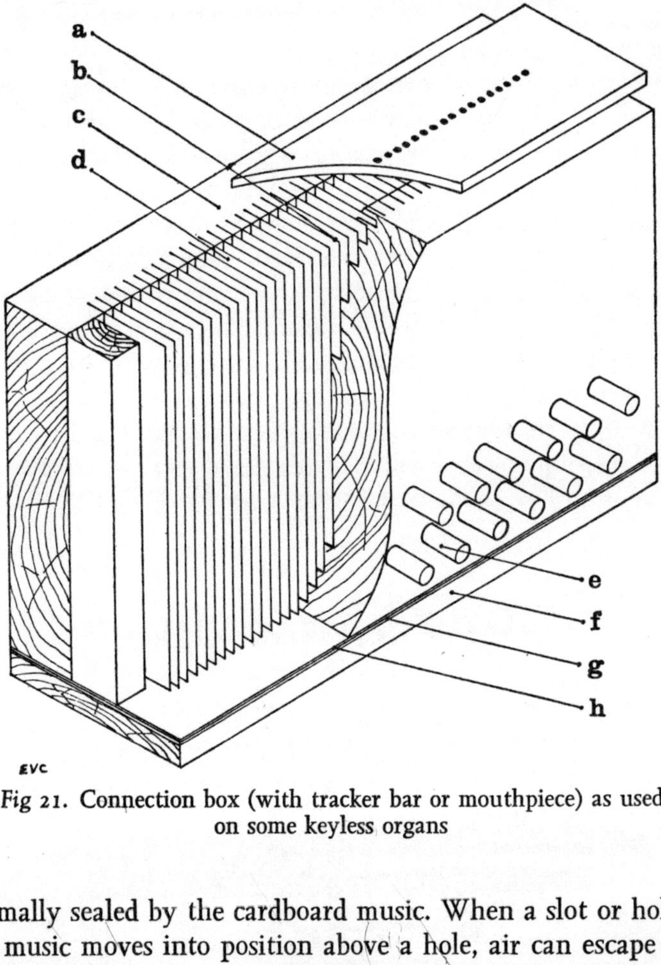

Fig 21. Connection box (with tracker bar or mouthpiece) as used on some keyless organs

normally sealed by the cardboard music. When a slot or hole in the music moves into position above a hole, air can escape into the atmosphere, via a corresponding groove in the metal roller which lies above it. The air pressure immediately falls, causing a pneumatic motor to operate. When the slot or hole in the music has moved on, the hole in the top of the box is once again covered by the cardboard and the air pressure immediately builds up again.

Connections could, of course, be made direct to the mouthpiece or tracker bar, as in instruments operated by perforated paper rolls. The box-type of construction, however, makes connection easier and also acts as a collector for dust which enters the holes and which would otherwise choke the pipes. The removable bottom of the box facilitates cleaning.

As stated above, organs using the exhaust pneumatic system have to incorporate a relay system between the key frame and the wind-chest. The relay pneumatics are sometimes referred to as the 'primary' system, and the wind-chest pneumatics as the 'secondary' system. The relay system to be described was devised, after a study of various methods, by a young Swiss enthusiast, who successfully used it to operate an organ of his own design.

The system is illustrated in Figure 22. It consists of a small wind-chest which is kept charged with compressed air from the main reservoir, via a port (*a*). The space inside the relay box will be referred to as space AA. Inside the box are a number of pneumatic motors (*b*), each of which connects by means of a tube (*c*) to a key frame outlet. The space inside each motor and

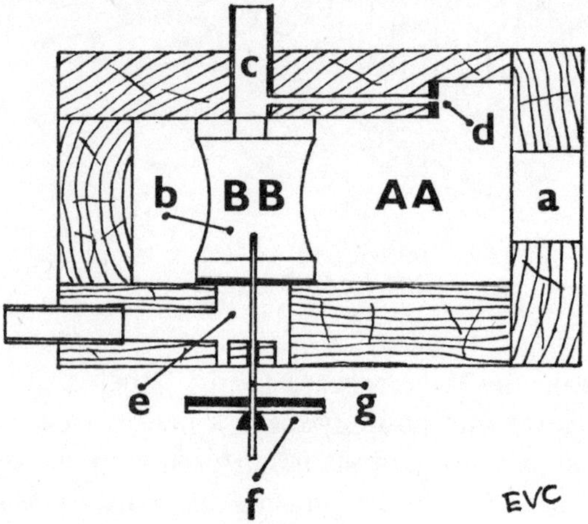

Fig 22. Primary pneumatic or relay system as used on some keyless organs

its tube will be referred to as space BB. A series of channels (*d*), about 5mm in diameter connect space AA with spaces BB.

The inlet to each channel is restricted by a metal plate in which a bleed hole 1·5mm (a little less than $\frac{1}{16}$in) in diameter is drilled. The size of the bleed hole calls for some experiment. The pneumatic motors are fixed by their upper parts to the roof of the chest. The lower parts are movable. Beneath each motor is an outlet hole (*e*) which connects both to the next part of the pneumatic system and to the atmosphere. The ports leading to the atmosphere can be closed as required by a valve (*f*) which is fixed to the lower part of the motor by a connecting rod (*g*). The method of operation is as follows.

When a pipe is silent the key frame outlet is sealed by the cardboard of the music. The air pressure in space BB is the same as the air pressure in space AA, that is, it is above atmospheric pressure, since the two spaces communicate by means of channel (*d*) and the small bleed hole. As the whole apparatus is in a state of pneumatic equilibrium the lower part of the motor rests, due to its own weight, on the bottom of the wind-chest, thus sealing the outlet hole.

When a hole in the music coincides with a key frame outlet, compressed air is released from the space BB into the atmosphere, until the pressure in space BB is the same as that of the atmosphere. The pressure in space BB is now lower than the pressure in space AA. The pneumatic motor (*b*) consequently contracts, lifting itself from the bottom of the wind-chest and uncovering the outlet hole (*e*). At the same time, by means of the connecting rod (*g*), it lifts the valve (*f*) on the outside of the chest and seals the channels leading to the atmosphere. Compressed air from space AA now passes to the main wind-chest.

It must be remembered that compressed air from space AA can enter space BB through the bleed hole. This happens all the time the key frame outlet is uncovered. The air, however, can escape as rapidly as it can enter, as the key frame outlet is larger than the bleed hole. Therefore no pressure is built up in space BB, which remains at atmospheric pressure.

As soon as the key frame outlet ceases to coincide with a hole in the music the escape route is blocked and pressure begins to build up immediately in space BB until a state of pneumatic equilibrium is again reached between spaces AA and BB. As this happens the lower part of the motor drops down under its own weight and seals the outlet hole, cutting off the supply of compressed air to the main wind-chest. At the same time the exhaust port opens. The main wind-chest is of conventional design.

Key Frame Muting Systems

Arrangements have to be made to mute the key frame when the music is removed, otherwise all the notes of the organ would sound at once.

A simple way of doing this was devised by Anselme Gavioli and patented by him (specification 11,044 of 1895). It consisted of a small lever attached to the key frame which was moved by the operator before a music book was removed from the frame. This cut off the air supply to the key frame and consequently muted the keys. The lever was moved in the opposite direction when the next music book was inserted, thus making the keys operative again. The efficiency of such a device obviously depended on the alertness of the operator and it is reasonable to assume that organs fitted with this device must have 'howled' badly at times.

A better method of muting the keys was by means of a small plunger. When the upper part of the frame was lifted the plunger rose, cutting off the air supply. When a new music book was placed in position and the upper part of the frame lowered the plunger was depressed and the key frame became operative again. A sophisticated version of this arrangement is now in more or less general use. With this arrangement one of the keys on the key frame is used to work an air valve which controls the air supply to the key frame. This is a much neater method and the key selected is usually one of the outermost keys of the key frame so that it is first to rise when the top part of the key frame is lifted.

Sometimes organ owners cut a small notch in the edge of the music so that the muting key rises a short time before the others, thus ensuring that the organ is muted in good time.

A similar arrangement is found on keyless organs. On these one of the holes is connected to the air valve. Cases have been observed where the muting hole is either slightly elongated or drilled out of line so that it comes into operation a little before the other keys.

Another method of silencing the key frame is by means of a lever which depresses all the keys at once, and keeps them in this position until it is moved in the opposite direction.

An elaboration of this method is found on Hooghuys organs. A metal bar of rectangular cross-section is fitted across the frame, just above the upper surfaces of the keys. A notch is cut in the bar above the key frame cut-off key. The bar is so pivoted that when the longer faces are horizontal the keys are able to rise. When the bar is turned through a quarter circle, so that the longer faces are vertical, all the keys except the key frame key are depressed and rendered inoperative. The key frame key can still remain in the 'up' position, due to the notch in the bar. When the key frame key rises it operates a pneumatic motor which is built into the key frame. This moves the bar through a quarter circle, from the position in which it allows the keys to rise to the position in which it depresses them all, except the key frame key. The bar can only be returned to its original position when the key frame key is depressed by the music. This cuts off the air supply to the motor and exhausts it. The bar can then be returned to its original position by means of a hand lever. It was not, apparently, practical or desirable, to make the return spring sufficiently strong to rotate the muting bar its required quarter turn in the opposite direction. In practice the keys are automatically muted at the end of a music book or when one is removed from the frame. The operator resets the mechanism by means of the hand lever, but this cannot be done until a new music book has been inserted in the frame and the bridge lowered. Part of this mechanism can be seen on page 53 (left) and Figure 20 (o).

Another mechanism is illustrated in Figure 23. This is an air valve which controls the supply of wind from the reservoir to the key frame touch-boxes. It consists of two hollowed-out wooden blocks (X and Y). Block X has two cavities in it, side by side, one of which (*a*) is connected to the key frame touch-boxes, while the other (*b*) is connected to the main air supply. A leather diaphragm (Z) is positioned over the cavities. It is glued only round the edges of the block, as indicated by the dotted lines, and not to the wooden division between the two cavities. Block Y has one large cavity in it and is secured to block X by screws so that the diaphragm is sandwiched between

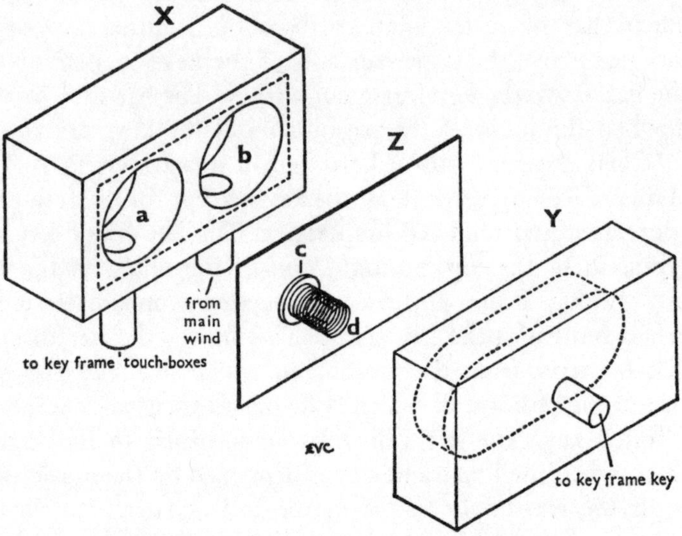

Fig 23. Device used to mute a key frame on removal of music

them. A spring (*d*) presses on the diaphragm, over the cavity (*a*) in block X. The diaphragm is suitably protected with a washer (*c*) of leather, cardboard, or similar material. The cavity in block Y is connected to the cut-off key on the frame. The device operates as follows.

When the organ is playing the music depresses the cut-off key. The air in the cavity in block Y is, therefore, at atmospheric pressure as no air reaches it from the key frame touch-box. This means that air from the reservoir, which is above atmospheric pressure, presses the diaphragm (Z) outwards. Air is thus able to pass from cavity (*a*) to cavity (*b*) and so supply the touch-boxes on the frame with air. When the key frame key rises, either because the music runs out, or because the bridge of the frame is lifted, air is fed into the cavity in block Y from the key frame as the valve for the cut-off key on the touch-box is open. The air pressure is now the same on both sides of the diaphragm and the pressure of the spring in block Y presses on the diaphragm and prevents air passing to the touch-boxes from the main wind supply.

The spring pressure obviously has to be very carefully adjusted so that the key frame wind cuts in and out as required. It would seem that the device is rather more suitable for small organs than large ones.

THE TRACKER BAR

Organs using paper roll music operate in a similar way to player pianos. The air in the pneumatic system which works the action is below atmospheric pressure and notes are sounded by the entry of air from the atmosphere into this part of the system, via holes in the tracker bar. This necessitates having a suction reservoir, for the action, and a pressure reservoir, for sounding the pipes and other effects.

The system to be described is found on a number of Wurlitzer band organs, including the 165. A description of the main wind-chest is included for two reasons. First, this pneumatic system is built as a whole, with the various parts interacting. Second, the system used on the main wind-chest is different from those already described.

As far as the action is concerned, the sequence of operations begins at the tracker bar where the music is read. It then passes to the primary pneumatic and on to the secondary pneumatic which operates the pallet, causing a note to play. The general layout is shown in Figure 24. Certain simplifications have been made in order to clarify the method of operation.

The music is wound from a supply spool (*a*) to a take-up spool (*b*) and in the process passes over the tracker bar (*c*). This is approximately the width of the music and is built up from two narrow strips of wood, one of which is faced with metal. Holes

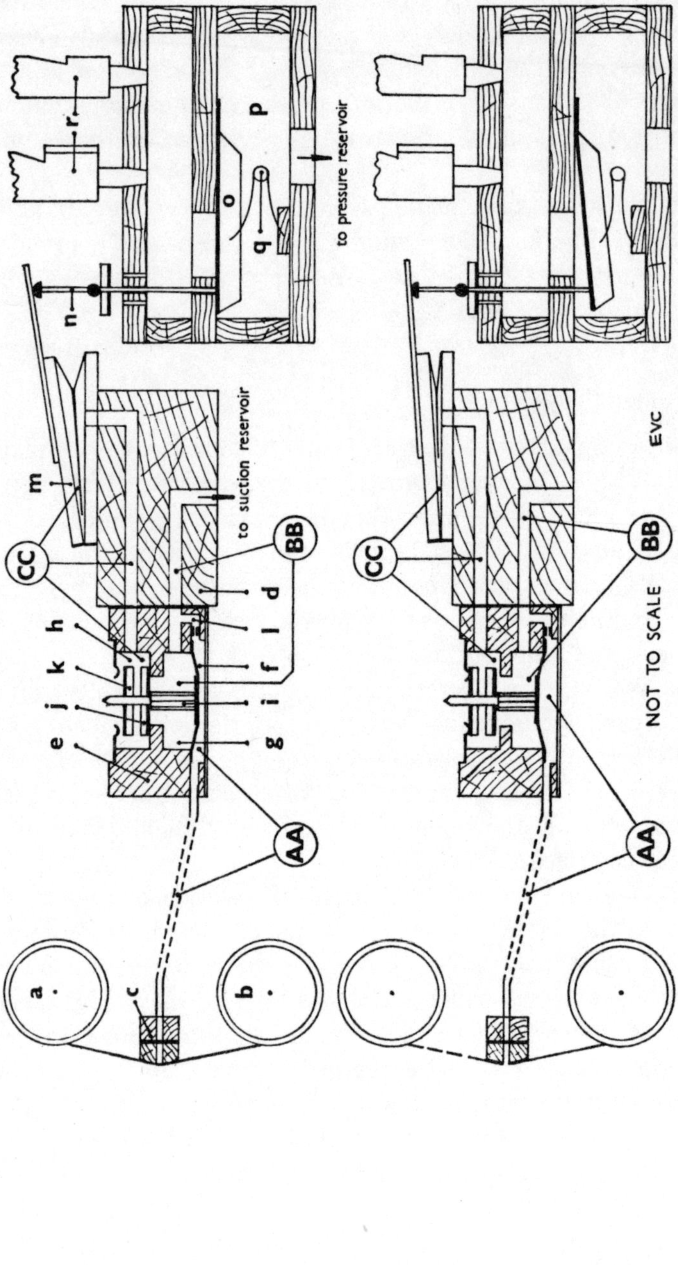

Fig 24. Pneumatic system used on some Wurlitzer organs (paper roll operated)

are drilled in the tracker bar to correspond with the perforations in the music. The two parts of the tracker bar are normally held together by bolts and knurled nuts. The inside faces are covered with thin leather. Sandwiched between them is a piece of very fine brass gauze which filters dust. If the knurled nuts are slackened the front part of the tracker bar can be removed, exposing the gauze, which can then be removed for cleaning. The 165 has twin tracker bars and this feature enables music to be played continuously, as one roll can be rewound while another is playing. The tracker bars are connected by tubing to a pneumatic switching device and this is connected in turn, by tubes, to the suction wind-chest.

The suction wind-chest consists of a channel board (*d*) and a number of unit blocks (*e*) which will be referred to as the primary pneumatics. There is one primary pneumatic for each hole in the tracker bar. The Wurlitzer catalogue makes the following note.

> On this new wind-chest each complete valve is built into an individual unit block. Each unit valve block is held to the channel board of the chest by two screws. Compression springs keep these screws tight and the constant pressure takes up any shrinkage. To remove the valve to clean or adjust it, simply loosen up the two screws. Be sure to draw them tight again when replacing them. The motion of each valve is adjusted to the thousandth of an inch, and should require no readjustment.

Each unit valve block, which is of wood, measures about 2in × 2in × 1in (5cm × 5cm × 2·5cm). In the base is a small pneumatic motor or puff (*f*) which is connected to a hole in the tracker bar. Above the diaphragm of the puff are two compartments, one above the other. The lower compartment (*g*) is connected to the suction reservoir via a duct in the channel board, while the one above it (*h*) is connected, in a similar manner, to the secondary pneumatic. The diaphragm of the puff actuates a push-rod (*i*) to which is connected a pair of valves (*j* and *k*). These are so arranged that when the puff is deflated the lower compartment is sealed, while the upper one is connected to the atmosphere. When the puff is inflated the upper compartment is connected to the lower compartment and the former's outlet to the atmosphere is sealed. A channel (*l*) drilled in the woodwork connects the inside of the puff to the lower compartment. The diameter of the channel is reduced by means of a brass nipple in which a small hole is drilled. The diameter of this bleed hole is critical and must be less than the diameter of the hole in the tracker bar. It will be seen that there are three connections to each primary pneumatic—to the tracker bar, the suction reservoir, and the secondary pneumatic, the latter two by way of the channel board.

The secondary pneumatic (*m*) consists of a small motor of the bellows type, measuring about 2½in × ¾in (6·35cm × 2cm). The upper part is free to move and is connected by means of a push-rod or sticker (*n*), about ⅛in (3·18mm) in diameter, to the appropriate pallet (*o*) in the main wind-chest (*p*). The lower part of the motor is fixed to the channel board. In the rest position the motor is at atmospheric pressure and is kept open by the pressure of the pallet spring (*q*) against the pallet. On top of the wind-chest are the pipes (*r*).

For purposes of description, the system will be divided into three sections as far as operating pressures are concerned. Section AA includes the inside of the tube from the tracker bar to the puff, and the inside of the puff. Section BB includes the lower chamber in the primary pneumatic and the inside of the duct in the channel board which leads to the suction reservoir. Sections AA and BB are connected by the bleed hole. Section CC includes the upper chamber of the primary pneumatic, the inside of the duct in the channel board leading to the secondary pneumatic, and the space inside the latter.

A cycle of operations begins when the music is in position. Assume that all mechanisms have been switched off for a short time. The air pressure throughout the system will, therefore, have adjusted itself to that of the atmosphere. The valve asembly in the primary pneumatic will have dropped down under its own weight, sealing the lower chamber and opening the upper to the atmosphere. The secondary pneumatic is kept open by the pressure of the pallet spring. This is the position shown in the upper diagram. We will now switch on the pumps and charge the reservoirs.

The pressure reservoir will fill the main wind-chest (*q*) with compressed air, ready to sound the pipes (*r*).

The suction reservoir will reduce the air pressure in section BB. This reduction in pressure will help to keep the lower valve closed. The air in section AA will also be reduced in pressure as this section is connected with section BB by the bleed hole. The suction exerted will draw the music against the holes in the tracker bar and seal section AA from the atmosphere. (This process is assisted by the natural tendency of the music to travel in a straight line from supply to take-up spool.) The air in sections AA and BB is, therefore, at less than atmospheric pressure. The air in section CC is at atmospheric pressure since this part of the system is open to the atmosphere via the opening in the top of the primary pneumatic.

We will now assume that the music is in motion and that a hole in it has coincided with a hole in the tracker bar. The position will be as shown in the lower diagram. Air from the atmosphere can enter section AA which will now be at a higher pressure than section BB. The diaphragm of the puff will be distended due to the increase in the pressure and it will lift the valve assembly. It must be remembered that sections AA and BB are connected by the bleed hole. As mentioned above, the hole in the tracker bar is larger than the bleed hole. Air can enter section AA through the hole in the tracker bar more rapidly than it can pass through the bleed hole to section BB. Air in section AA, therefore, remains at atmospheric pressure (or nearly so) and the diaphragm of the puff remains distended. As the valve assembly is now lifted the lower valve is open and sections BB and CC will be connected. At the same time the upper valve closes the outlet which section CC formerly had to the atmosphere. The air which is trapped in section CC is sucked out via section BB due to the suction exerted by the suction reservoir. The air in sections BB and CC is now below atmospheric pressure. The secondary pneumatic collapses. This is because the air pressure inside it is reduced and the pressure of the atmosphere can overcome the pressure exerted by the pallet spring. The sticker opens the pallet in the wind-chest and the pipe sounds.

When the hole in the music has moved on, paper prevents air from the atmosphere entering section AA. The position now reverts to that shown in the upper diagram. Any air left in space AA is sucked out via the bleed hole, and pressure on each side of the puff's diaphragm is equalised. It can no longer remain distended and the valve assembly drops down under its own weight. This motion is accelerated by the suction effect exerted by section BB and by the tendency of air from the atmosphere to rush into section CC. The lower valve seals section BB and disconnects it from section CC. The upper valve is now open and section CC is again connected to the atmosphere. The pallet spring can force both the pallet shut and the motor open, since section CC is disconnected from the suction reservoir and open to the atmosphere. The note ceases to sound. The system is now ready for another cycle of operations.

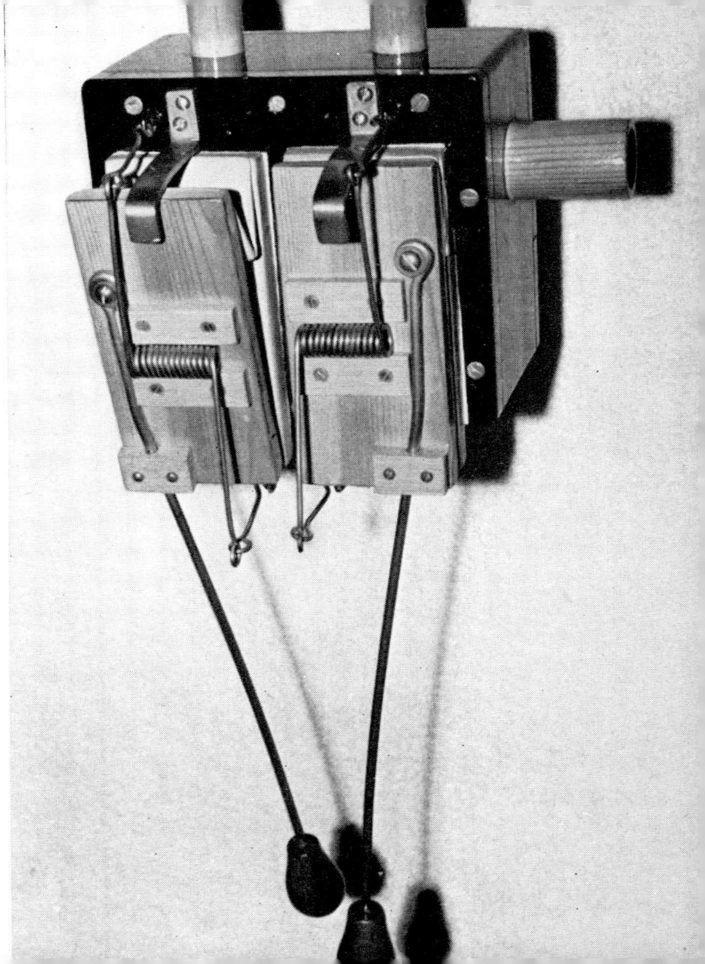

Page 89: (*left*) Part of a vox humana register—reeds backed by stopped flutes (on a 70 key Hooghuys dance organ); (*right*) side-drum mechanism

Page 90: *(above)* A set of four temple blocks (on the front of a 92 key continental dance organ); *(centre)* one of the famous Marenghi grelotphones, or 'sleigh bells' (on a 98 key Marenghi); *(below)* a vertically mounted xylophone (on a 70 key Hooghuys dance organ). Swell shutters, in the open position, can be seen in the background

4 Registers

ALL but the smallest organs, whether mechanical or otherwise, are fitted with a variety of registers or stops, the two terms being synonymous. At the risk of oversimplifying, a register can be defined as a rank of pipes, each pipe of which has a similar timbre and loudness to those on each side of it in the musical scale. Both timbre and loudness may vary, however, from one end of the scale to the other. The pipes differ from each other in pitch, as they play a musical scale. One register or rank differs from others in timbre, loudness, or pitch, or any combination of these factors. In certain circumstances every rank may not contain the same numbers of notes, that is, some may be 'short compass' ranks. By using registers on their own, or by using them in combination or contrast, tonal effects and variety can be introduced into the music.

In a manually played instrument the organist controls a register by means of a movable knob or tab. Movement in one direction sets the register and movement in the other cancels it. The rest of the operation is done by mechanical, pneumatic, or electrical means, or by a combination of two or all of these methods. The organ may have several keyboards, played either by the organist's hands (manuals) or by his feet (pedals). Each keyboard is named (great, swell, choir, etc) and it is connected to a group of registers. In all but the smallest of mechanical organs a similar arrangement is found, although the key frame takes the place of the key and pedal boards of a manually played organ. The keys in the frames of the larger mechanical instruments are divided into groups—melody, counter melody, accompaniment, and bass—and in one case known to the writer there is even a second counter-melody group. Each group of keys is connected to certain registers, the number and allocation of which depends on the size and type of the instrument. A large mechanical organ may have over twenty separate registers and these are sometimes changed every few bars.

Register changing is done entirely automatically and in accordance with the music marker's intentions. What registers an organ has, of course, is decided by the organ builder, and he allocates certain keys or outlets on the key frame or tracker bar to control them. The music marker ensures that the music he is preparing is punched with the necessary holes or slots to effect the register changes he has in mind. As the music passes through the key frame or over the tracker bar signals relating to register changes are sent to the register box, which is a form of relay or servo mechanism. In turn, the register box passes the signals on to other mechanisms which control the air supplies from the wind-chests to the pipes of each individual register. This, then, is the sequence of events by which registers are operated: music—register relay box—wind control mechanisms.

CONTROLS IN THE MUSIC

Using slots or holes in the music to change registers, at first sight, seems simple enough. Let us do what the organist does when he wants to set a register, that is, allow one of the keys on the key frame to rise when we want a register to play, and lower it when we want to cancel the register. This, however, would mean that a very long continuous slot would have to be cut in the music book while the register was in play—not a very practical proposition as the music would be seriously weakened. A slight variation of this method is used on some small keyless organs which operate from cardboard music perforated with round holes as opposed to rectangular slots. In these circumstances a continuous row of round holes appears in the music when a register is on. Sometimes, on small organs with only one register the opposite applies, the holes being used to disconnect certain pipes.

A second solution would be to use the same key for both setting and cancelling. Let the key set the register the first time it is raised and cancel it when it is raised for the second time. This is quite a possible solution—unless we remove a music book before it is finished, thus leaving some registers set and some cancelled. When a new music book is inserted registers will be set when they should be cancelled and vice versa. Anselme Gavioli patented an idea to solve this problem (specification 1083 of 1901). A special key was to be attached to the key frame, which could be worked manually by the organ operator. Before inserting a new music book he was to operate the key, the effect of which would be to cancel all registers. Registers would then be set as required by the new music book when it was inserted. The weakness of this arrangement was that it depended on the alertness of the organ operator—not always a thing to be relied on!

A third solution would be to have two keys for each register, one for 'on' and one for 'off'. This would make the whole process completely reliable but would mean, for example, that an organ with four registers would require eight keys allocated to register control. (Two keys are, in fact, used on small organs which have only one register, one key for on and one for off.)

A very effective solution has, however, been arrived at. Each register is allocated a key which sets it, but all registers are cancelled simultaneously by one common key. Thus, an organ with four registers will need only five keys to effect complete control, four for setting and one for cancelling. Slots are cut in the music book to operate the keys which bring the various registers into play. Another slot is cut to operate the key which cancels all registers. (This function is known in French as 'declanche' and in Dutch as 'afsluiter'. The nearest English equivalent is probably 'general cancel' or, colloquially, 'all off'.) The mechanism for register changing is so arranged that the setting mechanism is capable of overriding that of cancellation.

A cycle of operations is shown diagramatically in Figure 25. The organ is assumed to have three registers—violins, clarinets, and trumpets. At the beginning of the music book, before any notes are played, all registers are usually cancelled, as shown at (*a*) and the registers to be used, eg clarinets and trumpets, are set. Note that although the 'general cancel' or 'all off' key is operated at the same time as the setting keys, the operation of the latter overrides that of the former. If, however, the violins had been left in play because the previous music book had been removed halfway through, they would be cancelled, as the violin register is not required at the beginning of the music book now to be used. It should also be noted that the slots for setting are about twice as long as that used for cancelling. At (*b*) the clarinet register is cancelled and the trumpets are kept set. At (*c*) the violins are brought into play. The 'general cancel' is not used as it is not necessary to cancel any registers. Some music markers, however, make a habit of cancelling all registers at

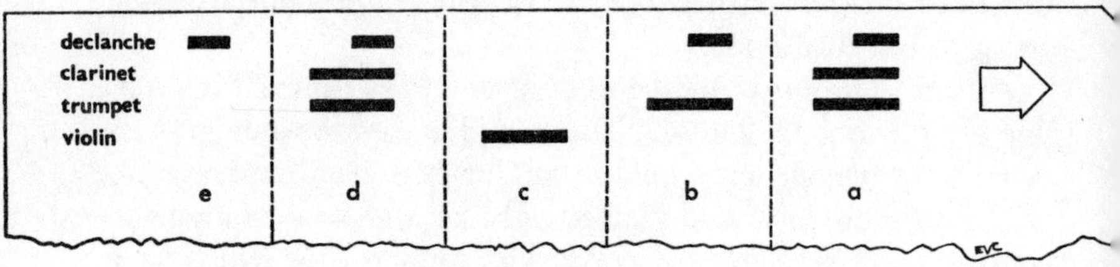

Fig 25. Method of making register changes by means of slots in a cardboard music book

every change and resetting them as required. At (*d*) three different manoeuvres are executed. The clarinets are set, the trumpets are kept set and the violins are cancelled. Finally at (*e*), at the end of the music, some markers cancel all registers ready for the next book.

On a manually played organ there are additional controls which, for example, enable the organist to play notes which are an octave apart from the same key ('octave couplers'), to play registers associated with one keyboard from another ('keyboard couplers') and to bring on and cancel certain prearranged groups of registers ('pistons'). The majority of these controls are rendered necessary because the player has only two hands of limited span, and two feet, and a limited amount of time at his disposal to effect the changes he wants. On a mechanical organ no such limitations apply as any combination of notes can be played at once. Similarly, the most complicated register changes can be carried out in a fraction of a second. The number of operational controls on a mechanical organ is, therefore, less than that on a manually played instrument of comparable size, as the controls do not have to be duplicated and grouped for easy operation by the player's hands or feet. Neither is it necessary to set up certain prearranged combinations of registers so that they can be operated simultaneously by one control. It is because of this, because of the speed and precision with which registers can be changed, and because of the great economy of pipework, that a mechanical organ can produce effects which one would expect only from a larger manually played instrument. To a certain extent, even the effects produced by second touch can be obtained.

REGISTER RELAY BOX

Register changing signals pass from the key frame, or tracker bar, to the register relay box. A typical box by which several registers are controlled is shown in cross-section in Figure 26. The valve arrangement is similar to that found on some types of keyed frames. It consists of a small wind-chest (*a*) connected to the main air supply at (*b*) and fitted with a pair of valves (*c*) and (*d*) for each register it controls. Beneath the wind-chest is a puff-board (*e*) with a puff (*f*) lying beneath each pair of valves. A similar puff-board (*g*) is fixed to the front of the wind-chest. A simple arrangement of levers (*h*) and (*i*) completes the apparatus. When the levers are raised the registers are engaged, or on. When they are lowered the registers are off. The method of operation is as follows.

A register is set when the appropriate key on the key frame rises. This inflates the lower puff (*f*) and lifts the horizontal part of the lever system (*h*), which in turn raises the vertical lever (*i*) to which it is connected. Pressure from a spring (*j*) latches it on to a catch (*k*). The lower valve (*d*) is now shut due to the pressure exerted by a flat metal spring (*q*), which is attached to the lever (*h*). As the lower valve (*d*) shuts, so the inside valve (*c*) opens. Compressed air can now pass from the small wind-chest (*a*) to the third and final part of the register control system, via the outlet channel (*l*). Thus, although only a short puff of air is received from the key frame, the mechanism is so arranged that continuous air pressure is applied to the last stage of the system.

The puffs on the front of the box are connected together by a channel (*m*) which, in turn, is connected to the general cancel key on the key frame. When this key rises air is admitted to all the puffs (*n*) on the front of the box, causing them to expand simultaneously. They push against any vertical levers (*i*) which are in the on position and force them off their catches (*k*), causing them to drop down. In turn, they lower the horizontal levers (*h*) to which they are pivoted. This allows the outside valve (*d*) underneath the small wind-chest to open. As this valve is coupled to the inside valve by a short metal rod (*o*) the inside valve (*c*)

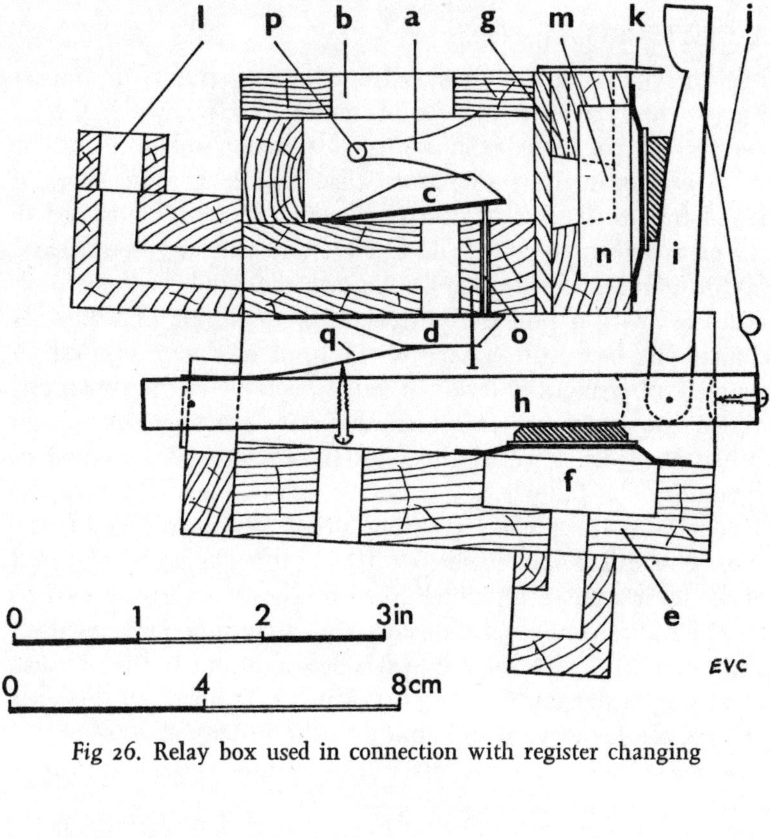

Fig 26. Relay box used in connection with register changing

closes, due to spring pressure (*p*). This shuts off the supply of compressed air to the final stage of the system and the register ceases to play.

Let us now see how we set, cancel, and keep set certain registers at the same time. As already mentioned, the setting mechanism overrides that of cancellation. Thus, if both upper and lower puffs are inflated at the same time the levers rise and open the inside valve. When the cancellation puff presses against the vertical lever, however, the lever cannot drop as it is kept lifted by the setting puff. As soon as the cancellation puff is deflated, the locking spring pushes the lever onto the catch, securing it in the on position. This works because the slots in the music for the general cancel and for setting the register begin at the same time, but the setting slots are longer, as it is necessary to hold up the lever (*h*) for a short time after the general cancel is exhausted, so that the locking spring (*j*) can latch the vertical lever (*i*) onto its catch (*k*). The box just described, and another are illustrated on page 54.

SLIDERS AND AIR VALVES

The third and final stage of the register control system consists of a means of shutting off and turning on the air supply to the pipes. Three methods will be described.

The first is sometimes used in small organs when the pipes to be controlled are mounted directly on the main wind-chest. It could, however, be used equally well in connection with off-note chests. Inside the chest and beneath the feet of the pipes runs a perforated wooden strip, rather like an outsize piece of Meccano. This can move a short distance lengthways. In one position the perforations in the strip coincide with the outlets in the wind-chest to the rank of pipes concerned. The register is then on. When the strip is moved lengthways so that the holes no longer coincide with the outlets to the pipes the register is off and, therefore, ceases to play. Large pneumatic motors move the strip as required.

The second method uses a ventil or air valve in conjunction with an off-note chest. Figures 14a–b illustrated an off-note chest

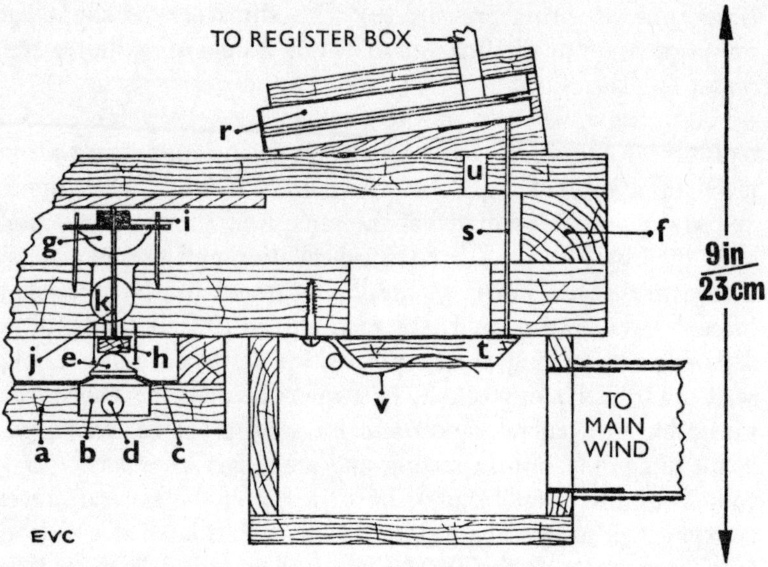

Fig 27. Ventil, or air valve, used in connection with register changing (cross-section along YY of Figure 14a)

used in conjunction with a xylophone mechanism, which incorporates a ventil. A cross-section along the line YY is shown in Figure 27. (The parts indicated by the reference letters (*a*) to (*i*) have already been discussed in Chapter 2 and need not concern us now.) The remainder of the mechanism comprises the ventil and has two component parts, the motor and the pallet. The motor (*r*) is mounted on top of the wind-chest and is connected to the register box. A push-rod (*s*) connects it to the spring-loaded pallet valve (*t*) which is boxed in and connected to the main air supply. When the xylophone register is on, a supply of air comes from the register box which inflates, and keeps inflated the pallet motor. The lower board of the motor is the one which is free to move and it carries out two functions. First, it opens the pallet by means of the push-rod (*s*) and, second, it seals the outlet hole (*u*). The under-surface of the motor's lower-board is faced with leather to make the seal effective.

When the ventil pallet (*t*) is opened, air at a greater pressure than that of the atmosphere enters the wind-chest and charges it with air. When the xylophone register is cancelled by the operation of the declanche the air supply to the ventil motor (*r*) is cut off. The pallet spring (*v*) is now able to close the pallet and shut off the air supply. Also, by means of the push-rod (*s*) it collapses the motor located above the wind-chest. This opens the escape hole (*u*) and any air remaining in the wind-chest escapes into the atmosphere. The hammer-striking mechanism is now rendered inoperative.

The action of this particular arrangement is slightly different when used in conjunction with pipes. In this case, when the ventil is shut the wind-chest is robbed of air and the pipes cannot sound, although the pallets continue to operate.

A third register control system is illustrated in Figure 28. The pipes are not mounted directly on the wind-chest. Instead, a block of wood (*a*) intervenes. A number of holes (*b*) and (*c*) are drilled in the block, two for each pipe. The lower hole of the pair

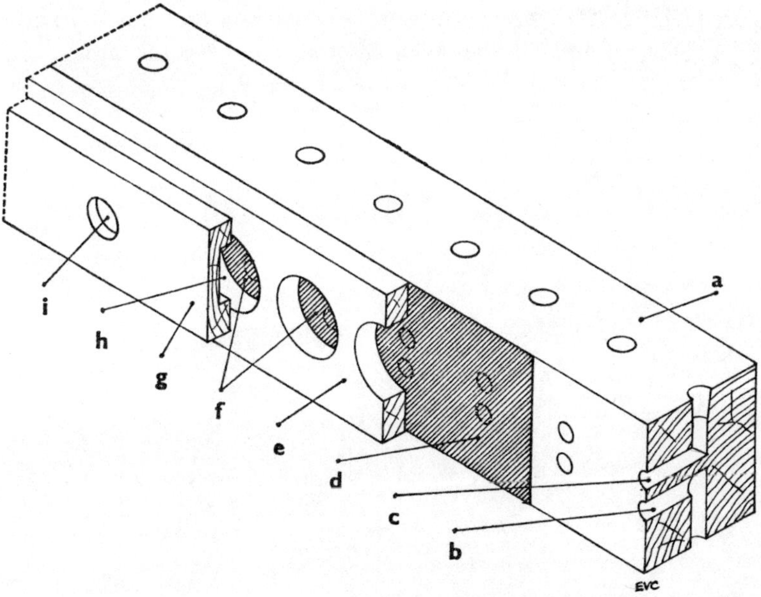

Fig 28. An unusual method of register control (believed to have been used by Ruth)

(*b*) leads to the wind-chest, while the upper (*c*) leads to the opening in which the foot of the pipe stands. A piece of thin leather (*d*) covers the side of the block in which the holes are drilled. This is held in place by a strip of wood (*e*) in which a number of circular holes (*f*) are drilled. This piece of wood is, in turn, covered by another (*g*), which has a channel (*h*) cut in it. The channel communicates with the main wind supply at inlet (*i*). The method of operation is as follows.

When the register is off, compressed air from the main wind supply is fed into the inlet port (*i*). It passes along channel (*h*) into each of the circular holes (*f*). The leather strip (*d*) is forced against the holes (*b*) and (*c*) and thus prevents air passing from one to the other. This means that the pipes cannot sound. When the register is on, the air in the device is reduced to atmospheric pressure. When this happens air can pass from hole (*b*) to hole (*c*) as it can move the leather (*d*) to one side to make a passage and thus sound the pipe. When the register is off the device is again charged with air. The leather now presses against each pair of holes and the connection between the two holes (*b*) and (*c*) is blocked and air is prevented from reaching the pipes.

5 Pipework—Percussions —Prosceniums

THE subject of pipework is wide and it is neither possible nor desirable, in a book of this size, to cover all aspects. The first part of this chapter, therefore, concentrates on mechanical organ pipework, with a minimum of technical background. Many books on the manually played organ contain a great deal of information on pipework which is applicable to the mechanical organ, as do books on the physics of music. The reader should, therefore, refer to these if he wants to explore the subject more fully.

Organ pipes can be divided into two types, flues and reeds, both of which are found on fair organs. As the fair organ is subjected to a considerable amount of movement and to very variable weather conditions certain pipes have been specially developed to meet these circumstances. Many of the more robust pipes found on church and theatre organs are also used.

FLUES

A flue pipe is like a large whistle. The body consists of a hollow tube narrowing at the bottom to a foot. A horizontal slot, known as the mouth, is cut in the lower part of the body. The top and bottom edges of the mouth are known respectively as the upper and lower lips. A block, or languid, closes the bottom of the pipe except for a narrow windway behind the lower lip. Air emerges from this as a narrow jet and meets the sharp upper lip. Eddies or edge tones are set up and the main column of air in the body of the pipe resonates in sympathy with some of these, causing the pipe to speak. Flue pipes can be made of either wood or metal, although the majority of flue pipes on a fair organ are wooden.

As a general rule the length of a flue pipe determines the note it plays. The shorter the pipe, the higher the note; the longer the pipe, the lower the note. If we begin with middle 'C', which is sounded by a pipe about two feet (sixty-one centimetres) long, we have to halve the length every time we raise the pitch by an octave; similarly, we have to double the length every time we lower the pitch by an octave. Various notations are used to indicate the pitch of a note when writing about musical instruments. One of these is shown in Figure 29 together with the appropriate length of an open pipe which will sound the required note.

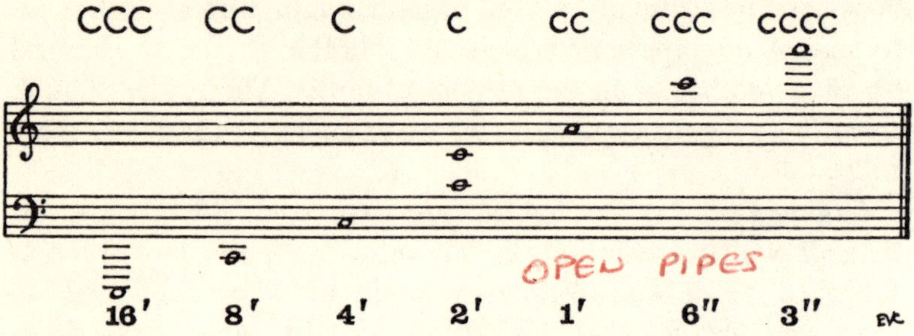

Fig 29. Relationship between pitch, pipe-length, and musical notation

If the end of a flue pipe is closed by a stopper the pitch is lowered by an octave and the pipe is known as a 'stopped' pipe. Middle C will, therefore, be sounded by a stopped pipe one foot long, and so on. Figure 30 illustrates this diagramatically. At (*a*) we have an open pipe sounding its fundamental. At (*b*) we have a stopped pipe sounding the same note as the open pipe at (*a*). A stopped pipe has a more 'fluty' timbre, as it sounds only the odd harmonics instead of the full range.

The tone of a flue pipe is affected by its scale, which is the ratio of its cross-sectional area to its speaking length. In general, large-scaled pipes give a less brilliant tone than those of small scales. On large-scaled pipes the diameter may halve every seventeenth or eighteenth note. With small-scaled pipes this cannot be done as the treble portion of some registers would be impracticably small. It will be found, therefore, that smaller-scaled ranks may halve on the twenty-second to the twenty-fourth note.

The pitch of a pipe can be raised if a small hole, known as a nodal hole, is drilled in the pipe. Figure 30 (*c*) shows the effect of drilling a nodal hole halfway along an open pipe, as indicated by the arrow. The pitch of the pipe is raised by an octave. As a stopped pipe sounds only the odd harmonics it is not possible to drill it so that it will speak the octave (or second harmonic) like an open pipe. It is, however, possible to make it sound the twelfth (the third harmonic) if a hole is drilled further from the mouth than the stopper, as at (*d*). An alternative position for the stopper is shown at (*e*); theoretically, the same note should continue to sound.

Nodal holes are drilled by organ builders to obtain certain

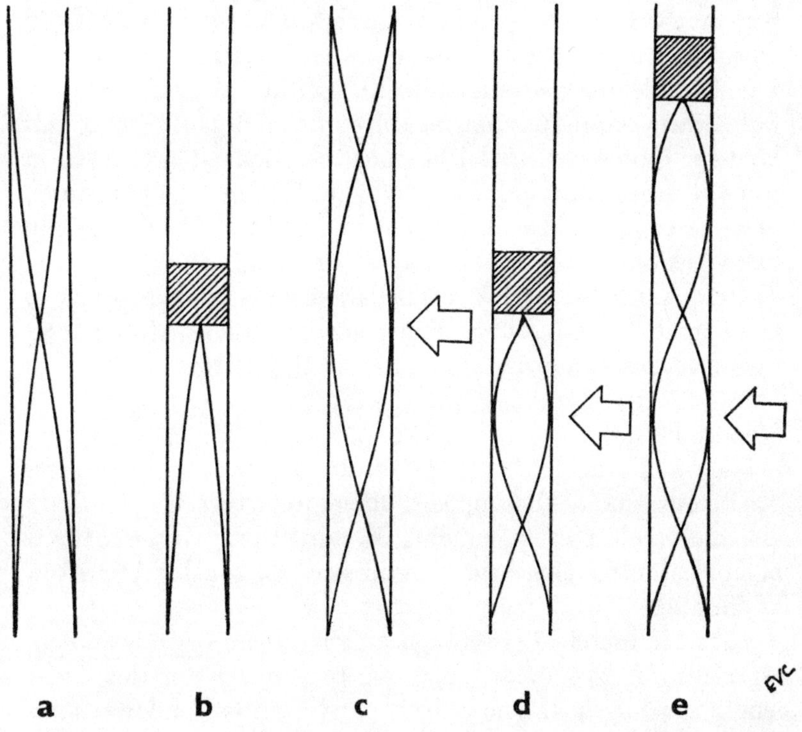

Fig 30. Effect of stoppers and nodal holes upon the pitch of a flue pipe

tonal effects which, although effective indoors, would not be particularly noticeable on a fair organ designed to play in the open air. Nevertheless, nodal holes are found in some fair organ pipes. A possible explanation is that, due to the high wind pressure with which fair organs operate, certain pipes would tend either to be unstable or to overblow, that is, sound the octave instead of the fundamental. By doubling the length of the pipe and drilling a nodal hole this could be avoided and the correct note would sound with certainty and promptness.

Open Flutes

The open flute is of reasonably large scale. It can be made of either wood or metal, though on the fair organ it is usually of wood. The fairground organ's open flute is a general-purpose pipe and is used with other flues and reeds to achieve a variety of tonal effects in all registers. It closely resembles its counterpart on the manually played organ, but it is not to be confused with the orchestral flute. Flute pipes are sometimes drilled with a nodal hole and, therefore, qualify for the name of 'harmonic flute', their counterpart on the conventional organ. Pipes of this kind are quite often found mounted nearly at ground level, in front of the organ. These are usually made of metal. Quite often, in some continental dance organs one of the registers (usually known as 'flute 8') consists solely of a rank of open wood flutes. These are usually used in combination with other registers to build up tone and volume. But sometimes they play on their own and their pure tones produce pleasing effects.

Stopped Flutes

Stopped flutes, like open flutes, are a general-purpose pipe. Their tone, due to the stoppers, differs from that of open flutes and they are useful for building up tonal effects. In mechanical organ parlance stopped flutes of all sizes are usually referred to as 'bourdons'.

They are useful in fairground organs, where space is limited, especially for bass notes. There are two reasons for this. First, length for length, the note they sound is an octave lower than that sounded by an open flute. Second, they can be mitred, that is, bent at right angles, without affecting the tone. The deep bass pipes are usually mounted beneath the organ case and, since deep notes are more or less non-directional, the musical effect is quite satisfactory. Figure 31 shows the way in which eight bass pipes are mitred so that they fit beneath the organ case. As a rule smaller pipes mounted elsewhere in the organ case sound with the longest bass pipes, building up a fuller tone as the smaller pipes supply the missing harmonics.

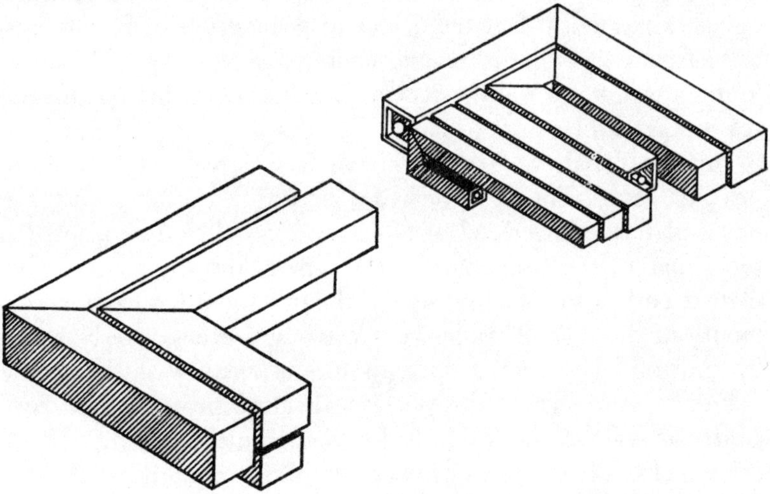

Fig 31. Method of accommodating long bass pipes beneath the case of 89 key Gavioli organ

Stopped flutes are often used in continental organs in the melody and counter-melody divisions of the scale. Two ranks of pipes are generally used and they are either identical in pitch, a fifth apart, an octave apart, or even a twelfth apart. Ranks of this nature usually have one rank in tune with the rest of the organ, while the other rank is tuned either slightly flat or sharp to produce an undulating effect.

Stopped flutes are sometimes drilled with a nodal hole.

Violins

The violins are open flue pipes of small scale and, as a consequence, they are much more slender, note for note, than ordinary open flutes. Their diameters usually halve on about every twenty-third note. The characteristic tone of the orchestral violin consists of the fundamental plus a generous supply of harmonics, both odd and even. To imitate this tone each pipe has to be of narrow cross-section compared with other pipes of similar pitch. This encourages the formation of harmonics but makes the pipe unstable, causing it to overblow. One device to prevent this happening is the roller-bridge, which consists of a wooden rod, of circular, elliptical, or rectangular cross-section fixed just outside the mouth. But the device in general use in fair organs is the harmonic brake or *frein harmonique*. According to Bonavia-Hunt, a well-known authority on church organs, this was invented by Charles Lemaire of Paris. The idea was patented in Great Britain on behalf of Messrs Gavioli & Company (specification 3013 of 1876). The *frein harmonique* consists of an adjustable metal plate the lower end of which is screwed to the cap of the pipe, that is, the front part of the pipe below the mouth. The plate is curved so that the edge of the other end lies close to the mouth of the pipe. This device effectively prevents overblowing by controlling the wind currents in the vicinity of the pipe's mouth. It also makes the pipe speak more promptly. A slot, nearly as wide as the inside width of the pipe, is usually cut in the top of either the front or back face of the pipe—normally the front. A metal plate, which runs in grooves behind this slot, can be raised or lowered to tune the pipe. As flue pipes are not as loud as reeds the necessary volume is built up by having several ranks of violins sounding in unison. The dimensions of each rank may vary slightly, so that minor tonal differences are created. Sometimes one or more ranks may speak an octave lower. The sounding of several pipes at once also helps to produce the characteristic singing effect of strings, due (among other things) to the fact that the various ranks can never be exactly in tune. The violin pipes are usually of varnished wood and they occupy a prominent position at the front of the organ. On some instruments, the sound produced is quite realistic. The deeper violins are usually known as cellos or bass cellos and on some organs the latter are used to reinforce the bourdon basses. The deeper string-toned pipes often have roller bridges instead of

Page 107: *(above)* Bass drum and cymbal mechanism. The bass drum plays on its own unless the pneumatic motor in the foreground is inflated. This operates the trip which causes the cymbal to sound with the bass drum (on an 84 key Mortier dance organ); *(below)* two bandmasters, with moving heads and articulated arms

Page 108: *(above)* An early roundabout (probably about 1880), rotated by horse power, with a small hand-turned trumpet barrel organ in the centre; *(below)* an early bioscope show, with a heavily carved front. A trumpet barrel organ is on the left. The bass drum on the left of the organ is played by hand, as are the brass bells on the right of the entrance. Note the electric light engine on the right, and compare it with the one illustrated on page 18 (lower). Notice also its extension chimney and carved screens. One of the films being shown is of the bombardment of Port Arthur, which took place during the Russo-Japanese war of 1904–5

freins to stabilise them. Two ranks of violin pipes are also used in the *unda maris* and *vox celeste* registers. One rank is tuned either slightly sharp or flat to produce an undulating tone which is effective if used with discretion.

Several views of a violin pipe are shown in Figure 32. At A is an isometric view without the *frein harmonique.* At B we have an enlarged view of the mouth of the pipe showing the *frein harmonique.* The top of the pipe is illustrated at C, which shows the tuning slot and slide. A section through the pipe is given at D with front and top elevations of the tuning slide and *frein harmonique.* The scale shown applies to sketch D and to the vertical scale of A. Sketches B and C are enlarged three times. The pipe on which the sketches are based is the top 'D' pipe from the violin register of an eighty-nine key organ. The front pipes on page 71 (above) are violins.

Piccolos

Piccolos appear on barrel, book, and paper roll organs of many different makes. They are found on Wurlitzer band and orchestral organs, and on other products of the USA. They are also found on the instruments made by Gaviolis, Marenghis, Limonaires, and Gasparinis. They have always been a popular feature of the trumpet organ. Piccolos are usually situated towards the front of the organ (possibly for acoustical reasons) and, although strictly functional, are of pleasing appearance. The piccolo pipe is not found in the same form on the church or theatre organ. Its origins are obscure but it was found on early street barrel organs in roughly the same form before it appeared in fairground organs.

The orchestral piccolo is the highest pitched instrument in the orchestra and, like the flute, is blown transversely, that is, as if one were blowing across the mouth of a bottle. Its tone, like that of the flute, is very pure with few overtones, the fundamental or first harmonic predominating. Organ piccolos, which are among the highest pitched pipes of the fair organ, are also blown transversely, the wind from the wind-chest being directed across the lower end of the vertical tube via a channel in the wooden base. The vertical tube is of metal or, occasionally, wood and

TOP D VIOLIN REGISTER

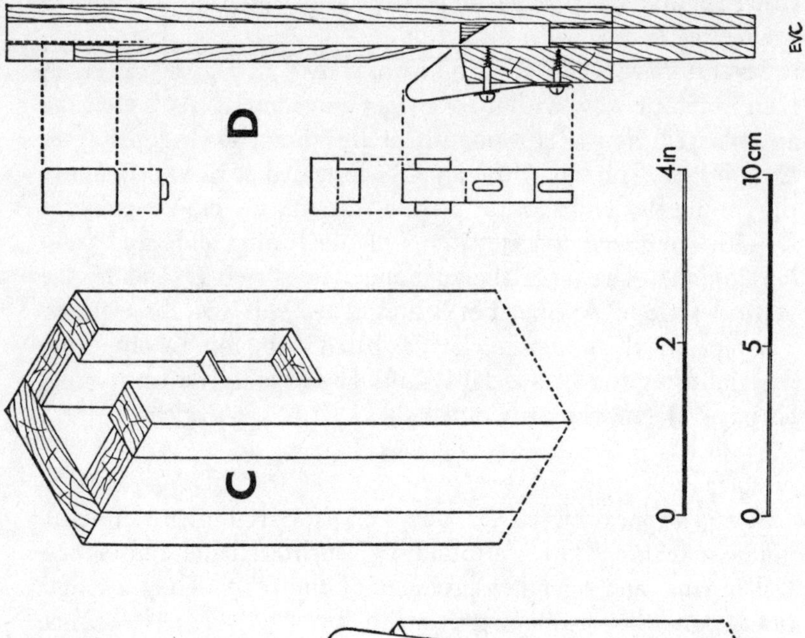

Fig. [illegible] Detail of a violin pi[illegible]

contains a plug. This is attached by means of a screwed rod to a wooden acorn at the top of the tube. Some piccolos have nodal holes drilled in them, usually at the back.

Organ builders may have thought that this unusual method of construction made the pipes sound as much as possible like their orchestral counterpart. Stopping certainly eliminates the even harmonics and may possibly, in this case, help to produce a purer tone. Today, however, some organ enthusiasts claim that no musical advantage is gained by this method of construction and are of the opinion that small wooden flute pipes would be just as effective. The range of the orchestral piccolo is shown in Figure 33, A. At B the range of the piccolos on an 89 key

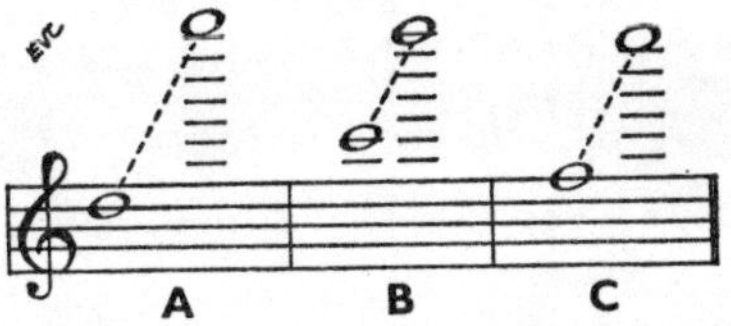

Fig 33. Range of orchestral and organ piccolos

organ is shown. There are seventeen notes, top D♯ being missing. The piccolos at C are those from a 65 key organ. There are twenty-one notes, top A♯ and D♯ being missing.

As a rule two wooden flute pipes play with each piccolo, sounding an octave or two octaves below it, or even a higher note than the actual piccolo pipe. These flutes may both be open, or one may be open and the other stopped. Both the open and the stopped pipes may be drilled with nodal holes.

Figure 34 includes two views of a piccolo pipe from a Marenghi organ. The note sounded is about top E on the piano. On the left is a side elevation, the wooden base of the pipe being about 20mm (¾in) thick. A nodal hole is drilled as indicated by the arrow, 43mm (1·69in) above the mouth. On the right is an exploded isometric view of the same pipe, to the same vertical scale. Piccolos, backed by stopped flutes can be seen on page 71 (below).

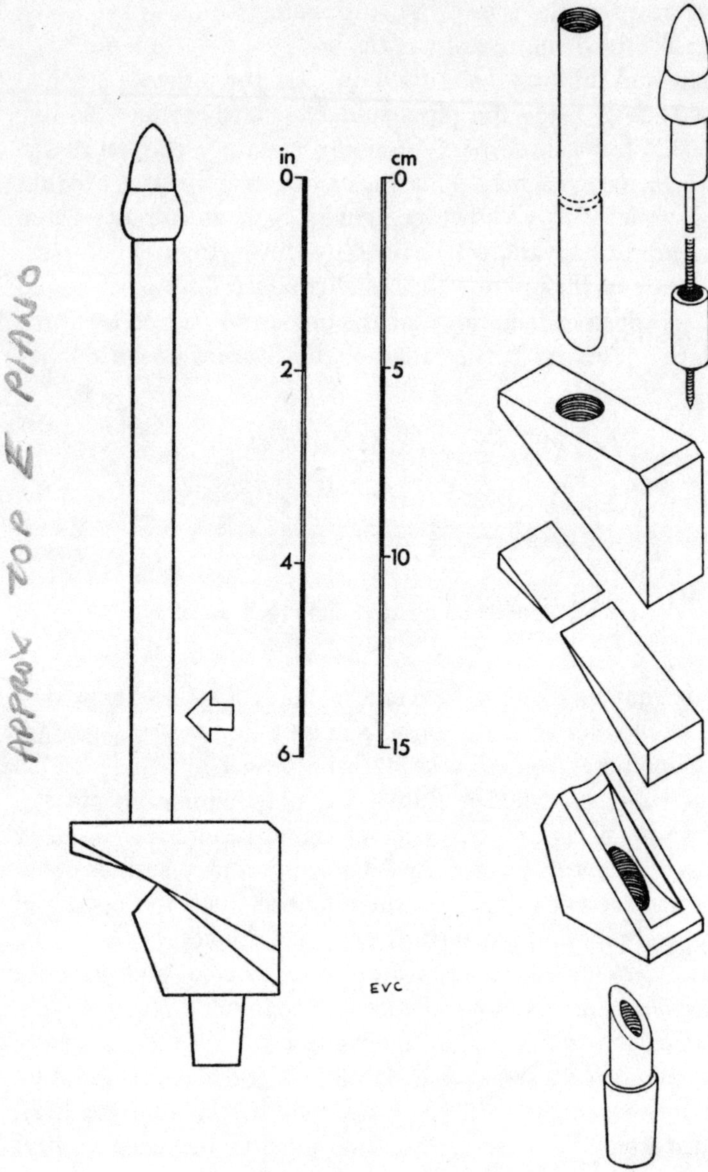

Fig 34. Detail of a piccolo pipe

Jazz Flutes

The jazz flute is common on Belgian dance organs and is an ordinary wood flute, either fully or half stopped—never open. In the fully stopped variety the stopper is of wood. On half stopped pipes the stopper is drilled and fitted with a metal chimney. The top of the chimney projects from the stopper and is fitted with a tuning collar.

The usual type of tremulant varies the wind pressure before the wind reaches the pipes. Jazz flutes, however, are fitted with a tremulant device which operates on each pipe and these can be brought into use as required by means of a special key. A hole is drilled in the back of the pipe and beneath the hole, built into the pipe, is a small puff. This operates a spring-loaded pallet valve which seals the hole above the puff when the tremulant effect is not required. When the tremulant effect is required the puff is fed with an intermittent supply of air from a special motor. The pallet valve is opened and shut in sympathy. Figure 35 illustrates the arrangement. In another system all the tremulant pallets are connected to a single movable bar. When this is agitated by means of a special motor all the pallets are moved simultaneously.

A friend of the writer, Dennis Chappell, who is well versed on church, theatre, and mechanical organs has supplied some comments on the jazz flute. He says that pipes of this name are unknown in church or theatre organs. He states, however, that the fully stopped version of the jazz flute, in various pitches, appears in theatre organs under the name of tibia. This type of pipe is not found in classical organs although the name is sometimes used in connection with pipes of a different timbre. The tibia tone, consisting as it does of about ninety-five per cent fundamental and five per cent windiness, is considered by many musicians to be very unmusical. This particular tone is produced from pipes of a very large scale with high-cut mouths. The pipes need to be copiously and heavily winded and are usually of wood, although metal can be used. To obtain the characteristic effect a tremulant must be used, which merely fluctuates the wind supply, giving a 'mock pathetic' effect which used to be much loved by cinema audiences.

Chappell then reverts to the tremulant on the jazz flute and comments that the effect seems to be no better than the conventional one and is, of course, much more expensive to produce. Strictly speaking, tremulants produce a variation in pitch as well as power. As used on Mortier organs, by certain music arrangers,

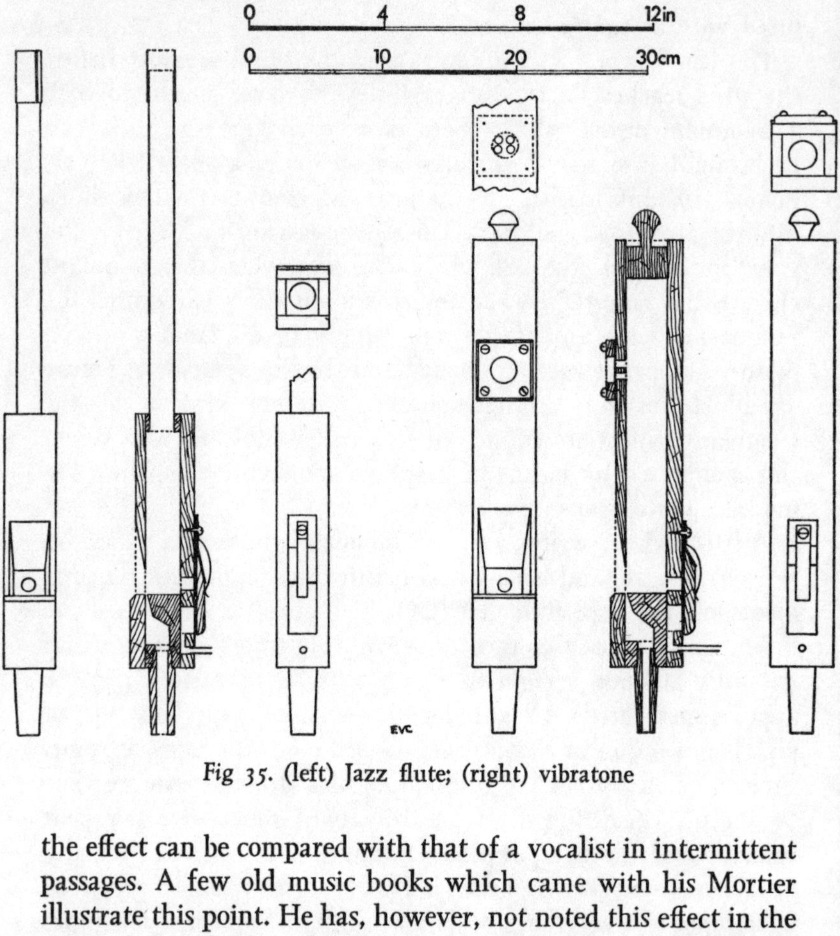

Fig 35. (left) Jazz flute; (right) vibratone

the effect can be compared with that of a vocalist in intermittent passages. A few old music books which came with his Mortier illustrate this point. He has, however, not noted this effect in the more modern books. The jazz flute is also used in combination with other ranks to give quasi-orchestral effects. The timbre of the jazz flute with the half stopper would appear to come somewhere between that of the tibia and the chimney flute which was introduced into England in the eighteenth century.

Vibratones

Like the jazz flute, these pipes are fitted with a tremulant device. It is usual for both jazz flute and vibratone tremulants to be operated by the same register key. The pipes resemble the ordinary stopped wood flute, with one difference. There is a circular opening about half-way along the body of the pipe. Covering the opening is a diaphragm of thin metal, plastic, or similar material. This is loosely secured by a block of wood in which another hole is drilled, corresponding to the one in the body of the pipe. When the pipe sounds the diaphragm vibrates in sympathy, giving a 'tizzy' sound. The arrangement is rather similar to that found on the child's musical submarine or 'kazoo'. Figure 35 refers.

REEDS

A reed pipe consists of two parts, the reed assembly and the resonator. The working parts of a reed assembly are housed in a hollow cylindrical tube known as the boot. This is made of wood or, sometimes, rolled paper. Air enters the boot at the lower end, through a neck which fits into the appropriate hole in the wind-chest. A wooden stopper, known as the block, fits tightly into the upper end. Two holes are drilled vertically through this. Into the underside of the larger of the two holes fits a brass tube or shallot. The lower end of the shallot is closed but an opening is cut in the side. The top is also open. A thin brass plate, or tongue, exactly covers the opening in the side of the shallot. The shallot and tongue are securely held in the block by means of a small wedge, but the lower end of the tongue is free to vibrate. A tuning wire passes through the smaller hole in the block. The lower end of the tuning wire is bent up at an acute angle and it presses on the tongue. As the wire can be raised or lowered, the length of the tongue free to vibrate can be regulated. This enables the reed unit to be tuned. At the lower end of the resonator is a neck which fits tightly into the upper end of the larger hole in the block, above the shallot.

Various views of a reed unit are shown in Figure 36. At A we have a cross-section of a unit, with top and bottom elevations

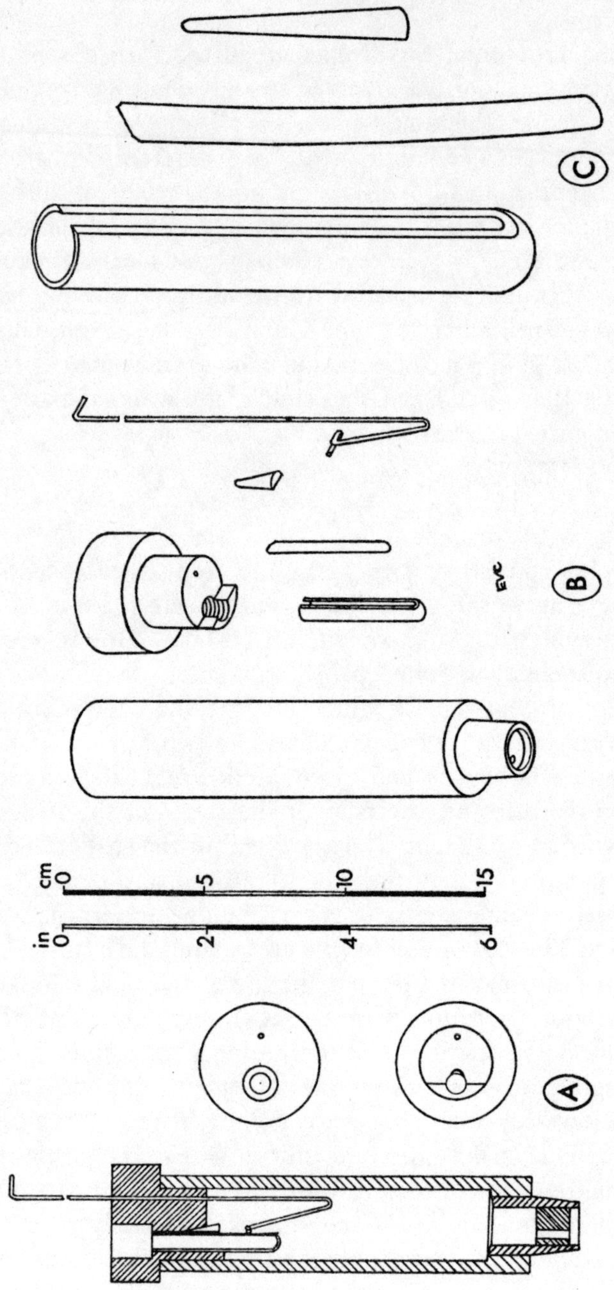

Fig 36. Component parts of a reed assembly

of the block. Isometric views of the component parts (to the same vertical scale) are given at B; from left to right is the boot and block; beneath the block is the shallot, tongue, wedge, and tuning wire. The shallot, tongue, and wedge are shown to an enlarged scale at C.

When air is admitted to the unit the brass tongue, which partly bars its passage, oscillates and this vibration sets the column of air in the resonator into sympathetic vibration. The pitch, quality, and loudness of the note depend basically on the shape and size of the component parts of the reed unit and on the wind pressure. The resonator, however, amplifies selected parts of the sound and thus helps to make the note more audible and give it its characteristic timbre. It will be found that a reed unit will continue to sound approximately the same note even if the resonator is removed.

Basically, the shape of the resonator can be either cylindrical or conical. A reed fitted with a cylindrical resonator will act in a similar way to a stopped flue pipe and produce only the odd harmonics (ie fundamental, twelfth, tierce, etc). With a conical resonator the full harmonic series is produced (ie fundamental, octave, twelfth, fifteenth, etc).

On a conventional organ certain reed resonators are hooded, that is, they are bent forward at the top rather like a ship's ventilator. This method of construction has two advantages without affecting the quality of the note. First, it throws the sound forward; second, it prevents dust and dirt from falling into the reed assembly. This practice is followed to a certain extent on fair organs. The bass reeds of fair organs sometimes have either the shallot face or the tongue covered with leather. This smooths out 'flats' on a badly curved reed and makes voicing easier. The making, voicing, and regulating of reeds is, however, a very skilled job.

The human ear is somewhat insensitive to the harmonics present in both high and low notes. The harmonic development of complex reed tones need not, therefore, be carried out at the upper end of the scale since, in general, significant harmonics will be above the normal limit of audibility. It is customary, therefore, on the conventional organ to make the upper octave of some reed registers from ordinary flue pipes of small scale, which satisfy the ear completely; they are also easier to tune than very small reeds. This practice is sometimes followed on fair organs. For example, the top few notes of the trumpet rank on a 46 key organ are often produced by small wooden flue pipes.

The reed pipes on most fair organs found in Great Britain tend to imitate their orchestral counterparts, the most common being clarinets, saxophones, trumpets, and trombones. Various types of wooden and metal resonators, together with boot, block, and tuning wire are shown in Figure 37. These sketches are not to any particular scale.

Clarinets

The orchestral clarinet sounds mainly only the odd harmonics. We find, therefore, that clarinet resonators, if made of metal, are cylindrical in shape but taper at the bottom to a narrow neck, which fits into the top of the block above the shallot and tongue. A sliding metal sleeve is usually fitted at the top of the resonator thus enabling its length to be varied. Wooden resonators for clarinets are box shaped, with a rectangular hole in the top of the front face. A movable metal regulating plate runs in grooves behind the hole. This plate can be moved up and down, thus opening or closing the aperture. On church organs the resonators for clarinets are half length and this practice appears to be followed on fair organs, whether the resonator is of wood or metal. Other pipes often sound with the clarinets to build up tone. The ensemble is referred to as the clarinet mixture and part of one such mixture can be seen on page 72 (above). The front rank of a smaller clarinet mixture can be seen behind the violins on page 71 (above).

Saxophones

The saxophones on a fair organ are fitted with straight-sided resonators. They are similar to those of clarinets, but larger, although in theory it would appear more logical to fit tapering resonators, as the orchestral saxophone sounds the full harmonic series. The wooden box-shaped saxophone resonator with the

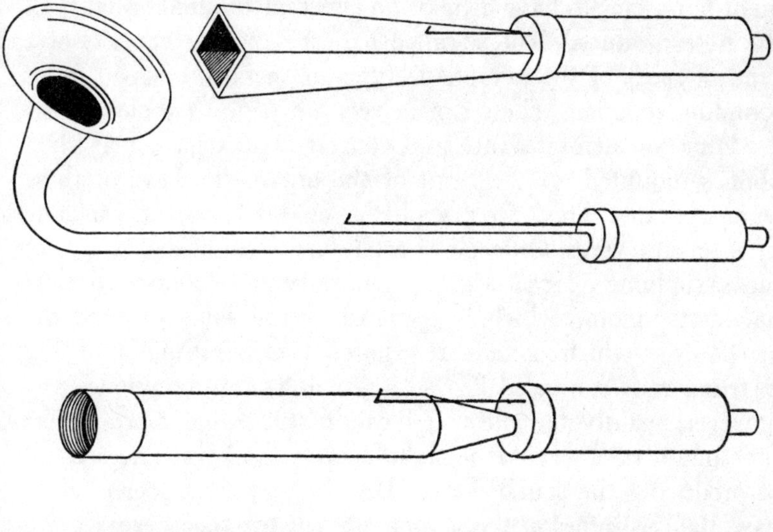

Fig 37. **Reed resonators of wood and metal: (left to right) clarinet, saxophone, and trumpet**

rectangular hole at the top of the front face is a very familiar feature of the fair organ. Sometimes the cover is set back slightly. This enables the metal slide to be removed for cleaning or adjustment but seems to have little or no effect on the tonal quality of the note produced. The so-called baritone register consists of a rank of reeds of the saxophone type and a rank of open flutes sounding together. These can be seen on page 72 (below).

Many continental dance and concert organs have real saxophones mounted on the front of the organ, the keys of these being actuated when the saxophone register is on. This is done by means of wires. One end of each wire is connected to one of the saxophone's keys, while the other end is connected to a pneumatic motor which is operated at the same time as the mechanism which sounds the note. The mouthpiece of the instrument is concealed behind a panel. These saxophones are, however, mainly for effect and would still sound more or less the same if no effort was made to operate the keys. The method of producing the sound varies. The simplest arrangement is to have the reed pipes of the saxophone register, together with the pneumatic motors for operating the instrument's keys, concealed behind a panel. A more elaborate arrangement consists of a series of reeds mounted on a baseboard in a similar manner to those on a reed organ or accordion. The baseboard is boxed in and the mouthpiece of the saxophone is connected to an outlet in one of the sides. With this arrangement the sound appears to come from the bell of the instrument if one is standing close to the organ. It is doubtful, however, if it is worth going to all this trouble as it is impossible to hear where the sound comes from when one is at a distance.

Trumpets

The sound produced by the orchestral trumpet is rich in all harmonics. In order to produce a similar sound the trumpet register on a mechanical organ is fitted with conical resonators, made either of wood or metal. Brass resonators have always been popular for these pipes, due to the tone they produce and also, as far as the fair organ is concerned, to their ornamental appearance. This type of resonator closely resembles its orchestral counterpart and is a familiar feature of the trumpet barrel organ. Metal resonators, especially brass ones, must have been fairly difficult and costly to manufacture. A tapering wooden resonator with an open top, and of square cross-section is much easier to make but sounds 'woolly', as it lacks the stridency of tone produced by a metal resonator. Neither metal nor wooden resonators have, as a rule, any means of regulating the quality of the note, possibly because their conical shape makes it difficult to fit satisfactory devices. On church organs a simple metal flap is sometimes fitted but this would not stand up very well to the hard wear and tear experienced by the travelling fair organ. A slightly different type of wooden resonator is sometimes found on continental organs. A wooden cap closes the top of the resonator and a sliding metal plate is fitted behind a rectangular hole cut in the top of one of the slides of the resonator. This enables the tone to be regulated in a similar way to that of the saxophone. Some brass trumpet resonators can be seen on page 71 (below).

Trombones

The sound produced by the trombone is, like that of the trumpet, rich in all harmonics, and similar but larger resonators are used. These may be made either of wood or of metal. As the resonator of a deep bass trombone may be over nine feet long considerable accommodation problems arise, as with the bass bourdons, and the way in which the wooden resonators are mitred so that they can be packed into the organ case is most ingenious. Figure 38 shows one way in which this has been done on an 89 key organ. Provision is rarely made for regulating the tone of trombones. The writer has, however, seen one simple method which can be used on wooden resonators. This consists of a hole about an inch and a half in diameter drilled in a side of the resonator, about six inches from the wide or open end. A simple wooden flap is screwed to the resonator so that it can be swivelled, uncovering as much of the hole as is required. Metal resonators for bass trombones are rarer than wooden ones and are usually looped round in a similar way to orchestral trumpets. Bass trombones with brass resonators are often found on old trumpet barrel organs and two such resonators can be seen on page 71 (below).

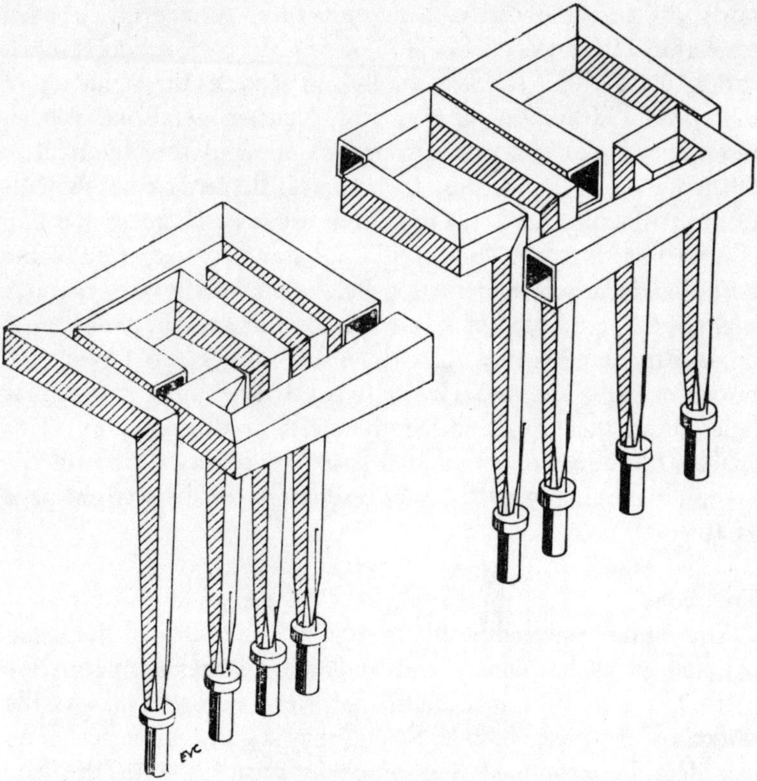

Fig 38. Method of accommodating bass trombones within the case of an 89 key Gavioli organ

V*ox humana*

The vox humana is rarely found on fairground organs, although it is sometimes found on dance organs. The resonators are usually short, which helps to give the sound emitted a series of intense overtones. Each resonator has a hole in the side, which matches a similar hole in the cap. Some vox humana pipes are shown on page 89 (left). These are on a Hooghuys dance organ and closely resemble their counterpart on the theatre organ. Mounted behind each reed pipe is a stopped wood flute. Both pipes sound together.

PERCUSSION EFFECTS

The percussion effects which are built into mechanical organs vary tremendously. On most traditional fair organs of up to and including 89 keys it is unusual to find anything more elaborate than a bass drum and cymbal coupled together, and a side- or snare-drum with two independently operated drumsticks. Thus, only three keys are devoted to percussion effects. In addition, but not working independently, one may find a triangle (coupled to the bass drum and cymbal) and castanets (coupled to the side-drum beaters). On 98 key instruments the castanets, when fitted, are usually operated by a separate key.

Rather more ambitious effects are found on some Dutch and Belgian organs. On Mortier dance organs, for example, it is not uncommon to find over a dozen keys allocated to percussion effects. These might include a side-drum (two keys—one of which may work a stick and one a brush), bass drum, single cymbal, double cymbal (hi-hat), temple blocks (four keys), an anvil, rhumba effect, etc. Quite often, by means of a special key, a tom-tom can be brought into play instead of the side-drum. Sometimes the side-drum action can be switched from sticks to brushes, as required. A set of temple blocks can be seen on page 90 (above).

An ingenious way of getting more variety into the rhythm effects without using too many keys is found on some Dutch street organs. They are equipped with what is known as a *trommel forte* key. In the off position the bass drum plays without the cymbal, and instead of the side drum we have two sticks sounding on a wood-block, ie a piece of hollowed-out wood. When the *trommel forte* key is operated by the music the cymbal is coupled to the bass drum so that the two play together. In addition, the wood-block is disconnected and play is transferred to the side-drum. This creates the desired *forte* effect. On some instruments of this type a further saving of keys is sometimes effected by coupling the *trommel forte* key to the bass trombone register, so that *forte* percussion effects are obtained automatically when the trombones are brought into play. This arrangement is often found on Mortier organs. The coupling mechanism by which the cymbal is made to play can be seen on page 107 (above).

An arrangement has also been seen whereby the distance the drumsticks travel is varied by means of a pneumatic motor, thus varying the volume of sound produced by the impact.

A typical side-drum mechanism is shown on page 89 (right). It will be seen that there is a pneumatic motor for each drumstick and that the amount the motor is allowed to open is governed by a metal stop. In the rest position the motor is open to the atmosphere and kept closed by the pressure of its spring. The head of the drumstick nearly touches the drumskin. When a drumbeat is required the motor is inflated and the drumstick moves away from the drumskin. The motor is immediately exhausted and it snaps shut, assisted by the spring. The head of the drumstick slightly overtravels, beats the drum and comes to rest a short distance from the drumskin. It will be seen that there are two inlets at the top of the mechanism. These supply air to a valve system which allows air to enter the pneumatic motors from the main supply via the large inlet at the side.

The bass drum motor operates in a slightly different manner. When the organ is playing, the motor is kept inflated all the time against spring pressure. The motor is exhausted when the drum is required to beat and is re-inflated immediately. It is quicker to deflate a pneumatic motor than to inflate it.

Several tuned percussion instruments are found. The most common is probably the glockenspiel, which consists of a series of tuned metal plates hit by small hammers. This is often referred to incorrectly as a dulcimer. The dulcimer is a *stringed* instrument played with hammers which are held in the player's hands.

Many Marenghi organs were fitted with grelotphones (from the French 'grelot', a small round bell). In English-speaking countries these are usually known as 'sleigh bells'. The grelotphone consists of a number of leather straps which can be agitated by pneumatic motors when required. Small bells are fixed to each strap, the bells on each strap sounding the same musical note. The bells are larger versions of the type which used to be found

Page 125: (above) An 89 key Marenghi organ in the centre of a motor-car switchback ride in about 1908; a close-up of some of the pipework can be seen on page 77 (above). The organ, unchanged, is now in preservation; (below) one of Pat Collins's elaborate show-fronts, photographed when new in 1905. Later photographs show further carving fronting the four vertical supports and along the top. The organ front bears Marenghi's name and is still in existence today, but with a different organ behind it

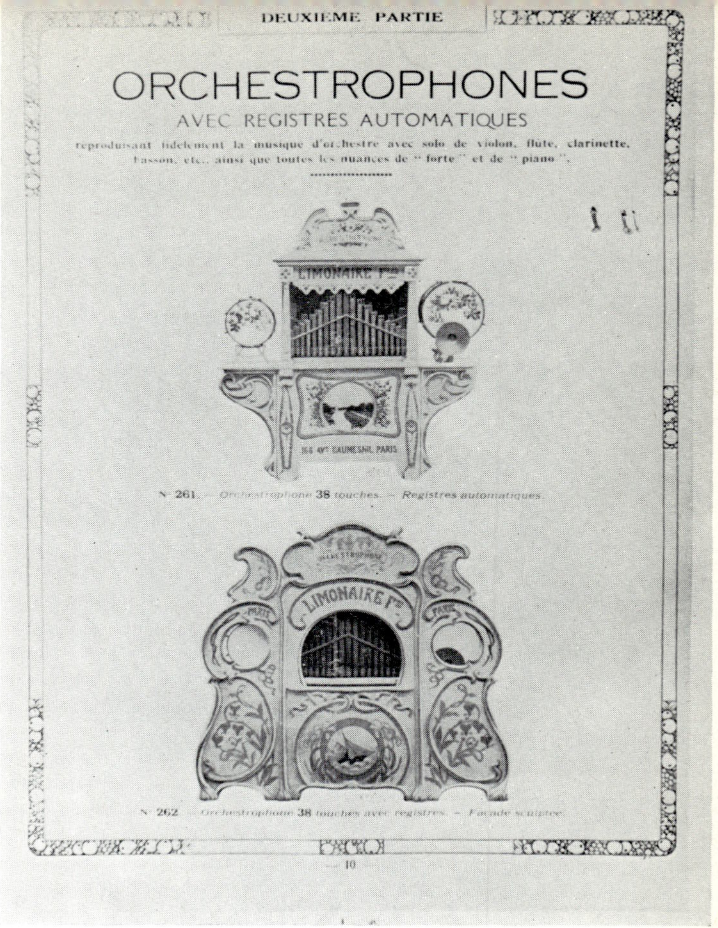

Page 126: Two pages from a Limonaire catalogue published not earlier than 1906. Organs of from 30 to 100

on children's reins. Sometimes as many as eight bells are used for the top notes. They increase in size as the pitch falls and there may be as few as two for the lowest note. The grelotphone is brought into play as required by a register key. The grelotphone proved to be a very popular attachment to fairground organs and many showmen had them specially fitted. Musically their use is rather limited and they are rarely found other than singly on theatre organs. Occasionally a tuned octave is found, although on one Wurlitzer known to the writer there is a two-octave set. A grelotphone is illustrated on page 90 (centre).

The xylophone is similar to the glockenspiel but it is made with wooden bars and struck with larger wooden hammers. Normally, on mechanical organs, the resonators beneath the bars are omitted. The action of a xylophone mechanism was described in Chapter 2, and illustrated in Figures 14a, 14b, and 27.

The bars of this xylophone are made from jarrah, although rosewood or a similar hardwood is often used. They are strung on a stout cord and kept the right distance apart by means of cylindrical wooden beads. The bars rest on hollow paper tubes which are fixed to the soundboard by screweyes with long shanks. The eyes also act as guides for the securing cord. The bars are positioned so that they are struck halfway along, and the holes for the supporting strings are drilled a quarter of the bars' length from each end.

With a constant cross-section, the length of a bar halves every time the pitch is raised by two octaves, not every time the pitch is raised by one octave as in the case of a flue pipe. To raise the pitch of a bar one semi-tone the length should be reduced by 0·0284 (or, approximately, 1/35). In the unit illustrated the bars appear to be a job lot and the cross-section varies slightly from bar to bar. The lowest seven bars have been made from thicker wood, presumably to enable slightly shorter bars to be used so that the unit can be accommodated more easily. A vertically mounted xylophone on a Hooghuys organ is shown on page 90 (lower).

Some mechanical organs are fitted with tubular bells, and sometimes mandoline attachments are found on Hooghuys dance organs.

PROSCENIUMS

A characteristic feature of the fair organ is its elaborately carved and painted proscenium, perhaps lit by coloured lights, and the carved figures which grace it. At one time efforts were made to make the proscenium as elaborate as possible. One can only hope that as much work and care went into the musical side of the instrument! The workmanship of the proscenium and figures varied tremendously and a great deal of thought went into the design of the better ones. The firm of Gavioli advertised organs with, for example, a 'Louis XV' or 'Renaissance' style front and made a point of referring to the number of figures on the front. The top canopies of some barrel organs were supported by as many as six pillars. Sometimes they were for show only and revolved by means of a drive from the crankshaft. Frequently they would be covered with twisted brass rod, giving the illusion that alternate pillars were continually rising and falling.

Chas. Marenghi & Cie filed a patent (specification 217 of 1907) coupling changes of lighting to register changes, each register presumably having its own lighting mood.

This idea was carried a stage further by the so-called Marenghi 'light books'. These were intended for use on the large organs fronting bioscope shows while a show was on. In order to keep the public interested, or to attract an audience for the next show, these books were 'played' on the organ and worked a series of lighting changes. No music was played and it would seem that the slots in the books merely operated the register-changing mechanism to which the lighting effects were coupled. One or two other keys may have been used exclusively for lighting changes but the author has no evidence of this. The idea had a short life, apparently, and does not appear to have been too popular with the showmen. One reason advanced for this is that the books caused unnecessary wear and tear to the key frame. This may have been so. It would seem that there was scope in the scheme to use an endless loop of 'music' which would repeat the required effects time and again. This would have been much cheaper than using the ordinary type of book.

It has not been possible to trace a Marenghi light book which is still in existence today. An old 100 key book has, however, come to hand with what appear to be some pointless register changes at the end, which is shown in Figure 39. The only reasonable explanation which can be offered for the register changes after the dotted line which marks the end of the music is that they caused lighting changes which rounded off the performance. The scale of the organ for which this book was made is discussed in Chapter 6.

Many of the more modern dance organs have lighting effects coupled to the register controls.

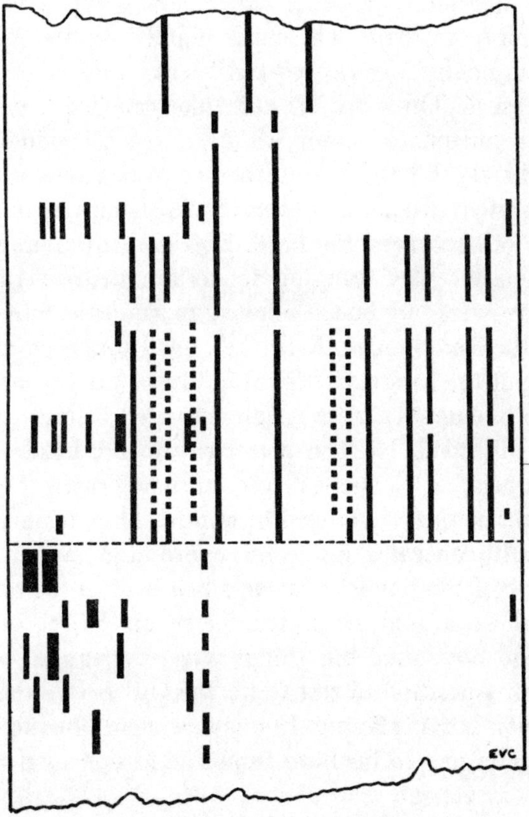

Fig 39. Marenghi music book (100 key), showing lighting changes after end of song (indicated by dotted line)

Organ figures can be nearly life-sized. Some are completely immobile and are used for decoration only. Others move and these are of two types. One type performs tasks such as conducting, bell-ringing, or drum-beating and the actions of these are controlled from and are in time with the music. The other type of moving figure attempts no synchronisation with the music and is worked from the organ's crankshaft.

The moving parts of synchronised figures are operated by metal rods connected to pneumatic motors. Movement is usually confined to the head and arms and where necessary joints are concealed with thin leather coverings. Quite often the wind supply to the motors is restricted to slow down movement and make it more realistic. The most popular figure is the bandmaster. Originally, he was worked by two independent controls from the music. One control, sometimes labelled 'chef' or 'bras', operated a pneumatic motor which moved a conductor's baton held in his right hand. The other control, sometimes labelled 'tete', operated two motors, one of which moved the left arm, while the other turned the head. This gave the impression that the bandmaster was bringing in certain instruments and his movements were, in fact, designed to coincide with, say, the entry of the saxophones. A further small touch of realism was the lifting of the bandmaster's baton just before the music began. The three pneumatics were usually situated behind the pedestal on which he stood. Next in popularity to the bandmaster were the bellringers, or 'clochettes', and on some organs there were as many as six of these, arranged in groups. The pneumatic motors were usually concealed inside the figures and caused a hammer held in one of the hands to strike a bell held in the other. Occasionally there would be a trumpeter on barrel organs. His trumpet did not sound but things were so arranged that it was raised from a position of rest to his lips just before the trumpets on the organ began playing. In one case mentioned to the writer the trumpeter moved his head from side to side 'as if to see how business was going'.

The non-synchronised figures either rotated on their pedestals or performed simple bowing and swaying movements.

Today, some organs have keys which still operate moving

figures exclusively. Most figures, though, are now worked either from a percussion effect or from a register control. It is quite common for the bandmaster to conduct only when the bass drum and cymbal are playing. Typical organ figures can be seen on page 107 (below).

6 Scales

When we discuss the 'scale' of an organ, we are referring to the function of each key on the key frame, or outlet on the tracker bar, and to its position. As readers will have gathered, a key can perform one or more of a number of functions. For example, it can:

(i) sound a musical note
(ii) sound a percussion effect
(iii) set a register
(iv) cancel a register or registers
(v) mute the key frame
(vi) operate a moving figure.

As regards (i) we must know the position of the note in the musical scale and to which group of pipes it belongs (eg bass, accompaniment, etc). For (ii) we must know which percussion instrument is struck. For (iii) the name of the register or its description is necessary; in addition we should know its pitch (ie whether 4′, 8′, 16′, etc) and of which pipe group it forms a part. Items (iv) and (v), generally, need no further details. For (vi) we need to know whether the key controls a bandmaster's baton, his head, a bellringer's hammer, or other effect. On some organs keys may work swell shutters, tremulants, lighting effects, or short compass fanfare ranks.

Full details of an organ's scale will be required by a music marker if he is not familiar with the organ. Unless the organ has its own scale book this information is often difficult to come by, although a lot can be learnt by studying some of the organ's music books. The remarks on the 100 key scale later in this chapter indicate how this can be done. Although music books will rarely yield any information about registers and their situation it is usually possible to work out the relationship of the musical notes fairly easily. It is impossible to give details of all scales but a representative selection has been made. The key to the symbols used in the diagrams will be found in Figure 42.

45 KEY BARREL ORGAN SCALE

The key frame of this 45 key barrel organ, which was probably made by Wright & Holmes, is marked with its scale, as shown in Figure 40. The letters and signs have been burnt into the wood with brands and the builder has conveniently arranged

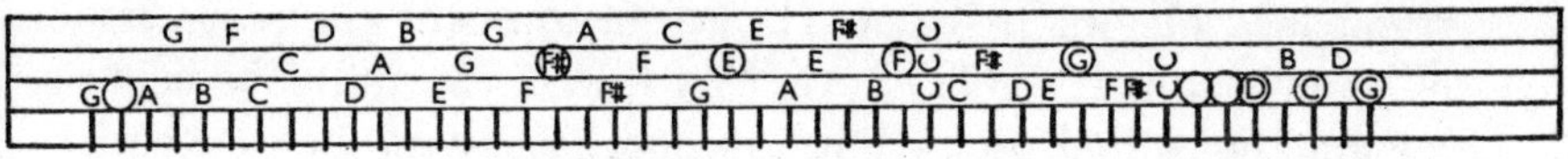

Fig 40. Scale of 45 key barrel organ, as branded on key frame

them in three rows, which has helped considerably with the task of deciphering the scale.

The top row of markings refers to the accompaniment group, which contains nine notes, from G to G, all naturals except F♯ The keys, like the pipes, are arranged symmetrically on either side of the lowest G.

The middle row shows which keys operate the small counter-melody group of brass trumpets. There are twelve of these and they range from E to G, again all naturals except for lower and upper F♯. They are arranged in a similar manner to the accompaniment, except that the top four notes are in the middle, alternating with the four lowest.

The bottom row of markings indicates the melody group, which has sixteen notes. This runs, in order, from G to F♯, and covers two octaves. Here again, all notes are naturals except for lower and upper F♯. On the right-hand side of the bottom row are the bass notes, C, D, and G. Three is the minimum number which can produce any worthwhile musical effect. The last key but one of the left-hand side of the key frame works the bass drum, while the two keys on the right, between the top note of the melody and the three basses, work the side-drum. These keys are indicated by circles. The keys marked CC and CCC operate the self-change mechanism which was described in Chapter 2.

46/48 KEY SCALE

The 46/48 key scale described here is the most common scale for small organs in Great Britain and is usually adopted when conversions are made. The 46 key scale is very straightforward and has no register keys (Figure 41). It is divided into three groups. There are eight notes in the bass group, which runs from F to E, the seven naturals and A♯. The pipework consists, usually, of either open flutes (with roller-bridges) or bourdons and bass trombones, playing together. The accompaniment group consists of twelve notes, from F to F♯, lower F♯ and G♯ being missing. Open and stopped flutes usually make up the pipework of this group. The melody group, of twenty-two notes, continues up the chromatic scale from the accompaniment group, extending from G to F, one note short of two octaves. Top D♯ is missing. The composition of the melody group varies, one of the more common arrangements being a rank of wooden trumpets with one or two ranks of violins. The division between the top note of the accompaniment group and the lowest note of the melody group is, up to a point, arbitrary. Three keys are used for percussion effects, one for a bass drum and cymbal coupled together, and the other two for the side-drum. The key frame cut-out key is in its usual position near the opening edge of the key frame and is between the two side-drum keys. It is normal for the side-drum keys to be separated, as the cardboard of the music would be seriously weakened if the keys were side by side.

The 48 key scale is similar, except that there is an additional key at each end of the scale. One of these keys brings an additional rank or ranks of pipes into play when required and the other cancels its action. By using these keys the music marker can put more expression into his music.

It will be seen that there is an important difference between the two scales just described. The keys of the 45 key barrel organ

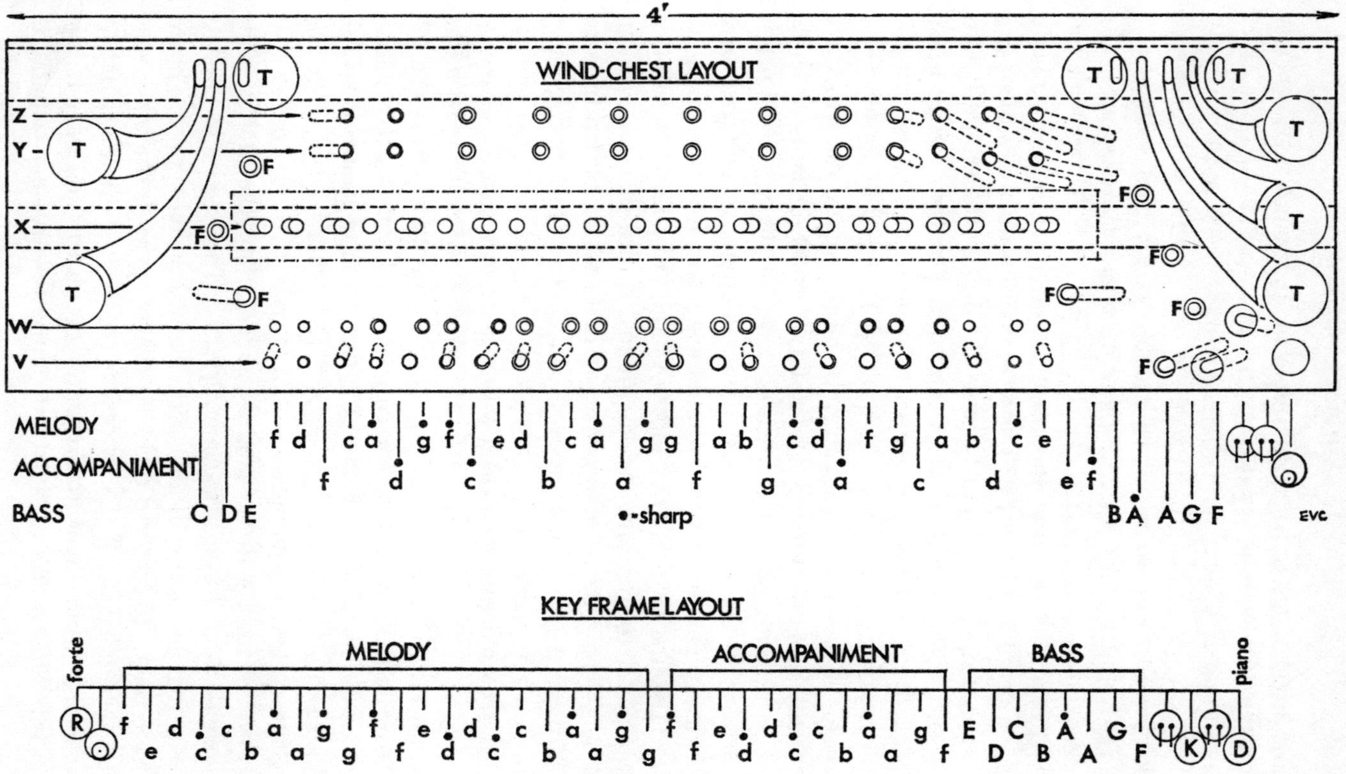

Fig 41. Pipe layout of 46 key organ and (below) scale of 46/48 key organ

are in the same order as the pipes on the wind-chest, whereas on the 46 key book organ they are arranged in the same order as the notes of the musical scale. This is the case in nearly all book organs, although an exception to this is the scale of the 52 keyless Ruth organ which is described in the next section.

It is much easier to get to know an organ if the layout of the pipework and key frame can be related. As a 46 key scale has just been discussed the opportunity will be taken to describe in some detail the layout of a typical organ with this scale.

Space is at a premium for any fair organ builder and he has to ensure that the pipes are arranged so that they can be heard properly. The builder also goes to some trouble to set out the pipework attractively and he quite often uses a dummy pipe or so to improve the symmetry. In small organs the pipes are usually mounted directly on the upper board of the wind-chest, or on an extension chest fitted on top of it. They are not necessarily mounted directly above the wind grooves which feed them with air. The upper board of a 46 key organ is shown in Figure 41. The first two ranks of pipes (V) and (W) are of twenty-two pipes each and are the melody violins. Notice that the pipes in rank (W) are arranged in pairs, and that each pair is fed from an adjacent pair of wind grooves. The intervening wind grooves are used to operate a different group of pipes. The organ builder has set each pipe in rank (W) more or less directly above its wind groove. He has, however, taken more trouble with the front rank (V) and has cut channels in the underside of the top board so that the pipes are evenly spaced. The channels are indicated by dotted lines. Behind the two ranks of violins is a rank of twenty-two wooden trumpets (X), which play with the violins. These are mounted on an extension wind-chest so that they are level with or slightly higher than the violins. This enables them to be heard more clearly. The extension chest is indicated by dotted lines. Notice how the holes in the board have been elongated so that they match up with the inlet holes on the underside of the extension chest. Beneath the trumpets is a slide which fits into a channel cut in the underside of the board. This makes it possible to mute the trumpets when the organ is being tuned.

Behind the trumpets are two ranks of accompaniment pipes, (Y) and (Z). Both ranks are of wood, one open and the other stopped. There are twelve pipes in each rank and a stopped pipe always sounds with the corresponding open one. The organ builder went to some trouble to arrange the pipes in a regular fashion but was not completely successful. He had to close up the pipes on the right-hand side rather more than those on the left. He also had to put the end pipes on the right-hand side of rank (Y) slightly out of line so that the channels leading to them on the underside of the board would not foul those leading to the end pipes on the right-hand side of the rear rank.

The eight bass trombones (T) have square-sectioned conical resonators and these have to be mitred so that they fit within the organ case. There are three trombones on one side and five on the other, and they are arranged at the back and ends of the wind-chest. Some of the trombones stand directly above their wind grooves, while others are connected to them by channels cut in the top of the board. The channelling is covered to make it airtight. This covering is not shown in the diagram. A slide runs in a groove as indicated, making it possible to mute the trombones in a similar manner to the trumpets.

Sounding with the bass trombones are open wooden flue pipes (F), some of which are mitred. These stand near the corresponding trombones. In some cases channels are cut to them in the underside of the board where it is not convenient to mount them directly over the appropriate wind groove.

Two outlets for the side-drum and an outlet for the bass drum and cymbal are on the right of the board. It will be seen that channels lead to the side-drum outlets. The layout of pipework on larger organs is more complicated and much use is made of off-note chests. It is well worth understanding, though, especially if tuning or maintenance is to be attempted.

52 KEY RUTH SCALE

This scale (Figure 42) belongs to a 52 keyless Ruth fair organ, type 33, and incorporates a number of interesting features. The layouts of the tracker bar (the organ is keyless) and pipework

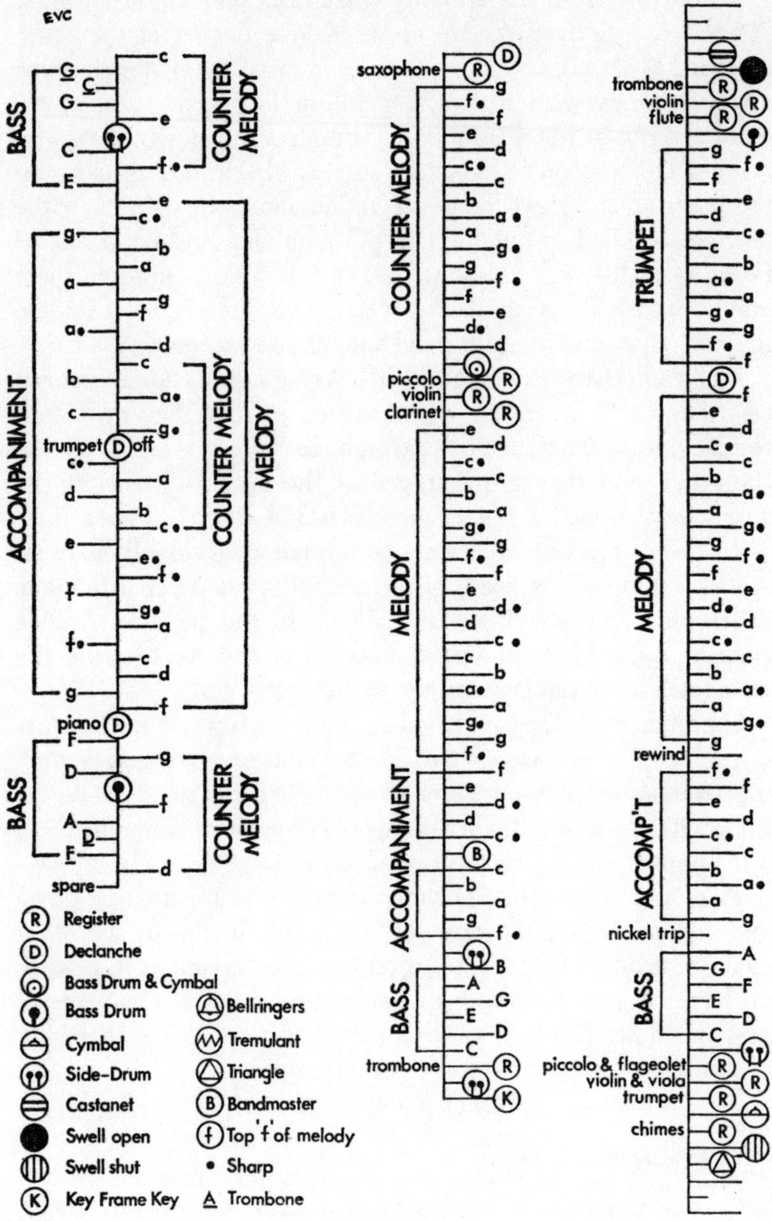

Fig 42. Scales: (left to right) 52 keyless Ruth; 65 key; 69 key paper-roll Wurlitzer (165)

follow the same order. As the pipework is, to a certain extent, arranged symmetrically, the music cannot be read at sight. Music markers consequently have a more difficult task, rather similar to that encountered by barrel markers, except that a book contains only one tune instead of, say, ten tunes all interlaced, as on a barrel organ.

The scale of the organ is far from chromatic. There are four bass trombones (C, D, F, and G) and six flue basses (A, C, D, E, F, and G). The basses are split into two sections, one at each end of the wind-chest, each consisting of three flues and two reeds, not arranged in any particular order. Between the basses is the accompaniment group. The eleven notes are arranged in order and run from G to G, G♯ and D♯ being missing.

The melody carries on from the top note of the accompaniment group and alternates with it. It has twenty notes, running from G♯ to F, one note short of two octaves, but with both lower and upper D♯ missing. The pipes are arranged alternately, with the longest, G♯ and A, in the middle, and the shortest, E and F, on the flanks.

The counter melody consists of brass trumpets and has, nominally, eleven notes but an economy has been effected with regard to the top five, which are borrowed from the melody. There are, consequently, only six independent notes, C, D, E, F, F♯, and G, and these are arranged in two groups of three, on either side of the melody group. The remaining five notes are the lowest five notes of the melody, G♯, A, A♯, B, and C.

There is one control for the bass drum. Another control works both sticks of the side-drum, a fairly common continental practice. As the organ is keyless and the music is punched with circular holes, the declanche can be dispensed with so far as register control is concerned. A continuous row of holes is used to operate each of the two register controls, which are described as '*piano*' and 'trumpets off'. Normally, all pipes play, but when a *piano* effect is required a continuous row of holes is cut in the music. This disconnects three ranks of pipes from the melody group and one rank of stopped pipes from the accompaniment. The other control silences the five trumpets which are connected to the lowest notes of the melody group.

65 KEY SCALE

There are not many 65 key organs in England and their scales vary. The scale illustrated in Figure 42 was used by several organ builders, including Gaviolis. For its size it is good, except that there are only six bass notes, C, D, E, G, A, and B, as opposed to the eight found on many smaller organs. Each note is produced by three bourdons, one sounding the fundamental and two helpers sounding the octave and super-octave. Six bass trombones can also be brought into play as required and these are controlled by a register key. The accompaniment group covers an octave, F♯ to F, G♯ and A♯ being missing. The melody group consists of twenty-one notes, F♯ to E, top A♯ and D♯ being missing. In one 65 key organ known to the writer, the melody group consists of two registers, violins and piccolos, each of which is controlled by a register key. On some organs a glockenspiel or xylophone also works on the melody. Unlike the 46/48 key scale, the 65 key scale incorporates a counter-melody group of seventeen notes from D to G, top D♯ being missing. The counter melody, like the melody, also consists of two registers, clarinets and saxophones, either of which can be brought into play as required. An organ with this type of scale can, therefore, have up to five registers (plus declanche), the flue bass and accompaniment (and possibly glockenspiel) being always in play. Percussion consists of side-drum (two keys) and coupled bass drum and cymbal (one key). In addition, there is the key frame key. Surprisingly, in view of the rather inadequate bass group, a special key situated in the middle of the accompaniment group is allocated to work a bandmaster. One would think that this key, with possibly one other, could be better employed working extra bass notes.

69 KEY WURLITZER BAND ORGAN SCALE

The term 'band organ' is used in the USA instead of 'fair organ'. There were many firms engaged both in manufacturing and importing these instruments from Europe, the most famous American manufacturer in the business undoubtedly being

'Wurlitzer'. One of the largest automatic organs built by Wurlitzers was the 165 band organ or, to give it its catalogue title 'The Wurlitzer Duplex Orchestral Organ (Style No 165)'. It was advertised as being suitable for the 'largest type stationary Carouselles, Roller Coasters and other Park Installations' and was also said to be used 'with great success in Park Dance Pavilions'. Wurlitzer's famous trade mark is shown in Figure 43.

The tracker bar has sixty-nine holes in it. The Wurlitzer Company contemplated building a larger organ having seventy-five holes in the tracker bar. The larger instrument, however, never materialised, due to the introduction of the electric gramophone and the consequent decline of the mechanical organ. Music for the 165 was arranged so that it would also play on

WURLITZER

Fig 43. Wurlitzer's one-time trade mark

the larger type of organ, if and when it was introduced. The three unlabelled controls at each end of the scale were intended for use on the larger organ.

The musical notes of the scale are arranged in the usual four groups (Figure 42). Three of these bear the conventional names used in Great Britain—melody, accompaniment, and bass. What would be known in England as the counter-melody group is described as trumpet or, alternatively, treble. The bass group consists of only six notes, C, D, E, F, G, and A. There are ten notes in the accompaniment group which is chromatic except for G♯ and D♯. The melody group consists of twenty-two notes, top D♯ being missing. The trumpet group is quite small and consists of fourteen notes, forming a fully chromatic scale except for the omission of top D♯.

The organ is fitted with swell shutters which are opened by one control and closed by another. It is not possible to vary the speed at which the shutters open and close, each operation taking probably about half a second. The swell shutters enable more expression to be put into the music but the arrangement lacks the versatility of the control fitted to the swell box of a manually-played organ.

There are two miscellaneous operational controls. One is for the rewind mechanism, which also mutes the tracker bar during rewinding. The other is the 'nickel trip', which was used in conjunction with a coin slot. Many automatic instruments were installed in cafés, bars, and restaurants and were similar in operation to the modern juke box. The instrument would play when a nickel was inserted in the slot and was cut off when a tune ended by a series of perforations in the music which operated the trip.

The six additional controls were intended for four extra registers and two extra percussion effects. Reading from top to bottom of the diagram these were as follows: violin and prestant, kettle drum, and side-drum *ff* (at the top) and uniphone bells, bass trombone and trumpet, and bass bells (at the bottom).

Some pipes are always in play and supply a foundation tone. There are seven registers controlled by slots in the music. Those for the melody division are flutes and piccolos, flageolets and open piccolos, violins *piano*, and chimes (or glockenspiel). On the trumpet division, naturally enough, there is a trumpet register. Violins *forte* (on melody) and violas (on trumpet) are set simultaneously by one control. There is one register on the bass division, trombones. There is also a declanche or general cancel.

The non-tuned percussion consists of a bass drum, a crash cymbal, a triangle, a pair of castanets and a side-drum. There are five controls for these. The side-drum mechanism, unlike most of those found in Great Britain, is worked by only one control. A similar system is used to operate the castanets.

86, 87, 89, 92, 94, AND 98 KEY SCALES

86/87 Key Scales

The first book organs to arrive in England were the 87 key Gaviolis and Limonaires. This scale underwent a number of

Page 143: Two pages from a Marenghi catalogue of 1906; key sizes vary from 60 to 100. *(above)* a 69 key organ, *(below)* one of 89 keys

Page 144: Two pages from a Gavioli catalogue published in English in the USA in about 1910; the catalogue

modifications as the years went by and formed the basis of the 89 and 92, 94 and 98 key scales which were eventually adopted as standard by many showmen when it became uneconomic to produce, or difficult to obtain, music of other sizes.

The scale is shown in Figure 44. The bass group consists of two sets of bass pipes. Each group has the same eight notes, all the naturals, plus A♯. One group consists of stopped flues (bourdons), with helpers, and the other of reeds (bass trombones). One advantage of having two entirely separate bass sections is that it is possible to introduce variety into the bass parts. Apart from sounding flues and reeds separately, or together, it is also possible to obtain *sforzando* (*sf*) or *forte-piano* (*fp*) effects by emphasising either the beginning or end of a note. These effects are obtained in the music cutting by arranging for one bass note to sound for approximately only half the length of the other, either at the beginning or end of a note. On some music the slots for operating the bass trombones begin a little before those of other notes, possibly to compensate for the slight time lag which occurs before these deep reeds speak.

The accompaniment group consists of ten notes, from G to F♯, G♯ and D♯ being missing.

The accompaniment continues into the melody group, which has thirty-four notes, and extends from G to F, one note short of three octaves. Top D♯ is missing. Note that the top F of this group is in rather an odd position, away from the group in question, and next to one of the side-drum keys. Apparently, in the prototype scale, the top F was in its logical place, and the bass drum (and cymbal) next to the side-drum. It was soon found, though, that with bass drum and side-drum slots next to each other, and very often sounding together, the cardboard music was seriously weakened. The positions of top F and the bass drum were, accordingly, reversed. As the top F is used much less than the bass drum, weakening the cardboard was obviated. The lower seventeen notes of the melody group are allocated to clarinets, while the top seventeen are allocated to piccolos. The counter melody has twenty notes, from A to F, top D♯ being missing.

The 87 key organs have no registers. They aimed at imitating

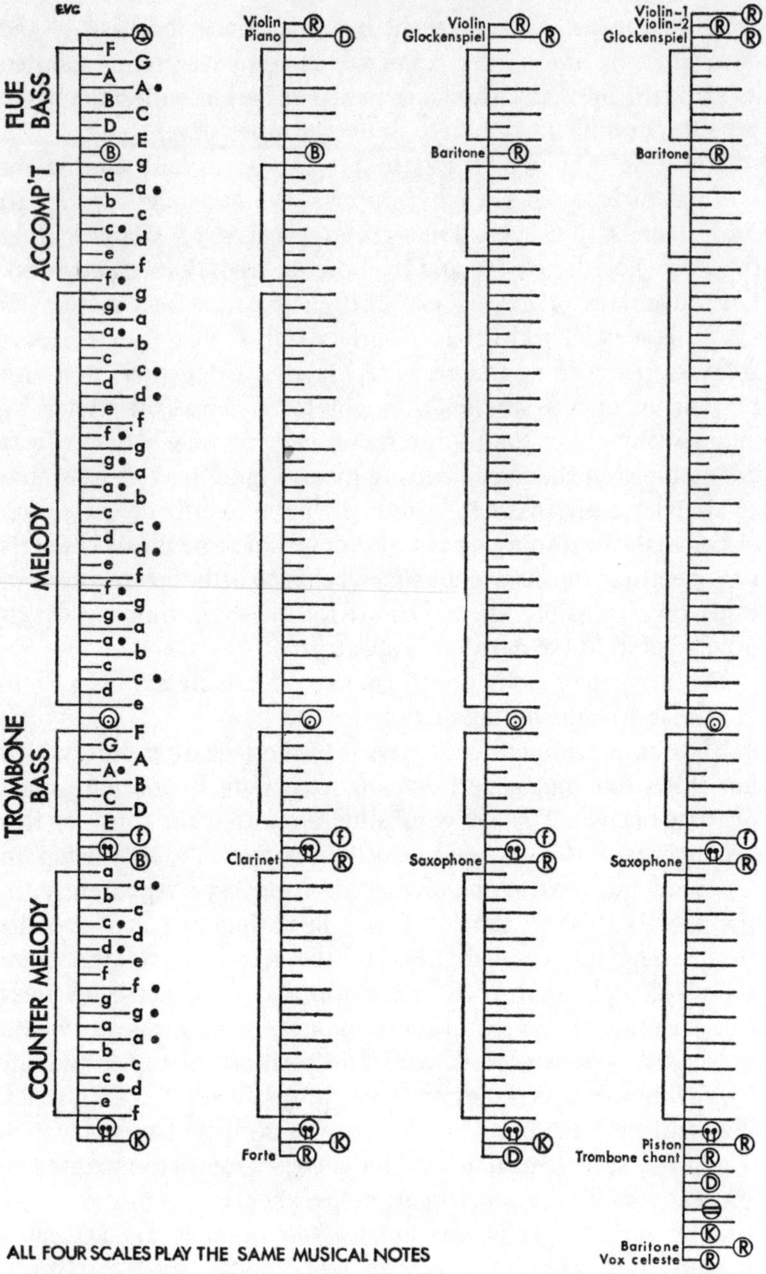

Fig 44. Scales: (left to right) 87 key; 89 key (G4); 89 key (VB); 92/94/98 key

a military band, despite their lack of trumpets. Their main melodic line is the clarinet, which predominates, even though the clarinet mixture usually includes at least one rank of violins. In any event, in part of its range, the clarinet is to most ears indistinguishable from the cornet, and can deal creditably with trumpet fanfares. Above the trombones the melodic sequence passes from saxophones to clarinets and thence on to piccolos.

These organs have the usual three keys allocated to bass drum and cymbal, and side-drum. They were originally of the six-figure type, but only three were operated from the music. One key operated a pair of bellringers, while the other two operated the bandmaster. On top of the organ, working independently of the music, from the organ's crankshaft, was a clown or jester, who performed a rotary swaying motion from the waist. On either side of him, at the ends of the organ, two ballet girls pirouetted. Limonaires made an 86 key model which had the same scale as the 87 key instruments, but the bellringers were not included.

89 *Key Scales*

With the introduction of the register system the 87 key scale underwent modification. Whether by accident or design there was room on the music for two more keys, one on each side. These were added. The keys which operated the figures also became available as the figures were now coupled to percussion effects. Two distinct scales emerged, the G4 and the violin-baritone (VB).

The G4 is illustrated in Figure 44. Notice that the key for the bandmaster's baton is still retained. Apart from the declanche there are three register controls—violins, clarinets, and *forte*. There are twenty-two violins, which use the same keys as the clarinets plus the five which operate the lowest piccolos. When the violins are on, the five lowest piccolos are silenced and the violins can play solo over the whole of their range. (Compare this with a similar arrangement on the 110 key Gavioli.) The *forte* key apparently added trumpets to the foundation tone of saxophones on the counter melody and added weight elsewhere. The declanche is sometimes described as the *piano* register since certain background or foundation pipes still continue to play throughout the organ's range when it is operated. There are less than half a dozen 89 key organs in Britain with a G4 scale.

It is the violin-baritone scale which has become the accepted standard for 89 key organs. As will be seen from Figure 44, the top two notes of the accompaniment have been transferred to the bottom of the melody, which now begins on F instead of G. This increases the number of clarinets to nineteen. The registers are usually arranged as follows: baritones—lower nineteen notes of melody; glockenspiel—upper seventeen notes of melody; violins and saxophones—twenty notes, each on counter melody. Arrangements differ slightly from organ to organ and some organs do not have all the registers.

Note for note, the G4 and VB scales are the same. The music is, to some extent, interchangeable, but the effect is unsatisfactory as the registration is completely wrong. Similarly, 89 key music will play on 87 key organs but the effect is not as the music marker intended. There is a noticeable lack of balance when passages intended for, say, violins are played by the saxophones. More obviously, when VB music is used, the bandmaster goes on strike, except when the slots for setting the registers pass through the key frame. The bellringers are similarly affected.

92, 94, and 98 Key Scales

The 89 VB scale was still further developed by Marenghis and other builders. There was room on the inside edge of the music for yet another key and this was added, together with up to eight keys on the outside edge. Various scales of 92, 94, and 98 keys evolved. The position of the key frame key and some of the registers varies according to the number of keys on the scale. The 98 key scale, which was the largest scale incorporating the basic 87 key arrangement, contains some spare keys (Figure 44). Possibly these were intended for some future development which did not materialise. The extra key on the inside edge of the music was intended to give additional expression to the violin register but this does not appear to have been used. Many so-called 98 key organs have only 94 or 92 keys and it is very doubtful if there is a 98 key organ in existence today which uses all available keys. Music arranged for 89 key organs can be played on 98 key organs provided the keys not covered by the music book are held down by a piece of cardboard. Needless to say, the result is not very satisfactory.

100 KEY MARENGHI SCALE

The scales discussed so far have all been non-chromatic and it was not until after the turn of the century that organs with fully chromatic scales began to appear in Britain. Among the earliest were the 100 key Marenghis. None of these organs survives, in its original form at any rate, and it has, therefore, not proved possible to obtain details of the scale direct from an organ. A 100 key Marenghi music book has, however, been unearthed which has yielded some interesting information about the scale.

Although the writer has had some success in arriving at the scales of organs from a study of music books, he had no luck with this one and passed it over to a musical friend. Apart from the fact that it bore a Marenghi label, two facts only were known about the music book and these were written on the front. First, the title 'Asleep in the Deep' (by H. W. Petrie) and, second, the key size '100 touches'. The French 'touche' was often used for 'key'. Unfortunately, the song was unknown to the writer's friend so he had little to work on, since the number of keys could easily have been established by measuring the music. The last few bars of this book are those shown in Figure 39, which illustrates lighting changes.

The first thing to do when 'scale cracking' is to mark the position of each key on a piece of card which is the same width as the music book. Certain keys can be identified by inspection. Start with the register keys, which are always approximately the same length and nearly always associated with the operation of the declanche. They are easily recognisable. Go right through the book and mark their positions on the card, together with that of the declanche. Next, locate the side-drum keys. The perforations for these are always of the same size and, often, a side-drum roll appears at the end of the music as it does in Figure

39. The regular beat of the bass drum can also be spotted easily, as the slots which operate it are always cut so that they begin in advance of the beat. Other percussion effects are also easy to spot and they should be marked on the card.

Quite often the keys will now divide themselves into obvious groups, which can be cross-checked by reference to the music. The bass group usually plays long notes, one at a time, while the accompaniment usually, but not always, plays a series of short rhythmic chords. The keys associated with these two groups should be established next. Normally this leaves the melody and counter melody to fit into place, the counter melody having fewer notes than the melody. With luck, the layout of the scale should be apparent. Snags do occur, of course, which can cause a lot of trouble. One snag encountered by the writer was the presence of a key for operating a bandmaster in the middle of the accompaniment group. This was on the 65 key scale illustrated in Figure 42.

The relationship between the musical notes is fairly easy to establish because many of the pipes play in unison or octaves. Find a passage where there is no counter melody being played and the counter-melody group is playing with the melody. The relationship between these two groups can then be established. A fairly elementary knowledge of harmony will help to establish the bass and accompaniment notes.

Working on these lines the 100 key Marenghi scale was built up. With only one book available there are, of course, one or two gaps as every key is not used in every book. A study of further books would probably fill in some of the gaps. As mentioned above the song 'Asleep in the Deep' was not known to the writer's friend, but on returning the music book, he played it correctly on the piano, reading the notes from the book itself!

And now to the scale, which was troublesome to establish as both bass and accompaniment groups were interspersed with register and percussion keys. It is illustrated in Figure 45 and guesses are shown with a question mark against them. The bass group has, most probably, twelve notes, F to E, while the accompaniment has only nine, F to C♯. The counter melody has probably twenty-five notes, C to C, while in the melody there

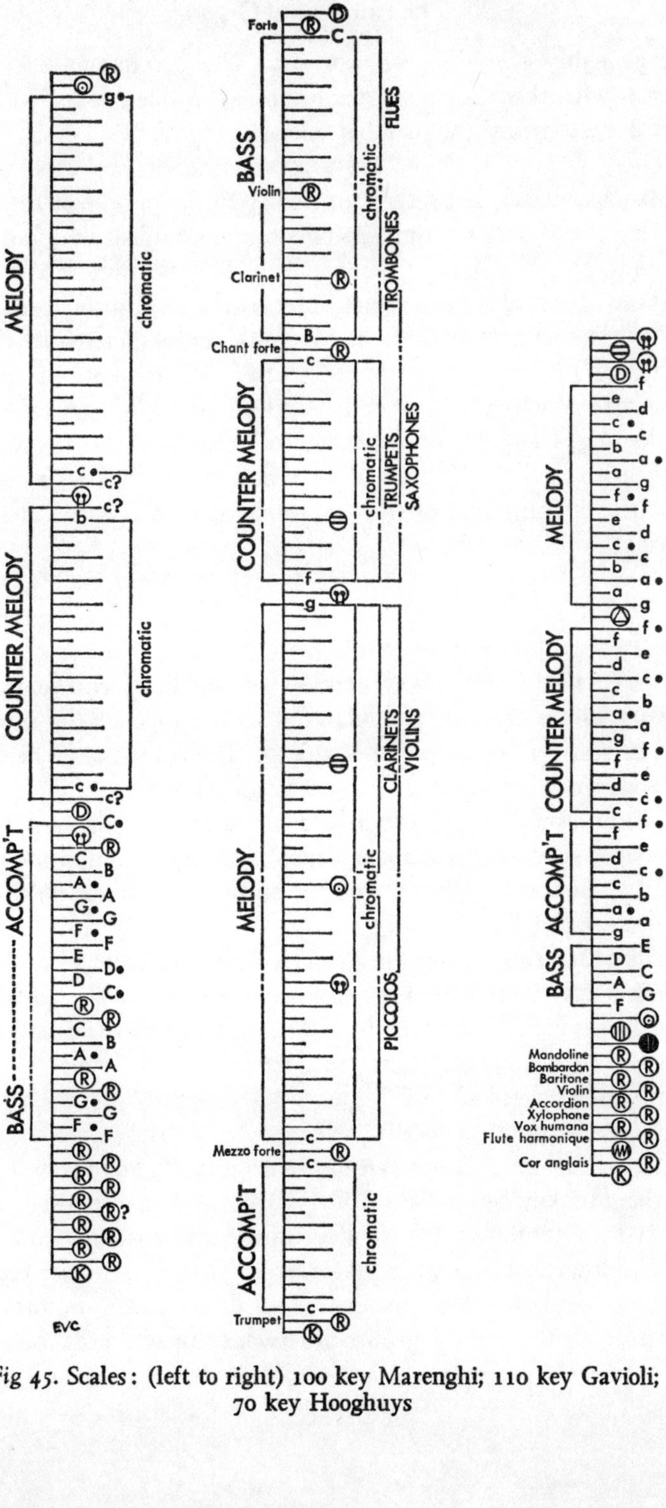

Fig 45. Scales: (left to right) 100 key Marenghi; 110 key Gavioli; 70 key Hooghuys

are probably thirty-three, C to G♯. The percussion effects on organs with this scale consisted of at least a side-drum (two keys) and a bass drum and cymbal coupled together.

There appear to have been about sixteen registers, plus a declanche, positioned rather unusually in the middle of the scale. With a bit of luck it might be possible to establish which groups of pipes certain registers belong to. This is possible if a musical passage is found where either the melody or counter melody is silent. The registers being used would be associated with the group of pipes playing; there is, after all, no point in setting registers which are not used. A close study of several music books might enable some guesses to be made as to the types of register in use. It is fairly safe to assume that the key frame key is at the opening end of the key frame as no slots are cut in the music to operate this.

110 KEY GAVIOLI SCALE

The 110 key Gavioli was another of the fully chromatic fair organs which arrived in England after the turn of the century, and its scale is illustrated in Figure 45. The compass of the organ extends from low C natural, a major third (four semitones) below E natural, the lowest note of the orchestral double-bass, to the C natural seven octaves above, the highest note on a grand piano and two semitones above the highest practical note (B♭) on the orchestral piccolo.

The bass group has a range of two octaves, from C to B. The lower octave consists of 8′ stopped flues, with the dominant added to create a resultant bass. The second octave of bass pipes consists of trombones. There are thirteen notes in the accompaniment group, from C to C.

What is now generally referred to as the melody group appears to be an enlargement of the original 89 key Gavioli scale. In the 110 key organ it has forty-two notes (as opposed to the thirty-four found on the 89 key organ) and extends from G to C. The lower twenty-three notes, from G to F form the clarinet register, while the top nineteen, from F♯ to C, are piccolos.

The counter-melody group has twenty-three notes, one note

short of two octaves, from G to F. The lowest five notes of this group overlap with the top five trombones. The F♯ above middle C is missing from both the top saxophones and bottom clarinets.

Six keys are allocated for register control. The clarinet mixture is controlled by two separate register keys, clarinets *piano,* and chant *forte.* Presumably three different tonal effects can be obtained, by using the registers separately or together. The violins overlap the lowest piccolos by seven notes. When the violins are brought on, these seven piccolos are cut off, allowing the thirty violins to play solo over the whole of their range. Apart from the seven lowest notes, the piccolos are not subject to any register control. The trumpet register, of course, controls the trumpets, while the remaining register controls, *mezzo forte* and *forte* successively add weight. The *forte* register would seem to bring the lowest five saxophones into play as there is no other key for their operation.

Five keys are allocated to percussion effects—one for a bass drum and cymbal coupled together, two for a side-drum and two, rather surprisingly, for castanets. The key frame key is in its usual position. On the outside of the key frame provision appears to have been made for two additional key spaces, possibly for registers which did not materialise.

Francis J. Buckley (who has contributed the barrel organ score and comments which appear in Appendix II) well remembers a 110 key Gavioli and has sent the writer some of his recollections.

He says that the clarinet *piano* register could be used as a solo voice, and with a light accompaniment was admirable. It was used thus in the tenor solo in the *Zampa* overture, where the accompaniment consists of short off-beat chords in the tenor range. The resultant bass was normally effective but tended to become rather overpowering in *piano sostenuto* passages, such as the well-known clarinet solo in the overture to *Oberon.* Additional cuts were made in the music to bring on the clarinet *forte* register. This improved the balance but detracted from the solo effect.

The high saxophones and the low clarinets have roughly the same timbre. This means that the music marker can extend the range of the clarinets downwards or the saxophones upwards by 'borrowing' notes from the other register. Long, sweeping chromatic runs can also be made. These effects were often used on 87 key organs. On 110 key organs, however, F♯ above middle C was missing from both the top of the saxophones and the bottom of the clarinets. If the music marker required this note he would borrow it either from the violins or the accompaniment.

Francis Buckley concludes by saying that the brass trumpets, which had the pitch and range of the clarinets, were voiced to a rather low volume, but were rich in timbre, as distinct from the dull wooden substitutes later used by Marenghis. There were also some very fine French horns in brass, which came on with either the *mezzo forte* or *forte* registers. As the trombones were chromatic they were often used effectively to underline a counter melody in the saxophones at *forte* repetition. Their more normal use was to play in octaves with the bass.

There are no 110 key Gavioli organs playing in Britain in their original state, although one or two are being restored. There is at least one, unaltered in any way, in playing condition in the USA and some information about its scale has been received. It differs slightly from the one just described. Nominally, at any rate, the organ is pitched in a different key, the lowest note being F, and not C. Part of the clarinet mixture is described as 'principal', which would indicate a different tonal quality. The clarinet *forte* register is replaced by a baritone register. This is situated in the lower part of the counter melody (or saxophone) group, which extends on this organ down to the bottom note of the trombones. The trumpet register coincides, operationally, with the upper part of the saxophones. The effect of the registers is as follows:

clarinets	adds clarinets
mezzo forte	adds principal and chimes
violin	adds a rank of violins
trumpet	adds brass trumpets to the upper register of the saxophones
baritone	adds baritones to the lower register of the saxophones

forte	adds a second rank of violins to the first rank and baritones to the trumpets.

70 KEY HOOGHUYS SCALE

This dance organ, which carries the serial number 595, was made in 1910 by the famous Belgian firm founded by Louis Hooghuys in 1880. Three organs were made with this scale. The one to be described is in England; there is another in the USA: the third cannot be traced. As will be seen from Figure 45, the scale of the organ is far from chromatic. Every D♯ and G♯ is missing, as are some other notes. This imposes considerable limitations on the music markers, who have scored most of the music in the keys of F, C, and G. The organ is in excellent condition and, despite its limitations, plays excellently.

The bass group has only six notes, all the naturals except B. The six large pipes which sound the fundamentals are mounted horizontally beneath the organ's case. There are helpers in the centre cabinet. The accompaniment group has ten notes, from G to F♯, both D♯ and G♯ being missing.

The melody group carries on where the accompaniment leaves off and has nineteen notes, G to F, one note short of two octaves. There are four missing notes, lower and upper D♯ and G♯. The counter-melody group has sixteen notes, from C to F♯. G♯ is missing, as well as lower and upper D♯.

There are eight registers. Five are on melody—violin, *flute harmonique, cor anglais,* accordion, and xylophone. Many dance organs have real or specially made accordions mounted on the front. This organ, however, has only a set of brass reeds, of French manufacture, fixed into slots cut in a panel. There are two reeds for each note, which are tuned celeste fashion to produce a slightly wavering effect. The main pipework of the organ operates on a wind pressure of about nine inches (0·324 psi; 25·7g/sq.cm) but the supply to the accordion reeds passes through a regulator which considerably reduces the pressure. The counter melody has two registers—baritone and *vox humana.* There is no foundation tone on either melody or counter melody. The accompaniment group is fixed, though, as are the bass flues. Bombardons can be added to the bass group by means of a register key. The usual declanche, styled *fermee*, shuts off all the registers.

The middle cabinet of the organ is fitted with swell shutters, which give expression to the pipes mounted behind them—the violins, accompaniment, bass helpers, and bombardons. One key opens the shutters and locks them in this position; a second key unlatches them and allows them to close. To prevent the shutters from slamming when they shut an ingenious air-cushioning device operates automatically and slows down the rate of closure.

Some Hooghuys organs were fitted with a mandoline register, but the one on this organ was removed in about 1914, only four years after the organ was built. A register of this kind would cause maintenance difficulties, due to the need for very regular tuning and to the delicacy of the operating mechanism. One such register, which is not in working order, is preserved on a 90 key Hooghuys organ (serial number 690). This organ is in the museum of mechanical musical instruments in Utrecht, Holland, and was built by Charles Hooghuys, the son of Louis.

Percussion effects comprise a bass drum and cymbal coupled together, a side-drum (two keys), a single-stroke triangle, and

Fig 46. Music label used by R. Charles Hooghuys

single-stroke castanets. The key frame key is the outermost key on the frame.

One key operates a tremulant, which is connected to two registers only, the baritone and the *cor anglais*. The *vox humana* has its own tremulant, which is always on when the register is playing, but can be cut out when the organ is being tuned. The *vox humana* tremulant operates at about six beats per second while the tremulant on the baritones and *cor anglais* operates at about four.

At the time of writing, the grandson of Louis Hooghuys, and the son of Charles Hooghuys is alive. He is R. Charles Hooghuys and his monogram is shown in Figure 46.

97 KEY MORTIER SCALE

The famous firm of Th. Mortier built some of the finest dance organs ever made and quite a few 84, 97, and 101 key models are in preservation in this country. Mortiers do not, to any extent, seem to have ventured into the fair organ field. The scale of one of their 97 key models is illustrated in Figures 48a–b and forms the subject of part of the chapter on tuning. The scales of 97 and 101 key Mortier organs are similar but the music is rarely interchangeable even between organs of similar key frame size. The specifications to which both the 97 and 101 key organs were built were very similar, but the arrangement of the keys was altered in nearly every case, presumably to prevent organ owners borrowing and 'pirating' each others' music.

The scale of the 97 key organ referred to above is typical of many Mortier instruments of this type. It is fully chromatic. There are twelve notes in both the bass and accompaniment groups, which run from G to F♯. The accompaniment group continues into the melody, which has twenty-three notes, G to F—one note short of two octaves. The counter melody has twenty notes and runs from C to G.

The melody registers include violins *forte* and violins *piano*, *unda maris*, baxophone, trumpet, vibratone, jazz flute, and xylophone. On counter melody there are cellos, bass cellos, *vox celeste*, flute 8, and saxophone. The accompaniment is fixed but

Fig 47. Music label used by Usines Th. Mortier, in conjunction with music marker Louis Somers

bass trombones can be added to the bass group. A declanche completes the register control system.

The swell shutters fitted to the centre cabinet are opened by one key and shut by another. (On some organs the swell shutters have a key to open them and are closed by the declanche.) In addition to the general tremulant a separate tremulant operates on the jazz flute and vibratone registers.

The percussion effects are reasonably comprehensive. There are a bass drum and a cymbal, both separately operated. The side-drum and wood block are each operated by two keys. There are single-stroke castanets and a reiterating triangle. Finally we have two spare keys and the key frame key.

This is a large organ, built into five cabinets, with the baxophone and xylophone registers on top of the main cabinet. It can successfully tackle most kinds of music. A Mortier music book label is illustrated in Figure 47.

7 Tuning

No organ—mechanical or otherwise—can play well unless it is in tune. There is no doubt that tuning is a skilled job and the technique certainly cannot be learned overnight. A keen amateur can, however, teach himself the basic principles of tuning and work wonders on an organ which would otherwise have gone untuned for lack of a professional tuner. It is a constant source of amazement to the writer that mechanical organs stay in tune as well as they do—especially those travelling with fairs or attending open-air rallies. How they survived, years ago, when they travelled on even rougher roads on trailers with metal-tyred wheels is an even greater mystery.

Every organ owner would be well advised to have a specially cut tuning and scale book. One part should show the complete scale of the organ in key frame order, with the function of each key clearly marked. Register keys should show to which group of pipes the register they control belongs, whether on melody or counter melody, for example. The other part of the book should be cut to facilitate tuning. Details will be given later. A tuning book is, of course, not absolutely essential as it is usually possible to sound the notes by hand, by operating the valve mechanism. On a large Gaudin organ known to the writer small levers are provided adjoining the wind-chests especially for testing and tuning. These enable any notes to be sounded at will. By hanging small weights on them a continuous note can be obtained.

Anyone who wishes to attempt tuning could, with advantage, study the appropriate chapters in any book on the conventional organ. This will give him far more background than the notes in this chapter can hope to supply. The first essential is to know the organ. Analysing the pipework on a large mechanical organ is a fascinating job, and the preparation of a diagram of the pipework and action to be kept for future reference is invaluable. The key frame drive should be disconnected and the section of the music book showing the scale (Figure 48a) should be turned through the key frame by hand. Registers should be set and cancelled as required manually at the register box. Sometimes whole ranks of pipes can be muted with sliders. These facilitate tuning and their positions should be noted. Every pipe should be accounted for when preparing the diagram. Establish the name of each register, checking it with the markings on the register box, and show to which group of pipes each register belongs. The scale part of the book mentioned above will help with this. This initial exploration may reveal that some pipes are not playing or are not connected properly, or that some register controls are not operating as they should. Defects of this sort should be rectified before tuning begins. Accordions pose special problems and these will be touched on later.

At some stage it will have to be decided which registers play at what is known as eight-foot (8′) pitch. With a mechanical organ this can be a somewhat arbitrary decision, but it is a good general rule to select a register on melody where the lowest C corresponds to middle C on the piano. The pitch of all other registers on melody should be related to this, specifying whether they are of 16′, 8′, 4′, or even 2′ pitch. Sometimes what should be the deepest pipes of a register sound an octave higher because, had they been full length, they could not have been accommodated within the organ case; their lengths have, therefore, been halved. This often happens with the bass pipes. In other cases, the lower pipes may change to half-length stopped pipes for the same reason. In this case the pitch will not be affected, although the quality will. Having established the pitch of the melody ranks proceed to the counter melody and nominate an 8′ rank here, preferably one which has the effect of carrying an 8′ melody register down the scale.

When one is familiar with the organ—and not before—tuning can begin. Before getting down to practicalities, however,

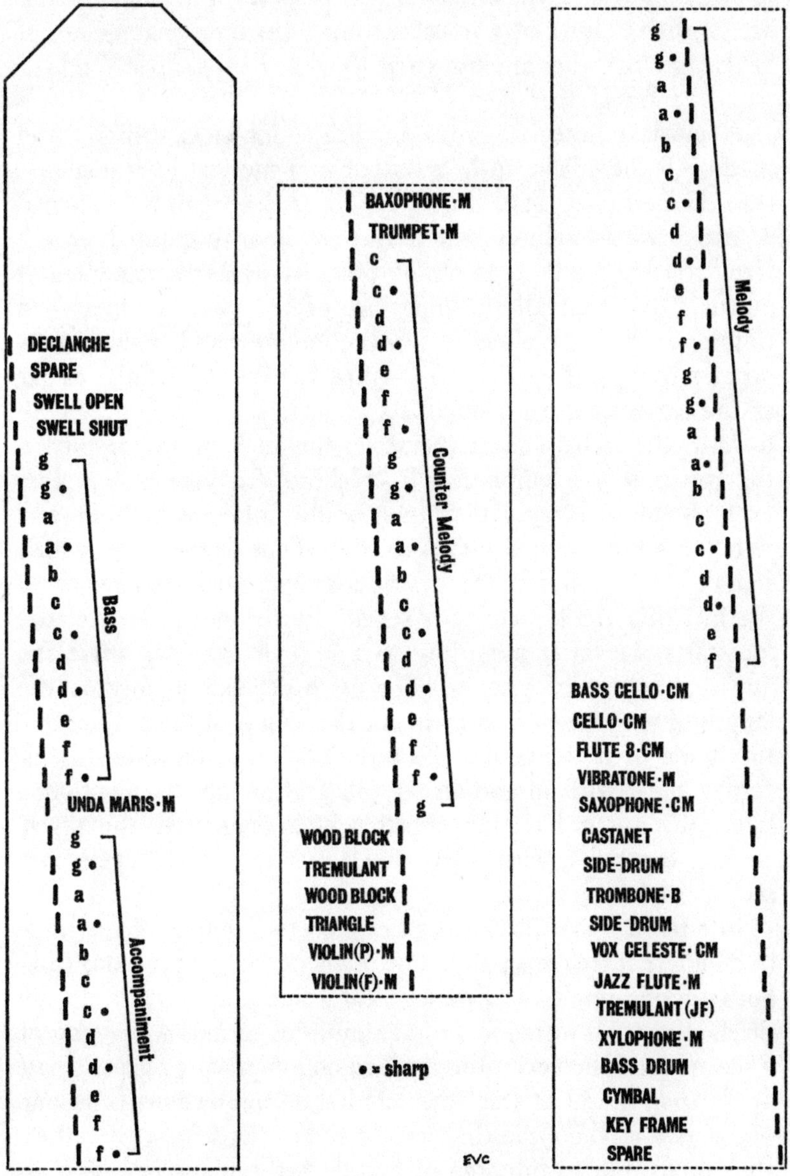

Fig 48*a*. Tuning book for 97 key Mortier organ (first part)

mention must be made briefly of three aspects of acoustics. These are (i) the qualities of a musical sound, (ii) the phenomenon of beats, and (iii) what are known as the *true diatonic scale* and the *scale of equal temperament.*

A musical note has three qualities—loudness, timbre, and pitch. All these have to be adjusted in a musical instrument so that the best effect is obtained. As far as the organ is concerned adjustment of loudness and timbre are jointly covered by the term regulation. If a group of pipes is properly regulated it means either that all the pipes are of the same loudness and timbre, or that any alteration in the loudness and timbre varies progressively, but slightly, from pipe to pipe. Generally, as far as the ear is concerned, loudness appears to increase gradually towards the treble end of the scale; this melodic rise results in the top note predominating in a chord. To give an extreme example of bad regulation, we would think something was wrong if a rank of violin pipes contained one or two pipes which sounded like trumpets. The position is complicated somewhat by the fact that the human ear's sensitivity to certain parts of the musical scale varies according to age. This can also affect the apparent timbre of a sound. The pitch depends mainly on the length of the pipe (if it is a flue) or the length of the tongue free to vibrate (if it is a reed). The tuner's job, theoretically, is concerned only with alteration in pitch although, as mentioned later, this often has side effects which may alter the pipes' timbre, especially with reeds. Pitch is measured in cycles per second, or hertz (Hz).

Interference may take place between two sounds of the same or of different frequencies. At one moment the compressions from both sounds reach the listener's ear simultaneously, as do the rarefactions. This produces a maximum of sound. A fraction of a second later, however, the more rapidly vibrating object is half a vibration ahead of the other, and the compressions from one will arrive at the same time as the rarefactions from the other, thus producing a minimum of sound. A throbbing or pulsating effect is produced, known as 'beats'. This is sometimes referred to as an additive and subtractive, or sum and difference effect. It is also described as constructive and destructive interference, as the vibrations alternately reinforce and annul each other. The number of beats per second is the difference between the frequencies of the two sounds which produce them. A good example is the undulating sound made by a twin-engined aircraft. This is due to the fact that the engines are not going at exactly the same speed.

In what is known as the *true diatonic scale* the ratio of the frequencies of any two adjoining notes is not always the same. The fourths and fifths (ie C–F and F–C, when the keynote is C) harmonise perfectly. There is no dissonance, as what are known as beats, pulsations, or discords are not audible. It is possible, however, to hear resultant tones which are produced by the combination of certain harmonics. (This phenomenon has a practical application in the production of a 'resultant' or 'acoustic' bass. The simplest way of achieving this is to sound simultaneously two pipes which are a fifth apart, say C and G. Pipes of 16′ pitch are usually used and this produces a note an octave lower than the lower note of the pair, in this case, C.) It would be perfectly possible to tune a rank of organ pipes to the true diatonic scale, beginning with, say, C as the keynote. If any attempt were, however, made to play in any other key, that is, to begin the scale on a keynote other than C, discord would result, which would be considerable when certain combinations of notes were played. Even the octaves would not necessarily be in tune. This is because of the irregular intervals. This situation does not arise, incidentally, with instruments such as the trombone, violin, cello, etc, where the player makes his own notes. Any fixed tune instrument (which includes keyboard instruments and mechanical organs) must be playable in any key and the intervals between the notes are 'tempered' so that all keys sound reasonable. The instruments are tuned so that the frequencies of adjoining notes always have the same ratio, $\sqrt[12]{1/2}$ or 0·9439 (about 17/18). This results in what is known as the *scale of equal temperament* and is, in the circumstances, the best compromise which can be arrived at. One result is that the *tempered* semitone is not identical with a *true* semitone. F♯ and G♭ are the same note, which is not so in the true diatonic scale. Another result is that whichever key is used beats are heard when fourths or fifths are sounded together, but not enough to distress the ear. (The octaves are, however, always in tune.) It is the general accumulation of this slight error which helps to produce a rich harmonic sound.

As may be expected, the phenomenon of beats follows a logical pattern. For example, consider the intervals from middle D up to middle A (a fifth), and down to tenor A (a fourth). If the upper A is tuned 'narrow' (ie slightly flat from 'perfect') and the lower A is tuned 'wide' (ie slightly sharp from perfect), each to the D, when the same beat rate is audible the two As are in perfect tune as an octave. In other words, the same beat rate applies to an upper fifth and its complementary lower fourth in any octave. Since any note is at twice the frequency of its lower octave, the beat rate gradually gets faster as the intervals are tuned up the scale. Tuning is carried out to a definite sequence of beat rates. The note being tuned is tuned slightly flat to its parent note. When this is done a fairly strong beat will be heard, its rate being the difference in hertz between certain upper harmonics of the two notes. In the case of fifths, beats are generated by the third harmonic of the lower note and the second harmonic of the higher note. With fourths, the beats are generated by the fourth harmonic of the lower note and the third harmonic of the higher note.

Before tuning is begun a reference frequency must be established. The standard frequency is A=440 Hz, or C=261·62 Hz. Some writers refer to the use of a pitch pipe but this is not necessarily accurate. It is more usual for a tuning fork to be used. This is an economical device within anyone's budget, and its accuracy cannot be surpassed. A piano can be used (if it is in tune), should the organ be located with other instruments in a museum or similar building. Complicated electronic tuning equipment is also available but it is not economical unless it is in more or less continuous use. The pipes and wind-chests are usually marked with the notes they play. This marking, which should coincide with that on the tuning book, may be purely nominal as organs are not necessarily built and tuned to play at standard pitch. They may, for example, be tuned as much as three semitones sharp and in this case a pipe marked C would sound D♯, and so on. According to R. de Waard in his book *From Music Boxes to Street Organs* all Gaviolis and most Carl Frei organs play a minor third higher than standard pitch. Once this is realised no confusion need result, but bear it in mind if an accordion is connected to the organ, remembering that the D♯ on the accordion keyboard may have to be connected to C on the wind-chest, and so on.

There are a number of systems for 'laying the scale' and reference to any book on the manually played organ will give details of these. Tuning books can be cut accordingly. The system to be described is one used on the continent and the illustrations are based on the tuning book supplied for a large Belgian dance organ.

The portion of the tuning book shown in Figure 48b (upper left) should be inserted into the key frame, with the key frame drive disconnected. The book should be adjusted so that the first note (A in this case) sounds on its own. Select a register of medium loudness and shut off all the other registers by hand at the register box, and with sliders if fitted. It is normal for organ tuners to set a scale at 4′ pitch. However, for the amateur, an octave lower (8′ pitch) makes it easier to count the beats and also gives a more accurate result. The note sounding should now be tuned to the frequency selected. When this has been done the tuner should proceed to 'set the scale', by moving the book into position so that E now sounds with A. The E should now be tuned until a perfect fifth is sounding. It is then flattened until the correct number of beats is sounding, in this case seven every ten seconds. The book is then moved on so the E now sounds with the B below. These notes are a fourth apart and the lower note, B, should first be tuned so that a perfect fourth is sounding. It should then be flattened until the correct number of beats is heard, in this case eleven. Note that once tuned, a note is not disturbed. It is always the new note of the pair which is tuned, and this is always flattened until the correct number of beats is heard. The tuner should now work his way through each pair of notes in this section of the book. Details are given overleaf.

Parent Note	*Tune*	*Beats in 10 seconds*
A	E above	7
E	B below	11
B	F♯ above	8
F♯	C♯ below	12
C♯	G♯ above	9
G♯	D♯ below	14
D♯	A♯ above	10
A♯	F below	16
F	C above	12
C	G below	18
G	D above	13
D	A below	20
A	E above	15

When the scale has been set, proceed to the next part of the job, which is tuning the rest of the register to this scale. This is done by tuning pairs of notes in octaves, using in each case a note which has already been tuned (Figure 48b lower left). The tuning must be perfect—no beats should be audible. One or two points arise. First, tune lower G to the octave *above* and, similarly, lower G♯ to the octave *above*. The As are the next notes to sound and they should already be in tune as a result of the first part of the exercise. If they are not, go back to the beginning and check the whole job. If the difference is very, very slight it will probably suffice to retune the top A. (As a general rule a slow beat rate is more acceptable than a fast beat rate.) A♯, C, and D should also be tuned to the octave *above*. The following should be tuned to the octave *below*: B, C♯, D♯, and F. The two Es should already be in tune. If they are not, check top E against the A below it (a fifth) and retune the E if necessary. No further adjustment should be necessary because the two As should already be in tune if the first part of the job has been carried out correctly. The other part of the tuning book (Figure 48a) now comes into use. Select the second register to be tuned and set it by hand. The register on which the scale has been set should be kept set. Work through the whole of the melody notes tuning the second register to the first. Do the same with the other melody registers.

Having tuned all the melody registers proceed to the counter

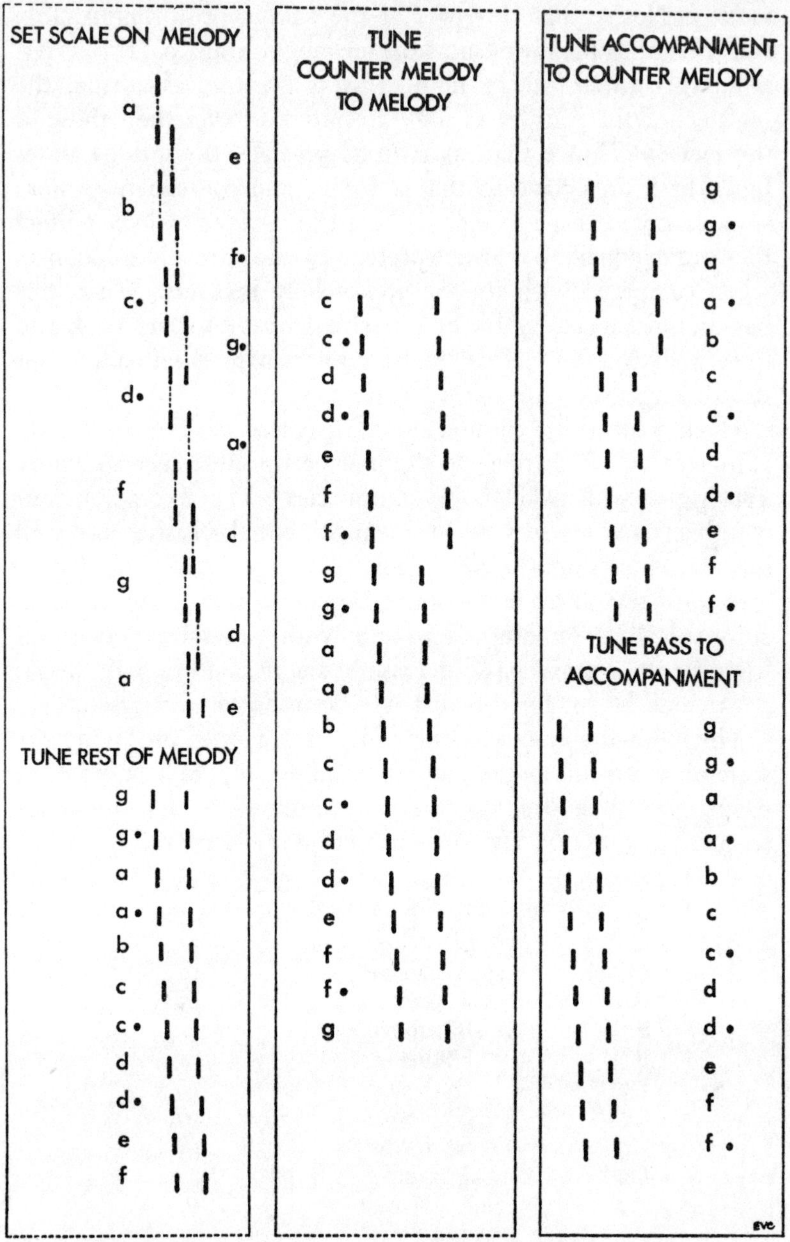

Fig 48*b*. Tuning book for 97 key Mortier organ (second part)

melody. Notice that this part of the tuning book (Figure 48b, centre) sounds the lowest possible melody note against the corresponding counter-melody note. This is because, as a rule, the registers of the counter melody are pitched lower than those of the melody. Notice that, as soon as possible, the melody notes break back an octave so that a lower, and consequently more suitable note can be sounded. Tune the counter melody perfect to a suitable melody register, preferably one of medium loudness when compared with the counter-melody registers. When this has been done change to the other part of the tuning book and tune each counter-melody register in turn to the first register tuned. These should be tuned perfect.

Having tuned the counter melody proceed next to the accompaniment and from there to the bass group. Reference to Figure 48b (right) will make the operation clear. The accompaniment is unlikely to have any register control, but the basses may well have trombones on a separate register.

A good test to see if the organ is in tune is to go up the scale chromatically, sounding each note with the third above and listening for a progressive increase in the rate of beats. A special book could be cut for this if it were considered worth while.

The following system is one which is suggested for laying the scale on electronic organs but it could equally well be used on mechanical pipe organs. Begin by tuning C to a reference frequency of 261·62 Hz, then proceed as follows:

Parent note	*Tune*	*Beats in 10 seconds*
C	G above	9
G	D below	13
D	A above	10
A	E below	15
E	B above	11
B	F♯ below	17
F♯	C♯ below	13
C♯	G♯ above	9
G♯	D♯ below	14
D♯	A♯ above	10
A♯	F below	16

Having tuned the last note (F) test it with the C below, which has been tuned to the reference frequency. The beat rate should be 12 in 10 seconds. If it is not, do *not* retune C. Start again at the beginning and recheck the whole sequence. On some organs, according to the number and arrangement of the notes on the melody group, it may be more convenient to begin on A. If so, use the following sequence:

Parent note	*Tune*	*Beats in 10 seconds*
A (220 Hz)	E above	7
E	B below	11
B	F♯ above	8
F♯	C♯ below	13
C♯	G♯ above	9
G♯	D♯ below	14
D♯	A♯ below	10
A♯	F above	8
F	C below	12
C	G above	9
G	D below	13

Test D, the last note, with the A below which has been tuned to the reference frequency of 220 Hz. The beat rate should be 10 in 10 seconds. If it is not, recheck the whole sequence from the beginning.

Other methods of laying the scale are shown in Figure 49.

And now for a few practical hints.

Choose a suitable day for tuning, as temperature is important —do not attempt the job when there is snow on the ground or during a heatwave. In the case of fair organs which perform mainly in the open air choose a day when the temperature is normal for the summer—about 60°F or 15·5°C.

Tune a register against one of similar loudness and timbre. Avoid trying to tune a very loud register against a very soft one.

Flue pipes of the open type should be tuned to the note required by knocking down the tuning slide to sharpen the pipe, or knocking it up to flatten it. An easy way to test if a pipe is sharp or flat is to shade the top with the hand. If this brings the pipe more into tune it needs flattening: if it makes it more out of tune it needs sharpening. Large open wood pipes usually have a rectangular slot cut at the top of one of the sides. This is covered by an adjustable wooden plate. The more the slot is

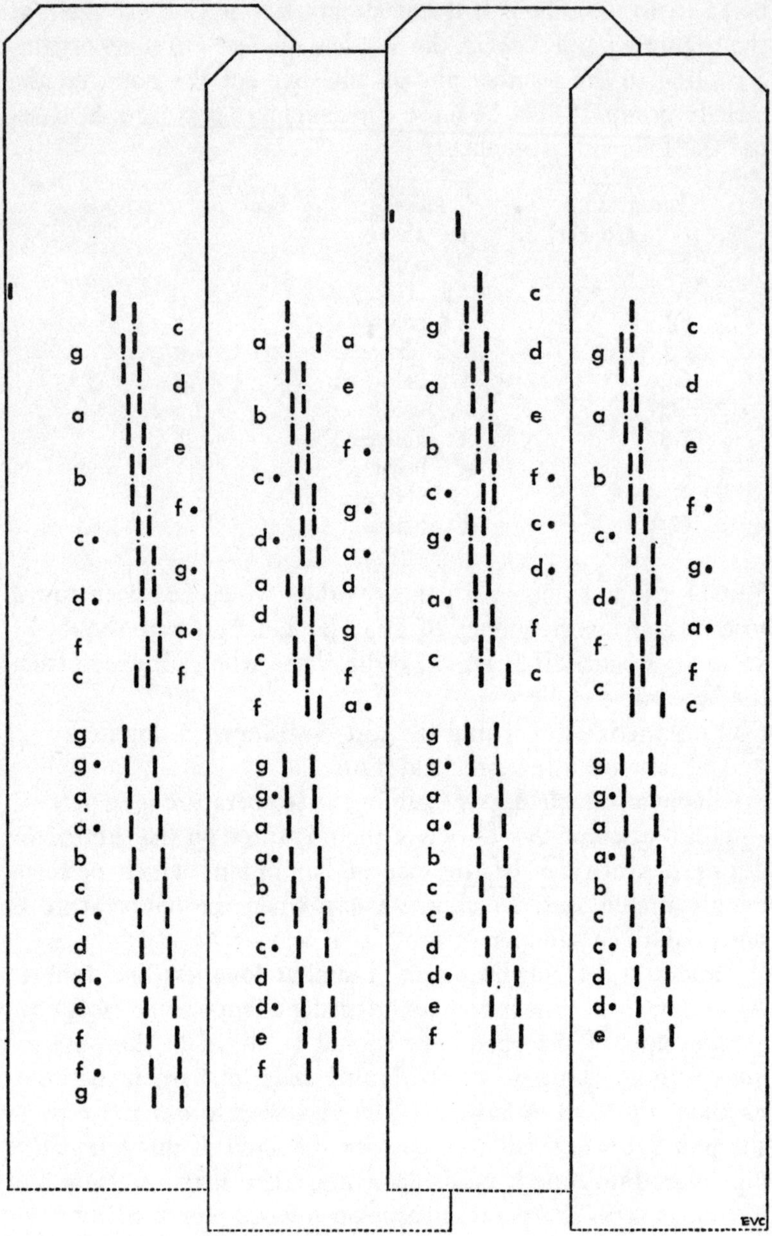

Fig 49. Various systems for 'laying the scale'

uncovered, the sharper becomes the pipe. Metal cellos (as found on Mortier organs), or other large metal pipes, have two parallel cuts made in them at the top, usually at the back. The metal tongue so formed can be rolled or unrolled to adjust the pitch of the pipe. A slight tuning of metal flue pipes, especially the smaller ones, may be effected by pressing or setting the ears of the pipes inwards to flatten the pipe and outwards to sharpen it. This method is, however, only advised when all else fails. Treble flues will probably need little attention. Quite often dust in the mouth of the pipe causes trouble and dusting with a feather will nearly always restore the pitch. Putting the stopper further into a stopped pipe sharpens it, while pulling the stopper out flattens it. The same procedure applies to half-stopped pipes.

Reeds are sharpened by knocking down the tuning wires; this shortens the length of tongue free to vibrate. Knock the wire up to flatten the pipe; this increases the length of tongue free to vibrate. Special tools, known as 'reed knives' are used for this purpose. If possible, loud reeds—apart from the initial octave—are best tuned with other octaves of the same rank, as the beats are easier to hear. On reeds the tone is affected as well as the pitch when the tongue is shortened or lengthened. The amount by which the tone is affected depends on the coupling of the tongue vibrations to those of the resonator. As a result, reeds can easily get out of regulation because of inexperienced tuning.

Registers consisting of more than one rank of pipes need special attention. The first thing to establish is the reason for having more than one rank. It may be to achieve loudness or to build up a special timbre—or for a combination of these reasons. On both fairground and dance organs, the violins usually consist of at least two ranks (sometimes as many as seven) playing in unison. Occasionally, a double-length rank is included which sounds an octave lower. Violin pipes sounding the same note or the octave should be tuned perfect. Do not confuse an *unda maris* or vox celeste register with a violin register, as they often look identical. One rank is tuned in unison to the rest of the organ while the other is tuned, usually, slightly flat and, less often, slightly sharp to produce the characteristic undulating tone of these registers. Listen carefully to the register before tuning it to establish the beat rate, which should get faster towards the top of the scale. Find out which rank sounds in unison with the rest of the organ and tune this rank first.

Some continental organs have a bourdon register on either melody or counter melody. This register usually consists of two ranks of stopped flutes, one rank of which is tuned either slightly sharp or slightly flat, as in the unda maris or vox celeste, and tuning should be tackled in a similar manner. Sometimes the ranks sound in unison; sometimes they are a fifth apart, an octave apart, or even a twelfth apart. The bass group may consist of up to five or six ranks of pipes—both stopped and open. Sometimes, on small organs, trombones are included. Normally, however, the deep reeds are on a separate register or are operated by a separate group of keys. All bass pipes should be tuned so that they sound in unison, without any beats being audible. It will be found that the deeper flues rarely need attention.

Complicated mixtures are not often found on mechanical organs. Sometimes what is known as a clarinet mixture is encountered on fairground organs and all ranks of this, like other mixtures, should be tuned so that no beats are heard.

Tune one pipe at a time when dealing with registers which contain more than one rank of pipes. If sliders are fitted, shut off the ranks not required. Otherwise, mute pipes as necessary with soft paper or cloth, or small mops.

An organ fitted with one or more accordions presents difficulties. The first thing is to establish to which groups of pipes the bass and treble parts of the accordion are connected. An amateur tuner will be unable to tackle an accordion—it is a job for an expert. If the accordion is more or less in tune do not attempt to adjust it. Tune the first rank of pipes to it. It does no harm to have the accordion very slightly sharp when compared with the rest of the organ as this adds a certain brilliance to the tone and makes it stand out when playing as a solo instrument. The same applies to other solo instruments such as xylophones and glockenspiels. If the accordion is badly out of tune, an accordion specialist will have to be called in to advise. He will undoubtedly take the accordion away to his workshop, where he will tune it to any required pitch. Because of their rather indefinite pitch, xylophones, glockenspiels, bells, and temple blocks are best left alone.

The example illustrated and discussed is of a large fully chromatic organ. The 87, 89, or 98 key fair organ with a Gavioli/Marenghi scale is not fully chromatic. Organs with these scales have only eight bass notes, two notes are missing from the accompaniment, and top D♯ from both melody and counter melody. Since, however, the melody is chromatic, except for the one note just mentioned, no particular problems arise. A scale can be set on melody, and counter melody, accompaniment, and basses (both flues and reeds) tuned in turn. Some organs may have considerably more missing notes, although the middle part of the melody usually contains a fully chromatic scale. If an organ with certain notes missing completely is encountered it will provide an interesting exercise to devise a system for laying the scale. One last word to the beginner—don't be too ambitious. Tackle a small organ first. This will cause enough headaches. Leave the 101 key organs until later! A selection of mechanical organ scales were illustrated and discussed in Chapter 6. The would-be tuner could well exercise his ingenuity by devising tuning books and procedures for these, especially for the 70 key Hooghuys.

8 A Short History

THE EARLY YEARS

THE preceding chapters have dealt with the way in which the organ works and with its music, and the reader should now be familiar with the various technical terms employed. It is, therefore, possible to deal with the history of the organ in the form of a simple narrative, uncluttered with technical explanations.

The mechanical organ has been part of the fairground scene for at least 150 years. The early instruments were not specially built for fairs, but were of the kind used by itinerant street musicians. Evidence for this is found in an oil painting entitled *A Village Fair* by Joseph Parry, who died in 1826. The picture is not dated but, obviously, it must have been painted sometime prior to 1826—perhaps round about the time of the battle of Waterloo! Included in the painting are three small barrel organs. Two of these are on the stages fronting side-shows, while the third is slung round the neck of its grinder. These instruments are the simple barrel organs of the period with flute pipes of wood or metal. None of the organs has any percussion effects. The organs on the side-shows are supplemented by what appear to be small drums, tambourines, bells or rattles, played by the show people.

Some years later Charles Dickens made several references to barrel organs in his story *Going into Society*. This was one of his *Christmas Stories* and was written in 1858. A showman had taken over an empty house for his activities and described it as follows:

> The front of the House was so covered with canvases, that there wasn't a spark of daylight ever visible on that side. 'MAGSMAN'S AMUSEMENTS', fifteen foot long by two foot high, ran over the

front door and parlour windows. The passage was a Arbour of green baize and gardenstuff. A barrel-organ performed there unceasing.

As well as fronting side-shows and being used by itinerant musicians working the fairgrounds, organs began to appear on rides, as on page 108 (above). At this time all organs would have been turned by hand. In due course, however, all but the smaller rides were converted from man-power, or horse-power to steam-power. The next logical step was to make use of the handy supply of steam which was now available, to drive the organs. As mentioned earlier, this was done by Soame of Marsham, when he introduced the steam organ engine in about 1865. As automatic tune-changing had not been introduced at this time, one can well imagine that tunes would have been repeated *ad nauseum* before the showman got round to shifting the barrel onto the next tune. In fact, a case was reported of a showman being summonsed for creating a nuisance by allowing his organ to play 'Won't you come home, Bill Bailey?' all day without stopping. As far as shows were concerned the organs did not, of course, play while a performance was on. With small circuses, however, there was often a small hand organ inside which played for the acts.

The exact date when organs were first built especially for the fairground is uncertain, but it was probably in about 1870.

The earliest type of fairground organ appears to have been the trumpet barrel organ, so called because of the fine display of brass trumpet-shaped resonators fixed to the reed assemblies. In addition to these there would have been a few similar, but larger trombone resonators. The remainder of the pipework would have been made up from piccolos of the now traditional design and, possibly, clarinets, with open and stopped wood flutes for bass and accompaniment pipes. These early organs were still without percussion effects, a refinement which had to wait until after the general introduction of pneumatic action. This simple box-type barrel organ, which survived for many years, was designed to imitate a military band. It was general practice for the sales catalogues and advertisements of the period to describe an organ as being equivalent to a band of so-many musicians. This was done not only to indicate, in the opinion of the maker, the musical capability of the organ, but also to give the prospective purchaser an indication of the money he would save by using a mechanical organ instead of live musicians! In the event, the standard of musical performance was probably in many cases superior either to that of a band of travelling musicians or the town band.

Most of the early organs were made by Gavioli of Paris. This is, without doubt, the most famous name in the mechanical organ industry. The family emigrated from Italy in about 1845 and set up an organ-building business in Paris. The fortunes and misfortunes of this firm have been well documented in the book *From Music Boxes to Street Organs*. Some organs made by the British firm of Wright & Holmes Brothers were also used at this time, but it is interesting to note that the man in charge of an organ was always known as a 'gaviman' regardless of the make of the organ he looked after.

By the mid 1890s steam rides were well established on the fairground and these included roundabouts of all kinds, horses, switchbacks, tunnel railways, and steam yachts. These all had their organs. In addition to the large rides a number of small-time operators toured a modest assortment of swings, boats, juvenile rides, and stalls. These would sometimes be accompanied by a truck on which was mounted a small trumpet organ, complete with boiler and steam organ engine.

No fair was complete without its shows, both large and small. The large shows included fairground menageries and circuses, marionette and ghost shows, and waxworks. These were known as 'walkup' shows, as a platform or stage was assembled across the entrance, with steps leading up on the outside and ramps leading down on the inside. All these shows had barrel organs mounted on the platforms and the most popular type would have been the wingless trumpet box organ with 50 to 64 keys. There is a photograph of Oldham Wakes, taken in the late 80s, showing three or four large shows in a line, seemingly all with organs of this type. These organs would have a foundation frame to which had been added permanent rollers to assist in offloading them from a general-purpose truck. The organ was usually placed on what is known as the opposite prompt side of the stage, that is, on the public's left as they see the stage. A typical show of this kind can be seen on page 108 (below). At this period most organs would be hand-turned by means of a large cast-iron wheel, some 15–18 inches (38–45cm) in diameter, manipulation of which required the full efforts of a hefty male for long periods. Percussion effects were added by two assistants, one of whom performed on a full-sized bass drum with cymbal attached, while his companion rattled a side-drum. Sometimes, in addition, a cornet player or similar instrumentalist would be employed. There would also be a couple of pairs of resonant brass bells to which anybody connected with the establishment had access. These were the days of uninhibited noise and the competition of raucous steam sirens and deep-toned whistles from the roundabouts had to be met.

The smaller type of show had no stage or platform and was known as a ground booth or, sometimes, a 'peep show'. These, too, would have had organs on the front and instances have been recorded of organs being driven either by an organ engine fed with steam from a small vertical steam boiler or by a small oil engine.

THE COMING OF THE BIOSCOPE AND BOOK ORGAN

'. . . the steam organ attached to a small roundabout filled the air with a pungent flavour of oil and with equally pungent music'. So wrote H. G. Wells, when describing a village fair in *The Invisible Man*. This book was written in 1897—an important date in the history of the fairground as, at about that time, two inventions appeared which had far-reaching effects on the fairground scene. These were the moving picture and the book organ, the latter having been pioneered by Gaviolis in about 1892.

The showmen were not slow to exploit the possibilities of the moving picture and shows of all kinds were quickly converted into cinemas, or bioscopes, as they came to be called. At first, there was little change externally; inside, of course, projectors and screens replaced the former contents of the booths. Electric arc lights, both for external illumination and for the projector, now began to come into general use, superseding carbide and limelight as the illuminants in the latter. The organs were now almost invariably driven by electricity and it was usual for either an electric-light engine or a showman's road locomotive, complete with generator, to be drawn up on the opposite side of the stage to the organ.

Book organs first arrived in any quantity at the beginning of the bioscope era. These were 87 key Gaviolis and they were soon installed on the fronts of shows and in rides. The first in the British Isles went to Toft and Turnbull of Belfast. The second (which was the first in England, Wales, or Scotland) went to Harry Wallis of Seaforth, Liverpool. Under an arrangement Limonaire produced similar instruments with 87 keys or, later, a kind of economy model with only 86 keys.

Soon after the turn of the century, and not for the first time, Gaviolis suffered a financial setback. Staff were laid off and Charles Marenghi who occupied a responsible position with the firm, left to open his own business, taking other key workers with him. In due course Marenghi organs began to arrive in Great Britain. The first of these had 89 keys, like the later Gaviolis, and with a similar scale, but different register arrangements. A very fine Marenghi organ of this type can be seen on page 125 (above).

There is no doubt that these 86, 87, and 89 key organs were some of the most successful and popular ever made and many have survived and are still playing today. Many 86 and 87 key organs were converted either to the Gavioli or Marenghi 89 key scales by the addition of baritone and violin registers. Marenghi, while keeping the basic 87 key scale more or less unchanged, increased his range in due course by producing 92, 94, and 98 key sizes.

The race was now on, and showmen vied with each other to see who could have the most elaborate show front and the best and largest organ. Up until about 1905 show fronts had been built up around two wagons, with a central entrance, and were known as either 'wagon fronted' or 'two wagon' shows. The organ, which now began to be decorated with incandescent lamp bulbs, was promoted and moved to a central position, with entrances for the public on each side. This type of show became known as an 'organ fronted' show and it underwent considerable elaboration in the next few years.

THE PEAK OF THE BIOSCOPE ERA

By 1907 the bioscope show had reached the peak of its popularity and the organs and fit-ups, both inside and out, had attained an excellence that was never to be equalled as can be seen on page 125 (below). The bioscope shows were, however, now competing with the picture palaces which were springing up all over the country—and it was the latter which eventually won.

Until now the notes played by the organs had not formed fully chromatic scales and this imposed certain limitations on the music markers when it came to key changes, or when the bass or accompaniment sections were required to play the melody. This shortcoming received the attention of the makers, and organs with fully chromatic scales became available. Each maker, of course, ensured that his own products played only his own music, and a bewildering series of key frame sizes appeared.

The largest and most elaborately fronted organs were those imported from Paris, the three biggest firms there being Gavioli & Cie, Ch. Marenghi & Cie, and Limonaire Frères. The main British firms were Chiappa & Sons (of London), Wright & Holmes Brothers, and A. Varetto & Sons (both of Manchester). Small excursions into the fair organ field appear to have been made by Imhof & Mukle and The Harper Electric Piano Co (1910) Ltd. (both of London), Jaconelli (of Birmingham), Antonelli (of Manchester), and Walker & Sons (of Tewkesbury). These firms acted as agents for their continental rivals. Savages (of King's Lynn) were at one time agents for Gaviolis and had a special organ showroom; they were able to supply new riding machines, complete in all respects, with carved work and organ.

The history of the fair organ from 1907 onwards is very much tied up with the history of the makers, especially the three big firms in Paris.

Despite a very extensive publicity campaign extending over many years Limonaires were not particularly successful so far as the British market was concerned. They claimed to have been established since 1840 and stated in their advertisements that they were 'actually the oldest firm, not electricians', and relied 'on the musical parts of their organs' to recommend them to travellers at large, 'not on electrical effects'—presumably a dig at some Marenghi organs which had elaborate lighting effects on their prosceniums. Limonaires' products bore the trade name of *Orchestrophones,* and part of their monogram is shown in Figure 50. In 1908 they were advertising a 92 keyless paper organ, guaranteed to have the simplest and most perfect system introduced at that date in this country. The organ was 'put in

Fig 50. Part of Limonaire Frères monogram

motion by an entirely new style French electric ¾hp motor'. Limonaires made organs with a variety of key frame sizes, from 35 to 118. The smallest was recommended as being suitable for cakewalks and in 1908 they claimed that six had been sold for this purpose. They tried to compete with both Gaviolis and Marenghis in the provision of show fronts. They made at least one specially large organ for a bioscope front which had, in addition to the usual percussion effects, a large 'thunder' drum, which occupied pride of place in the centre of the proscenium.

Although Marenghi did not set up in business on his own account until after the turn of the century, the firm became well established, respected, and well known within a surprisingly short space of time. Gaviolis must, indeed, have suffered a severe blow when Marenghi departed. There is no doubt that Marenghi used many of Gaviolis' ideas, but he also introduced many of his own. His products bore the trade name of *Ideal Orchestre* and the range included fully chromatic organs of 100, 102, and 104 keys. The 104 key model had the air feeders mounted on top of the organ case, doubtless to allow room for the many ranks of violin pipes which were now becoming an established feature of the large organs and which produced remarkably good tonal effects. Other characteristic features of the 104 key organs were the two three-quarter-life-size figures on pedestals, one at each end of the organ's front. One of the figures operated a bass drum and the other a side-drum. These were in addition to the bass and side-drums installed inside the organ's casing. One very large Marenghi organ went to the well-known showman, Pat Collins. On 25 April 1907 he wrote to Ch. Marenghi & Cie in Paris as follows from Walsall:

> Gentlemen,
>
> A line to say I am delighted with the new organ you sent to Wrexham for my show front. I think you have excelled all others. I consider it the finest orchestra that has ever been built, both for the music and tone it is so perfect, the workmanship is thoroughly well done, and the artistic work and decorations are magnificent. I may say that when we opened it thousands stood around daily to hear it—it was the talk of everyone in the district.
>
> Thanking you for your prompt and safe delivery of same.
>
> Yours truly,
> P. Collins

The ensuing popularity of the show and organ was very great and the following paragraph appeared in *The World's Fair* in September of the same year:

> Probably the greatest attraction at the Wakes has been Mr Collins' monster mechanical organ, costing no less a sum than £2,000, which forms a beautiful frontage to a first-rate cinematograph show. It is reputed to be the largest of its kind ever built; it certainly is an extremely large one, which can be gathered from the fact that there are over 1,200 instruments in it. At different intervals the organ has been illuminated by hundreds of vari-coloured electric lamps, which continually change in tint, forming designs at each change, and together with the rich gold and white frontage to the

> show, it is an artistic sight, altogether removed from what one is accustomed to meet on a fair ground. It is elaborate in the extreme and the music it sends forth is extremely fine.

Gaviolis' largest *Gavioliphones* (as their products were known) were at that time their 110 key models, the first of which was delivered in 1906 through their London Agents, Chiappas. By the middle of 1907 Chiappas advertised saying that eight out of ten orders for this type of organ and show front had been met. They still had two orders in hand but were prepared to take further bookings. These organs were described as having

> been made with 110 keys so as to have a complete scale, making it absolutely unnecessary to have any larger size than this latest model, which is absolute perfection in tone and artistic design of front. These organs are Messrs Gaviolis' masterpiece and result of six years careful study.

This type of organ which had two side-drums was certainly very popular, both in Great Britain and in the USA, where it was advertised as being suitable for both indoor and outdoor use. The scale of this organ has been dealt with in some detail in Chapter 6.

Despite the claim that no larger scale was necessary Gaviolis produced, a year or so later, their 112 keyless model. This appears to have been a last effort to capture the market, but it did, in fact, help to bring disaster to the firm. The model incorporated two novelties. One was an attempt to reduce cost and wear of music. The second, indirectly connected with this, was a new system of feeding wind to the bellows reservoir.

For the first, recourse was made to the Gavioli patent (specification 855 of 1891) which covered the use of two wind pressures. The high-pressure wind passed directly through the perforated music and operated the primary relay system of pneumatics. The low-pressure supply served the reservoir in the usual way. This system was quite different from the keyless exhaust pneumatic system described in Chapter 3, which is now in more or less general use on keyless organs. The early 112 keyless models used paper roll music, although later ones may have been fitted for cardboard books ex-works.

The firm's patent of 1907 (specification 5888) covered the replacement of the usual hinged feeders by two air compressors in the form of rectangular wooden chambers. Wooden pistons reciprocated in these. The pistons were made airtight by grooves which were both unpacked and unringed, in emulation of the labyrinth gland piston. The claim was advanced that by operating these at sufficient speed the eddies of air produced in the channels were sufficient to oppose the passage of air from one side to the other. The curious thing was that, contrary to all expectation, the system *did* produce the necessary quantities and pressures. Neither of these novelties was, however, successful in the long run and the cost was a heavy one. The air pressure on the music roll tore it far more quickly than keys, and the roll had to be rewound at the end of its repertoire with consequent interruption to the performance. The timber air compressors soon developed all sorts of troubles and attempts to put them right resulted in further breakages. Possibly the organs were sold under some sort of guarantee, for legal actions and claims for damages were numerous and may have accelerated Gaviolis' financial failure.

Owners had their 112 keyless organs converted to the 110 key scale or, later, to the 98 key Marenghi scale which came to be one of the accepted sizes when some form of standardisation became necessary for economic reasons. The owners also had the timber air compressors replaced by the normal triple feeder wind supply system. After the sad record of failure it is pleasant to record that the modified organs were thoroughly satisfactory.

The general makeup of pipes and other speaking units in the 112 key organs followed closely those of the 110 key scale, including a fine deep bass, trombones, clarinets, piccolos, trumpets, saxophones, and, in particular, violins and their lower pitched strings. There were seven ranks of violins, with lower strings in proportion and the result was an increase in the sweetness, and a strengthening of timbre which produced a magnificent balance of tone and volume unequalled by other organs.

Over the years much confusion has arisen about which organs were made by which firms. Further confusion has arisen as to the key frame sizes and scales used by the various makers. Confusion on these matters has been caused, in part, by the vast amount of conversion and rebuilding that took place from time to time. A case in point was the arrival from Marenghis' works of Gavioli organs with Marenghi fronts. It seems that when Gaviolis went out of business Marenghi acquired some of the former's unfinished organs and later resold them with Marenghi fronts. Apparently some 110 key Gaviolis appeared in this guise as Marenghi himself did not make any 110 key organs. To confuse matters still further, Gaviolis' goodwill is reputed to have been taken over by Limonaires. One of Gaviolis' famous music labels is reproduced in Figure 51. Some pages from the catalogues of Limonaires, Marenghis, and Gaviolis are reproduced on pages 126, 143-4.

Two of the main British firms operated in Manchester. Pietro Varetto was foreman for Gaviolis at their shop (in Blossom Street, Ancoats, Manchester) and took over the business on the failure of the French firm, running it with his sons. When he died, in 1910, his widow, Angela, carried on the business as A. Varetto & Sons. Upon her retirement four of the sons carried on as Varetto Brothers, employing mainly their own sons and nephews. In 1909 the firm took over a large furniture warehouse (in Milton Street, Lower Broughton, Salford) the rear part of which had been successively occupied by Gaviolis and Chiappas. Varettos adapted the building by strengthening the first floor and installing a manually-operated lift capable of handling the largest organs. The three floors of the building provided storage space and workshops, which were equipped with lathes and other machine tools for working in wood or metal. In addition, there were specialist machines for carrying out all the operations associated with the production of book and barrel music.

Varettos' ingenuity appeared to have no limits and the firm was sought out for many specialist jobs. These included designing and constructing very small mechanisms for self-playing concertinas used by music-hall artists, and the three one-manual trumpet organs featured by the Elliot Savonas, a bill-topping variety musical act of the 1920s. Peter Varetto invented and constructed a successful machine which turned out finished barrel organ pins and staples of any chosen lengths straight from the

Fig 51. Music label used by Gavioli & Cie

wire at an hourly rate reckoned in the thousands. Portable electric motors were wound to Varettos' own specifications so that they operated with maximum efficiency whether they were in continuous use at full speed or being run slowly for tuning and other adjustments.

The firm's output of organs was restricted to the smaller types but they overhauled, reconditioned, converted, and rebuilt instruments of every kind. Their craftsmanship and musicianship were always first class.

Sometime in the early 1920s they came to an agreement with Chiappas to market the latter's music from 89 keys upwards; for their part Chiappas passed on to Varettos all barrel organ work from London and the South. Varettos went out of business in the mid 1930s as a result of competition from amplified music.

The other Mancunian firm was Wright & Holmes Brothers. Prior to the formation of the firm both these names were associated with organ building in the district but the family relationships—if they existed—are unknown.

Wright was a first-class craftsman and musician, and handled the outside business, including tuning and repairs, with an efficiency which inspired confidence. One of the Holmes brothers, John, took charge of the works in Forest Street, Rochdale Road, Manchester. This was an establishment similar to Varettos' shop, but it employed a rather larger staff, mostly sons and relations. The other brother, James, was the 'bandmaster', in charge of all the major arranging and marking. He possessed a musical memory that was phenomenal and an innate sense of harmony and theory that characterised his work. (One of his arrangements forms the subject of appendix II to this book.)

After years concerned with barrel organs the firm swiftly took on everything connected with the maintenance and supply of music for the new 87 key book organs as soon as these appeared. The lilting settings of Boer War songs like 'Goodbye, Dolly Grey'—a revival from Crimean days—are imperishably implanted in the memories of elderly enthusiasts.

In 1905 Wright & Holmes Brothers converted an 87 key organ from book to barrel operation. This was done on the insistence of the owners and not without qualms of conscience by the firm at such vandalism. The idea caught on among show folks in the North and similar orders piled up. Such a clientele was developed, that eight years later, maintenance and provision of music for these conversions was keeping this side of the firm fully occupied and as a result of this they confined their book music to scales below 87 keys. The firm ceased business in the 1930s, another victim of amplifier competition. Like Varettos they made only small organs and their output was very much less than that of the French makers. Also like Varettos they left behind a reputation for first-class work and straightforward business dealing.

Although some organs were supplied by the makers with prosceniums which included entrances and pay boxes, much of this work was done by George Orton, Sons & Spooner Ltd (as they are now styled) of Burton upon Trent. A showman would order an organ from Paris and it would be delivered direct to Ortons, where it would be mounted on a truck. The rest of the showfront, including pay boxes and entrances, if not already incorporated in the organ's proscenium, would be built up round the organ. The whole of the front would be elaborately carved to match the organ—Ortons employed specialist wood carvers for this work. When ready for the road, the organ truck together with the dismantled show front, which packed into it, weighed several tons and was sometimes over thirty feet long. A first-class show front must have been very costly. Exact figures are difficult to come by, but *The World's Fair* of June 1909 carried the following paragraph under the heading 'Cost of Mechanical Organs':

> There is, of course, a great deal of elasticity of prices about organs. The old fashioned wheezy machine that can only grind out a few tunes costs between £25 and £50, but the up-to-date Paris-made organ, operated by an electric motor, fed by paper rolls of music, and illuminated by hundreds of electric globes, may easily cost £1,500 to £2,000. The music supplied by the latter type is excellent, and is beyond all comparison with the nerve-racking performances of the old-time organ.

THE SLOW DECLINE

With increasing competition from the cinemas in the towns, the bioscope shows faced a slow decline, and when the First World War broke out in 1914 those that remained were nearly all taken off the road. The showman was now faced with the problem of how to use the organ, probably the most valuable part of his show. Many organs saw a new lease of life in the elaborate scenic railways which were now reaching the peak of their popularity. The steam centre engine and driving frame in switchback rides were dispensed with and electric motors installed beneath the cars. The centre of the ride was now left free for elaborate scenic effects and larger organs. Some showmen had organs specially built for them while others adapted bioscope organs. The organ fronts were drastically cut down in size and much of the carved work was dispensed with. In some cases, of course, this necessitated alteration to the pipework. Pipework was altered, too, when many of the organs were converted to the 98 key Marenghi scale. This was probably largely due to the cost of and the difficulty in obtaining music. The establishment of the 89 and 98 key scales as a standard meant that, basically, the same musical arrangement could be used for both scales. Allowance had to be made, however, for differences in register arrangements. A further standardisation was forced on organ owners when 87 key music was more or less discontinued.

The Harper Electric Piano Co (1910) Ltd began a fairly extensive advertising campaign in 1912 directed towards fairground operators, for their paper roll operated orchestrions and fair organs, the prices of which ranged from £150 to £750. Whether or not these were of their own manufacture is not known. Harpers do not appear to have had any great success as far as fairgrounds are concerned.

At the end of 1912 the now well-known firm of Gebrüder Bruder (of Waldkirk, Germany) made an effort to enter the British market. Their agents were Walker & Sons, well-known makers of fairground equipment, who also supplied music for Gavioli and Marenghi organs. Northern outlets were arranged through Antonellis and A. C. Boyce (of Dunford Bridge, near Sheffield).

The Bruder family had been in the mechanical organ business since the early years of the nineteenth century and, in Germany, occupied a somewhat similar position to that of the Gavioli family in France. (One of the Bruders did, in fact, work for Paviolis' German branch.) Bruders were very much a family business and operated as a number of small firms—Gebrüder Bruder, Ignaz Bruder Sohn, Wilhelm Bruder Sohn, and Alfred Bruder. Bruder organs were keyless and initially four types were advertised: *Appolo, Sirene, Jubilaum,* and *Pompadour.* The proscenium of *Appolo,* with its swell shutters, was identical in appearance to the Wurlitzer 165 Band Organ made in the USA. The outbreak of war in 1914 put a complete stop to the import of Bruder organs for some years. Later, Chiappas became Bruder agents and sold many 46 key models for use in chairoplanes. Oddly enough, this popular model does not appear to be listed in any of Bruders' catalogues.

In the early 1920s Charles Marenghi died and his business was carried on for a few years by the Gaudin Brothers, who had worked for Marenghis. The business was now on the decline and not very many of their organs came to Britain.

During the war 'Jimmy' Verbeeck came to England from Belgium, probably as a refugee. He had worked with his brother Pierre in Antwerp as an organ builder and set up on his own account after the war in Birmingham and, later, in Islington. British-built Verbeeck organs were available from 1920 onwards. Initially the firm offered a year's guarantee that its key frames would not 'crush' the music, claiming to have had twenty-five years' experience in the business; this was presumably on account of its Belgian associations. Verbeecks built organs with a variety of key sizes. In later years as many as three accordions were added to the fronts of some organs, a practice much favoured by the builders of continental dance organs. It has been said that Verbeeck organs were popular with some showmen because they played with a staccato effect. Verbeecks ceased trading in about 1942 and the assets were taken over by Chiappas.

The woodwork of Verbeecks' organs was often branded with the design shown in Figure 52.

Another firm connected with the organ business was the Bristol Showmen's Stores (of Bristol). They described themselves as the sole British agents for Marenghi organs (in 1920) and offered to supply music for 87, 89, 92, 94, and 98 key organs.

Fig 52. Brand used by Verbeeck (actual size)

Mention of an 87 key size is interesting as it is generally accepted that the last firm to make this size of music was Wright & Holmes, who stopped producing it in 1912. The 94 key size was later omitted from the advertisements of the Bristol Showmen's Stores.

A late entrant into the field—too late to be successful—was F. C. Hands of Nottingham. Hands was an ingenious mechanic and was interested in the practical side of fairground machinery, and especially organs. He arranged and supplied a few music books but specialised in converting continental dance organs (probably Bruders) to a paper roll system. From 1929 to 1932 he filed some patents of mechanisms which ensured that the musical programme was not interrupted during the rewinding of the music rolls.

THE LINK WITH THE PAST

Increasing costs and labour difficulties steadily reduced the number of organs on the road. When the electric amplifier became a commercial possibility its loudspeakers quickly sounded the last post for nearly all the organs which remained. With the coming of the Second World War all but one of the organ firms had gone or were on the point of going out of business. Chiappas remained, and are still in existence today.

The firm was founded by Guiseppe Chiappa when he left the Gavioli works in 1864. After a few years in England he tried his luck in the USA. In 1877 he returned to England and set up the business on its present site in Clerkenwell, in what is now known as Eyre Street Hill. During its existence the firm has handled all types of mechanical musical instruments, street barrel organs and pianos, clockwork public house pianos, besides fair organs, both book and barrel operated. They have held the agencies for Gaviolis, Marenghis, and Bruders and, at one time, had a staff of over forty. The business passed from Guiseppe to his son Lodovico and then to his grandson Victor, who runs it today with but a handful of the staff which were employed in the firm's heyday. The firm's well-known music label is shown in Figure 53.

This firm provides, in Britain, the only link between the mechanical organ industry of the past and the present. It struggled through the late 1930s and through the war years with an ever-decreasing amount of work, provided by the few showmen who still had organs on the road—repairing them, tuning them, and supplying new music. Today, however, Victor Chiappa is a busy man, due to the revival in popularity of the fair organ. Many showmen have realised that, nowadays, a mechanical organ is a great attraction and have brought out organs from their stores, where they have lain dusty and unplayed for many years. There has, in fact, been a great revival in the public's interest in the mechanical bygones—whether they be musical boxes, tramcars, toys, paddle steamers, or mechanical organs.

Some of the credit for this must go to the Fair Organ Preservation Society of Great Britain. This society was formed in 1958, when the fairground organ seemed threatened with extinction.

Fig 53. Music label used by Chiappa Ltd

A handful of enthusiasts in the North of England decided that steps should be taken to preserve these instruments and from this small beginning the Fair Organ Preservation Society had (in 1970) about 1,200 members. Its quarterly journal *The Key Frame* goes to members all over the world. There are well over a hundred organs in preservation in Britain, in addition to those travelling with showmen. The organs in preservation are mostly mounted on trucks and throughout the summer can be seen at outdoor events of all kinds, entertaining the public and in some cases collecting large sums of money for charities. Throughout the country there are also a number of museums, both publicly and privately owned, where collections of mechanical musical instruments can be seen and, more important, heard playing. One such museum is in the author's home town of St Albans, Hertfordshire, where every weekend a varied collection of mechanical musical instruments plays to visitors from all over the country and abroad.

APPENDIX I

Restoration

(by Ronald Leach, ARIBA, M Inst RA)

ACTION

AN organ can only play well if the action is correctly adjusted, and if the puffs and associated valves give the right amount of movement when they get their signal of air from the key frame or tracker bar. Several different actions have been explained in the earlier part of this book and the following notes deal with some of the defects which arise and how they can be rectified. For example, the leather used on the puff may be stiffer than it should be. The fibre disc could be stuck to the puff over the whole of its surface. The rod passing through the wind-chest could be corroded, causing it to bind in its bearing. The pallet could be binding on its guide pins. The pallet spring could be slightly corroded and the small channel in which it rides could be indented where the spring rests, or even clogged with dirt. Any of these defects will prevent the pipes sounding promptly or fully, and they must be rectified.

Puff-boards

First, examine the puffs. Make sure that you have the correct grade of leather for repairs. The only suitable leathers are pneumatic skiver or split skin. Both are good and both are costly. Indifferent quality leather is not suitable as it does not respond quickly enough to the air signal transmitted from the key frame. Even the best thin skins from the local tannery are not suitable as they can be full of holes, barely visible to the naked eye. Before removing the old leather, it is well to make a small tool to assist in forming the new puffs to a standard depth. This is quite simple and is shown in Figure 54. Make sure that the depth of the face of the tool is the same as the depth of the old puffs before you strip them down. Next, remove the fibre or card discs and clean off the old glue. Note that the glue does not cover the whole of the discs' surface, thus allowing the discs to move as much as possible and to adjust themselves to the wooden heads of the push-rods.

When the leather has been stripped off, clean the air channels and cavities in the puff-board. Do not leave this until the board has been releathered.

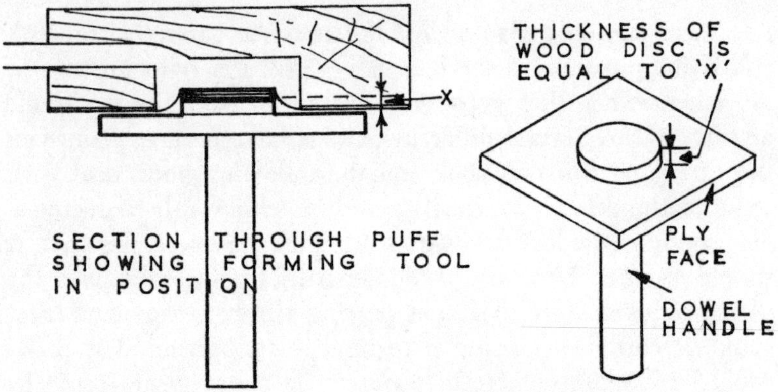

Fig 54. Tool for regulating depth of puffs

The new leather can now be cut to shape. Make sure that you allow plenty of spare, as the leather has to be worked into the cavities in the wood. Use thin hot Scotch glue. As you spread the glue it will tend to run down the sides of the cavities in the puff-board. If this happens the leather will stick to the side of the cavity and prevent the puff from inflating properly. No amount of adjustment will cure the fault and the work will have to be done again. Guard against this, and if necessary coat any glue that does run down with talcum powder. Do not attempt to releather the whole of any puff-board in one go, however small it may be. You will only end up with a lot of tacky glue and crumpled leather. Begin at one end and tackle two puffs at a time.

As you place the leather on the board, work it into the cavities with the fingers. When it is fairly well arranged and the outside edges are lying flat on the surface of the board, take hold of the tool you made. Place a fibre disc on the dish of leather, and work the leather across the surface of the hot glue, keeping it flat on the board. At the same time form an even pocket in the puff cavity with the tool. It is essential to place the fibre disc in the dish when doing this to ensure that the correct amount of play is obtained.

When the first two cavities have been releathered properly, do the next two, and so on until the whole of the board has been releathered. Keep the glue hot and running.

Allow the glue to set, which will take twenty-four hours at least. The discs, which should have been cleaned, can now be replaced. The glue should be a lot stiffer for this job as it must not run. Using a small brush, carefully coat the central third of the disc's surface with a thin layer of glue. Place the disc on the leather puff, inflating the latter by means of a short length of plastics tube. At the same time press the disc firmly onto the inflated leather, taking care not to puncture the puff. Ensure that the disc is centrally located on the puff. It is wise to leave the puff inflated until the glue is set. This prevents the glue spreading under the disc and sticking the whole of its surface to the leather.

When you have completed this job, and the glue is dry, inflate each puff separately. The discs should rise up on the top of the leather and, if their edges are gently flicked, they will tend to oscillate very slightly. Remove and reglue any that do not.

Wind-chests

The next job is to take out the push-rods for cleaning. It is wise to clean out the exhaust holes that are drilled under the discs attached to the bottom half of each rod. These sometimes get choked with dust and can cause the pipes to cipher. The rods run through holes drilled in the top of the wind-chest. These should be carefully cleaned out.

The rods are generally of brass and, therefore, should not be rusty. However, even brass can become tarnished and the rods should be polished with a metal polish of the wadding variety. Do not use steel wool as this will roughen the surface. Make sure each rod runs smoothly in its sleeve and that the rod is straight. Also check that it has not been broken and is still the right length. Replacements can be made fairly easily but they can be obtained commercially if required.

The pallets must be checked for loose hinges or leather faces which do not make good contact with the surface of the wind-chest. Any pallets which are removed for releathering must be replaced exactly as they were. The leather used on the pallets is thicker than that used for the puffs and is fixed with its rough side towards the surface of the wind-chest. All pallet leathers must be checked to see if the surface is indented where the push-rod makes contact. They generally are and this can cause trouble. It is advisable to replace any that are badly damaged.

The steel guide pins which are fixed on each side of each pallet are nearly always corroded and should be replaced where necessary. Make sure that each pin is slightly splayed out from the edge of the pallet, thus ensuring that the pallet slips back into the correct position when it closes. The pins must be set just on the edge of the pallet and driven in at an angle of about seventy degrees to the surface of the wind-chest. Do not drive the pins in straight and then bend them, as the pallet is certain to bind. There is a small groove in the underside of each pallet. A spring runs in this and, after years of use, tends to make a notch where it rests. Also, the groove becomes rough and clogged with dirt. Sharpen a 2H pencil to a long but blunt point and run this back and forth in the groove until the three surfaces forming the groove shine with blacklead. This graphitic form of lubrication is the best you can give the wood and metal spring surfaces to run on.

The springs should be inspected to see if they are mis-shapen or too weak, or even too strong. New ones should be made where necessary, and the brass wire for this job can be obtained quite easily. Make sure it is of a similar quality. New springs should be made as follows. Take out an undamaged spring and lay it on

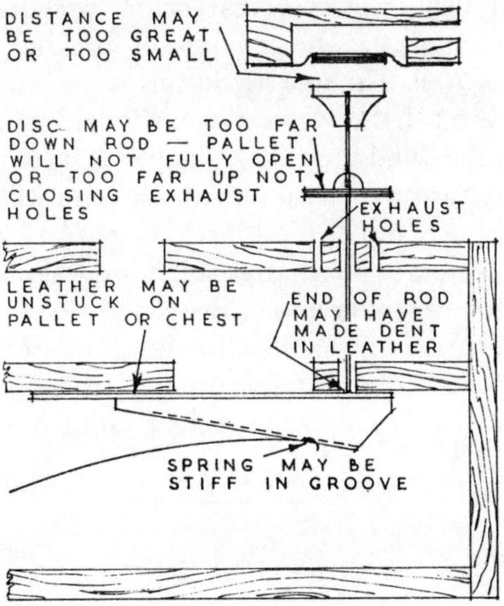

Fig 55. Defects likely to be encountered in the pneumatic action

a piece of pine or similar wood. Make up a jig with pins or screws. Using this you can quickly wind a good many springs which exactly resemble the original.

Before reassembling the pallets and springs, make sure that the windways to each pipe are clear of dust.

Ensure that the faceboard on the side of the wind-chest is securely sealed with a leather gasket. In many cases a stiff cardboard panel is glued onto the wind-chest before the faceboard is fixed on. This is very satisfactory, but if fitted with care, a leather gasket is just as good, and simplifies access to the inside of the wind-chest. A leather gasket is made from strips of the same leather as that used for facing the pallets. Glue the leather to the faceboard with thin hot glue. When this glue has set, coat the leather with lard to keep it soft and improve the seal.

Reassembly

In theory you should be able to screw the puffboard to its supports which are on the top of the wind-chest and be assured of a perfect job. However, cardboard packing pieces will generally be required. The amount of packing can only be determined by trial. The time to do this work is now, not when you have re-erected the whole organ. Couple an air hose from the organ to the wind-chest and then, with a length of plastics tubing, inflate each puff separately. Each valve will be opened in turn and if there is any dirt left inside, it will be blown out. This will also allow you to see if any pallets are leaking. If they are, the wooden mushroom on top of the push-rod should be screwed down, thus shortening the effective length of the rod between the puff and the surface of the pallet. If this adjustment does not suffice you may have to adjust the position of the disc which

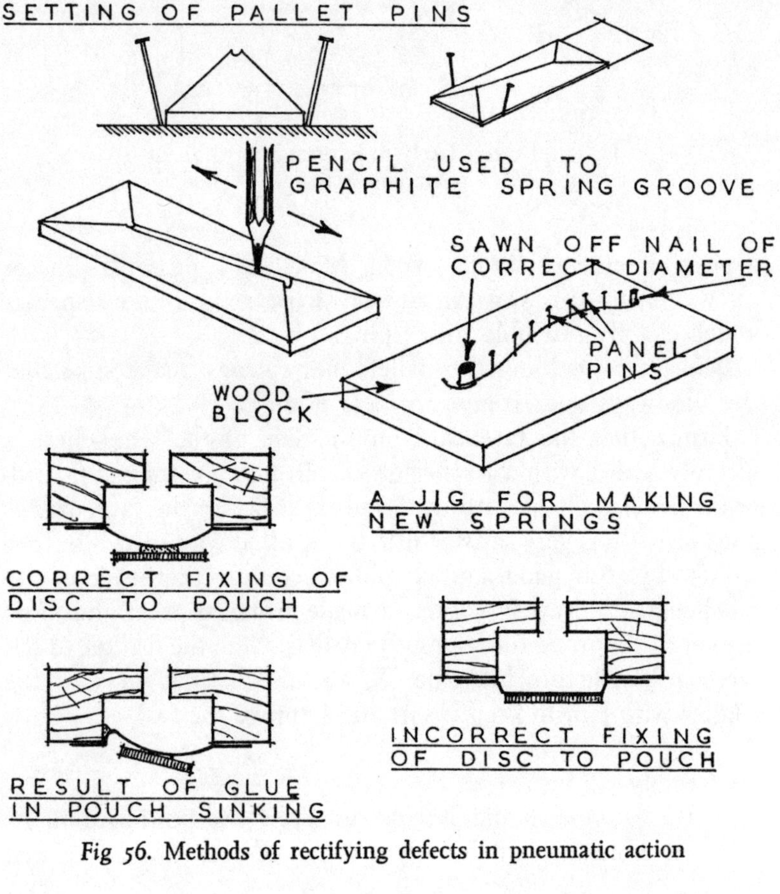

Fig 56. Methods of rectifying defects in pneumatic action

seals the outlet holes. Obviously, if this is too high it will not close the exhaust holes in the top of the wind-chest when the puff is fully open. If it is too low it will allow neither the puff nor the pallet to open fully and the pipe will be starved of wind. Figures 55 and 56 illustrate a number of faults and show how they can be put right.

PIPEWORK

Generally speaking, when an organ is acquired for restoration, the pipework is mostly in speaking order. There are, however, a number of faults which prevent the pipe from producing either its full or its correct sound. Sometimes a pipe will not speak at all. It can generally be accepted that the pipes need correction because of neglect, dirt, or maltreatment. Normally, they will not require revoicing. If they do require this take them to an expert.

Before repairs can be undertaken it is essential to understand what is happening in a pipe when wind is fed to the foot. Figure 57 illustrates the sequence of events when wind enters a flue pipe. In A the wind has passed the block and is forming a wind

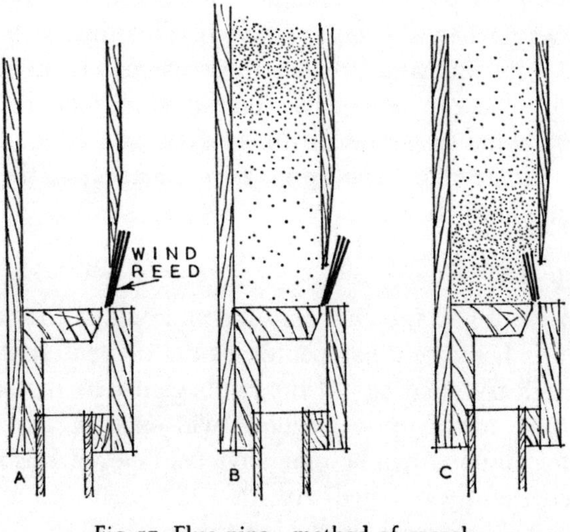

Fig 57. Flue pipe—method of speech

reed which you will notice is moving up the outside of the lip. As the pipe is already full of air at atmospheric pressure this continues until the equilibrium of pressures in the air column in the pipe is disturbed. Then, in B we see that the wind reed, being at higher pressure than the atmosphere, tends to suck the air out of the pipe at the lower level, thus reducing the pressure in the pipe. As this happens we see in C that the atmospheric pressure outside the pipe takes over and forces the wind reed back into the pipe until pressure is built up again and the cycle of operations begins once more. The whole cycle takes but a fraction of a second and the movement of the air generates the harmonics which cause the pipe to speak. A pipe does not speak because a lot of air is blown through its body. This can be illustrated practically by blowing a mixture of air and tobacco smoke through the pipe's foot. Very little will come out of the top of the pipe but you will see a considerable quantity at the mouth.

Having analysed the method by which a pipe is made to speak, we shall see that some of the faults that prevent it from speaking properly are easy to cure. Try to arrange your sequence of work so that you are not held up for work while glue is drying.

The windway may be blocked with dust, or there may be dust in the cavity between the foot and the block which only rises to the windway when the pipe is blown. This dust will partially block the windway and prevent the true pattern of wind reed developing. The cap may have come unstuck and be allowing some of the wind to escape, or it may even have been incorrectly replaced at some time. The lip may be damaged, or the foot not stuck firmly into the base.

Bodywork

One cause of bad speech, or no speech at all, is that the joints of the pipe's body may be opening at the corners. If the pipe is large enough try opening out the joints gently by inserting your fingers at the top. Any weak joints will open up and any that are already unglued will become obvious. Pipes in this condition should be carefully repaired with thin hot Scotch glue. This can very often be done without taking the whole pipe apart. Clean out the old glue with a razor blade. The new glue must not be too runny. Hold the pipe with the open joint perpendicular to the floor and allow the glue to penetrate into the joint. Bind the pipe with a string tourniquet; do not clamp it as this can easily damage a thin pipe. As soon as the string is in position clean out the surplus glue with a piece of wire of about ⅛in diameter, sharpened to a blunt point at one end. It should be just sharp enough to cut away the unset glue. Run the wire up and down inside the pipe holding the pipe upside down to prevent any surplus glue falling into the windway. Make quite sure you do not cut the wood as this will be as bad as leaving surplus glue in the pipe. Remember that a pipe is built to a scale, or set of dimensions which allow a certain quantity of air to be contained within it. Large blobs of glue inside a pipe will affect its timbre. Leave the tourniquet on for at least twenty-four hours; remove it, and carefully sand off the surplus glue which is bound to be on the outside.

Caps

The cap may have come off or have been refixed incorrectly. This is fairly simple to rectify. However, to ensure that you have it in the right position, it is vital to reglue the cap while the pipe is standing on its wind supply. The importance of correctly positioning the cap cannot be stressed too much. If it is too low the wind from the windway will be directed too far outside the pipe, and if it is too high the wind will be directed inside the pipe. It is important to see that the top edge of the cap is set level with the top of the block; if it is not so adjusted the wind may not reach the lip.

Clean the old glue off both surfaces making certain that no wood is cut away in the process. Invariably, with old pipework it is a fairly simple job to see exactly where the cap was from the dirt which is ingrained into the exposed surfaces of the pipe. Even so, I advise you to reglue it in position while the pipe is standing on its wind supply. Get your glue hot and a little thicker than that used for repairing pipes, otherwise you will find that you cannot get a good tight joint. Then, having made ready the wind supply, place the foot of the pipe in its hole in the sound or pipeboard. Put the cap in position. As the glue is hot you will find that you have plenty of time to adjust the cap correctly on the pipe while listening to the speech. However, you may find that the first attempt takes too long. If so, start again. Clean off the glue and repeat the process. After repairing one or two pipes you will become adept. When the cap is in its correct position clamp it in place, first packing the bearing surfaces of the clamp, and tightening it up to ensure that the resulting joint of glue is as thin as possible. Clean off all surplus glue. Incidentally, this particular piece of work is not recommended if one's neighbours are allergic to the pipe organ. The noises that can be produced, while getting the cap into its right place, are indescribable.

Windways

It is generally possible to see if the windway of the pipe is damaged. If it is, a new piece must be made to match the damaged piece. Remove the offending piece. If the windway and the block are in one piece it will mean taking the pipe to pieces. You may prefer to have this job done by a professional. If, however, you decide to tackle it yourself, the glued joints can be steamed open, but this is difficult without experience. It is better to ease the joints with a veneering iron. The new piece should be made as accurately as possible, and from similar wood. This is not always easy nowadays. Oak, teak, birch, mahogany, and parana pine are not suitable. Spruce and straight-grained Columbian pine are, however, both suitable and available. When the replacement piece exactly matches the original in finish the pipe can be rebuilt. Proceed in this order. Glue the back of the pipe onto the block, then the two sides, front and cap. Leave each section to harden off before attempting the next. Do not use nails or screws. Use only fresh, hot Scotch glue and whenever possible use a string tourniquet to hold the various parts together while the glue hardens.

Feet

The foot of the pipe may be damaged or missing. A new foot is simple to make if you have a lathe and are adept at wood turning. However, for those having neither the skill nor the tools the following method is suggested. You will require a roll of brown gummed postal tape as wide as the overall length of the foot. Get a piece of dowel which just fits inside the foot. If the dowel is too loose build it up to the right size with tape. Now wind on the tape to form the foot. Wet the glue on each turn after, say, the second and build up a foot of the required thickness and length. When the glue has set, give the new foot two coats of varnish. When this is dry, glue the foot into the base of the pipe. Make sure that no surplus glue gets into the cavity under the block and keep the pipe the right way up during the glueing and setting.

Tuning Slides

Over the years tuning slides become tight and when moved split the pipes along the grooves in which they are located. Sometimes a slide is bent or has the top edge broken off. If this is so, a new slide can easily be made. Get brass of the right gauge. If it is too thin it will slip in the grooves; if it is too thick it will force the pipe apart. If the side and front of the pipe have already parted company in the vicinity of the tuning slide groove you will have to decide whether to make a new front, to reglue or to patch the top. Whichever you do, make sure that no glue is left in the tuning slide slots as it is very difficult to remove afterwards. If you are making a new slide, clip the bottom corners at an angle of 45 degrees, and smooth the edges. It is important to see that the slide fits tightly to the inside face of the front of the pipe. If it does not, tuning will be difficult and in extreme cases the same note will sound even if the tuning slide is completely removed.

Stoppers

The stoppers must be an airtight fit, otherwise their purpose is lost and the pipe will not speak properly, or may not sound at all. Removal of the stopper is not always easy. This is especially so for the bigger basses as the stoppers of these have probably not been moved for many years. The stoppers are generally covered with tallow before they are inserted in the pipes, and this, mixed with dust, causes them to become quite well fixed. Care must be exercised when removing them otherwise the pipe will split. Generally the small 'handle' at the top of the stopper will not stand too much pulling and it is best to work at it gently. Having removed the stopper inspect the leather covering. If it is fairly sound do not re-cover it. Take the edges of the leather which are nearest to the top of the stopper and pull them away from the sides of the stopper for about half an inch. In this way you loosen up the material so that when you replace it, it makes a good tight fit to the sides of the pipe.

If you decide to re-cover the stopper make sure your leather is of the right thickness. If it is too thin the stopper will sit in the pipe quite well but the pipe will soon go out of tune; if too thick, you will split the pipe when you insert the stopper. Re-covering stoppers is not difficult. It is important for the leather to be fairly tight over the sides. If it is bunched up at the corners the stopper will not enter the pipe properly and may even split it. It is best to apply glue to two opposite sides first, but not to the underside at all. Take the leather, which should be cut well over size, and apply it to one side, stretch it over the bottom very slightly and then apply it to the other side. As soon as this is done, glue the other two sides and repeat the process. You will begin to see that there is a surplus of leather at the corners and it will be necessary to work this out by gently pushing and pulling the leather over the four surfaces until no creases are left. It is surprising where the surplus leather goes. However, much of it is worked out to the underside which was not glued. After the glue has set, trim up the top edges but leave about half an inch of surplus all round. Before inserting the stopper apply a thin coat of ordinary household lard with a finger to all surfaces. This helps to keep the leather soft and also makes for a good air-tight joint.

Woodworm

Woodworm is a common cause of incorrect or complete lack of speech in a pipe, especially if the organ has been standing in a barn for many years. If the damage is not too serious treat the wood with paraffin or one of the patent liquids which are on the market. When it is thoroughly dry tap out all the old dust. Take a pipe to your local ironmongers and get a filler which is a good match for the wood and fill the holes left by this infuriating insect. The work is tedious and, depending upon the amount of damage, can take a long time. When repaired, the pipe will not sound as the maker and voicer intended it to. In fact, in extreme cases, it may sound very different from those which have not been attacked. In addition, the appearance of this work is not first class as the filler never matches the wood exactly. Whether or not you have the pipe remade depends upon how much of a perfectionist you are and the size of your bank balance. I have carried out this treatment when restoring my own organ and in only one case was the result unacceptable. In this case, I had a new pipe made.

Appearance

The appearance of the pipes may be improved, especially if they are nearly black with age. There are preparations on the market which will bleach them but their use is not recommended. If appearance is vital, and the pipes are grimy, a very light sanding with a wet and dry paper will have to suffice. Do not use a sanding disc or any other type of mechanical sander as this will take too much material off the sides and may ruin the timbre. After the sanding has been gently carried out each pipe can be stood in a rack, or on the sound board, and given a coat of varnish. Use a light one, and not one which is plastic based. Some pipework which has been treated with a proprietary varnish looks as though it had been dipped into a barrel of treacle and left to dry! This type of treatment does nothing to improve the tone. It should be borne in mind that the pipemaker would have decided on his materials, the scale of the pipes, and finish to produce the timbre he desired. If you add a thick coat of 'treacle' you cannot expect the pipes still to have the same timbre.

Pipe Supports

The pipe supports may need attention. These are the strips of wood which run across the faces of the pipes and to which each pipe is screwed. If you are not removing the rank, the support need not be unscrewed. However, if you are tackling an organ which has been neglected for a long time take the supports off and inspect the face of the pipes underneath. Sometimes the screw hole is bigger than it need be, and sometimes the hole has been badly plugged, and the plugging material projects into the pipe. Sometimes the end of the screw projects into the pipe. All these defects will affect the speech of the pipe. If the holes need plugging, do this with softwood, using a sharp penknife to cut small pieces to fit each hole. When the plug is ready, coat it with Scotch glue and insert it in the hole, making sure that it does not project into the inside of the pipe. Leave the surplus sticking out of the front of the pipe until the glue has had at least twenty-four hours in which to dry out. Then, trim off the surplus with a sharp chisel. Before putting the support back, drill a pilot hole for the screw. It is well to renew all the screws if you are doing the job. Use small brass screws with raised heads and, before inserting them, dip the ends in 'Vaseline'. This will allow the screws to be withdrawn easily at a later date.

Reeds

Defects in reed pipes are generally fairly easy to trace. Loose joints between boot and block can easily be dealt with by using masking tape, tightly wrapped round the shank of the block until it is a tight fit in the boot. Inspect the wedge which holds the reed in place. This may have worked loose, or it may have been knocked in too far. If the wedge is damaged, make a new one of the right length from beech or pine. The reed may be set too high, leaving a gap between its end and the end of the opening in the shallot. If this is the case, wind will enter the shallot through the gap and the reed will not vibrate correctly. The foot of the resonator may be a bad fit in the top of the block. This can be cured by building it up with masking tape if it is a regular difference. If the difference is irregular an oversized piece of wood can be glued on and then carved with a sharp chisel until it is an exact fit. The use of a medium-grade glasspaper is allowable here but only for the final finish. Incidentally, do not fix wood on with panel or cabinet pins. This will not help matters as both the foot of the resonator and the piece you are trying to attach may split.

Tuning wires are generally in a bad state if the organ has been in the open air most of its life. They are usually rusted, making it impossible to move them, and sometimes the end has broken off leaving only a short piece projecting. Sometimes, the foot of the tuning wire, which should be in contact with the reed is broken, making it impossible to tune it.

Making new tuning wires is not easy. The best way is to take the next pipe, inspect the tuning wire and make a copy. I know of one organ, which belongs to a very famous showman, where the tuning wires are being replaced with new ones of stainless steel. This is, of course first class from the point of view of corrosion. The amateur restorer may, however, find one or two failures on his hands if he uses this material. A good quality steel wire can be used and it does not matter if it is a little thicker than the original. Do not form the top curl on the wire until the wire has been inserted through the block. The length of wire must be governed by the position of the pipe in the organ. When dealing with pipes which are well hidden by other ranks, the wire needs to be as long as possible, so that you can reach inside the ranks of pipes and tap it easily. Make the top curl as bold as you can and with a little hook on the end. This helps a lot when tuning the more inaccessible reeds, as the tuning tool can be got under the hook and the wire pulled upwards. It is also important to leave a reasonably flat surface to the top of the wire so that when tapping it down the tuning tool does not tend to hit the wire and slide off.

In some cases the boot is secured to the block with one or two small screws. If so, it is as well to renew these while you have the assembly dismantled. It is advisable to plug the screw holes before inserting new screws. Glue the plugs in place and trim them off as for the pipe supports.

Finally, the reed itself should be inspected. Put the pipe on its wind and listen to the result. Every care should be taken of the reed if it is removed for any reason as the profile to which it has been formed is vital. If the pipe does not speak as it should, first, make sure that you have reset the reed correctly. It is possible that you may have put it in back to front. The reed always curls up and away from the shallot. If this is not the trouble, look at the curve on the reed. This should start approximately two thirds of the way along the shallot from the wedge. It is impossible to give a set distance for this as voicers vary their setting and curvature. The reed should be completely parallel to the shallot and gently curve away from it at an ever increasing distance until it finishes just level with the end of the shallot. Do not adjust the curve of the reed unless you feel convinced that you can correct a tiny fault. If you break a reed the replacement is bound to be different, especially if your organ is a very old one. This can affect tone and pitch. If you are really in trouble go to an expert for help. In conclusion, may I stress how delicate reeds are. However, in case I have discouraged you, let me say that I was able to correct nearly all the bad reeds on my organs by using care and by studying the next pipe reed which was in working order. With this caution I can do no more than suggest that you try to repair one which is really bad. If you succeed, the experience you get will be worth more than all the words that can be written.

Violins

The remarks on the renovation of flue pipes apply, of course, to violin pipes. The *frein harmonique,* however, needs special attention. Test the violin pipe on its wind and see if you are getting the correct string tone. This is easily recognisable and you will have no trouble in deciding whether or not the frein is working properly. Most freins are fitted to the cap with two screws, as shown in Figure 32. The screws may be in bad order and the slots burred. If this is the case, replace them. The holes in the cap should be inspected to make sure that they are in reasonable order and, if not, the usual practice of plugging and glueing, then drilling just undersize, must be undertaken.

If the test reveals that you are not getting true string tone, the frein must be adjusted. First grip the blade of the frein with bull-nosed pliers and gently move it backwards, away from the mouth of the pipe. Do not make the adjustment too great as a little movement can make a lot of difference. Try the pipe on its wind again, moving the pliers away from the mouth. If this has not improved matters try a slight adjustment towards the mouth, and finally try lowering or raising the blade; if this is not right, start again, moving it upwards and towards the mouth. In this way you will soon find the position where you can finally tighten up the bottom screw to fix the frein in place. It will then be necessary finally to adjust the position of the frein either by tightening or screwing in, or loosening the top screw. The point at which your pipe begins to speak after your preliminary adjustments is the time to tighten up the bottom screw. After this you can finally trim the speech up with either the top screw or the pliers, carefully adjusting the angle of the blade to the windway. During the whole of this operation do not attempt to adjust the tuning as this will only tend to confuse the issue. Once you have the string tone you can tune the pipe to your heart's content without spoiling the effect you have achieved with the frein. Finally, it is essential that you set the frein after any other repairs to the pipe as, if there are defects, especially those which affect the speech, your efforts on the frein will be wasted.

Piccolos

The piccolo, which is illustrated in Figure 34, is generally easy to deal with. The windway can be troublesome and it is as well, therefore, to check that it contains no dirt. Make sure that the windway is not chipped or damaged and that the cap, which in this case is set at an acute angle, is correctly positioned. The acorn, on top of the pipe, should be a reasonably tight fit. Check that the rod below the acorn is not loose and, therefore, incapable of supporting the plug. If the plug is loose on the rod it may be as well to make a new plug either from wood or cork. This must be an accurate fit.

Trumpets

The trumpet can have a resonator of either wood or metal. If of metal, the resonator is either spun from one piece or made with a brazed joint. With wooden resonators the only points you have to look for have already been dealt with. Brass resonators should be polished. Not only does this improve the appearance, but a well-polished interior also helps to develop the 'clang'-like dissonance which is voiced into this reed stop to give it its characteristic timbre. Some trumpet resonators are literally black with age. I have found, in the case of both my Mortier and my Welte, that polishing the outside is relatively easy, although of little importance musically. Polishing the inside of the horn is more difficult and needs hard work. The larger resonators are easiest; the smaller the pipe the more difficult it is. I have dealt with forty-four resonators on my own organs and find that perseverance is necessary. Do not use any of the proprietary preparations for the removal of corrosion and similar patinas as these can have a detrimental effect. Incidentally, I have been recommended *not* to lacquer the inside with a clear cellulose or other preparation to prevent further tarnishing. Although I have no proof that this advice is correct I would not use any liquid of this type on my own trumpets except on the outside and well away from the bells.

Metal Flutes

The open metal flute is more often found on street or dance organs than fair organs. Inspect it for defects as follows. Examine the position of the bottom lip in relation to the edge of the languid. You may find that the two pieces are not parallel to each other. If this is so, *carefully* ease the bottom lip in or out to straighten it. Next look at the languid and see if this is level with the edge of the bottom lip. If it is not, some careful adjustments will help here. Either defect will affect the pipe's speech. Next inspect the foot. I cannot guide you on the size of the hole in the foot as this is adjusted by the voicer. If it is too small the volume of sound produced will be reduced and it may improve matters to open it gently. However, before deciding to enlarge the hole check the pipe against at least three or four others. If the upper lip has been pressed inwards, rectify the fault as follows. Bend a piece of thin steel flat, no more than, say, a quarter of an inch by one sixteenth of an inch in cross-section, into a right-angle. The shorter leg, which should be about a quarter of an inch long, is inserted into and behind the upper lip and gently pulled. The object is to bring the bottom of the lip forward but to preserve the slope of the lip as it was set. Sometimes the body of the pipe is dented. Correcting this can be difficult. Take a piece of dowel or broom handle and, with some pressure, ease this down into the pipe against the dent. After repeated applications the dent will gradually disappear.

KEY FRAME

Several types of key frame have been described in the earlier part of this book. The keyless frame is, of course, easier to renovate than the keyed variety as the mechanics are much less complicated. The paragraphs which follow deal mainly with the faults I encountered when I overhauled the keyed frame on my Mortier. This particular frame works on the pressure pneumatic system and the method of construction is very similar to that used by several other makers. Many of the features are, in addition, common to most types of frame.

Touch-boxes

Each key on the frame operates a pair of valves, one of which is inside and one of which is outside the touch-box. They are connected by a small rod which passes through a hole in a wooden guide. The following defects can arise.

The leather faces of the pallets may be damaged. The leather where it extends from the pallet to form the hinge, may be unstuck and thus prevent the pallet from seating properly when it is closed. The spring which closes the pallet may be damaged or have lost its tension. The rod which connects the two pallets may have cut into the leather face of the pallet, or it may be binding in its guide channel or sleeve if one is fitted. To get at these rods you will have to remove the top springs from the frame. This is fairly easy, but time-consuming, and can try one's patience. Removal of the rods is best left until later as it may prove to be unnecessary.

Inspect the gasket between the faceboard and the inside of the touch-box. Any dark patterns will indicate a leak. Replace the gasket if necessary, using a fairly thick leather with the rough side towards the inside of the touch-box. If the faceboard is no more than a few inches deep, cover the whole surface with leather rather than just the area which is in contact with the frame of the touchbox. Coat the rough surface of the leather with household lard before reassembly. Ensure that the screws and screw holes are in order; if necessary plug and redrill the holes. Any leak here will prevent the organ from playing properly.

Manifolds

Beneath the key frame you will find the tubes which connect it to the puffs and register box. The tubes are connected to the frame by manifolds, which are held in place either by wire cleats or screws. Disconnect the outer faces of the manifolds. This operation needs care, as it is easy to disconnect the flexible tubes, either at the puffs or the manifolds. The tubes are probably connected to the manifold by short lengths of lead pipe. Check that the lead pipes are both securely glued into the manifold and into the ends of the flexible tubes. It is easy to repair or replace any which are missing. If you are rebuilding the organ remove all the tubes. If you are only renovating, it may suffice to reglue the loose ones.

Keys

The keys should be straight and move freely between the teeth of the metal combs. See also that the keys move freely on their pivots, but do not remove the hinge pin unless absolutely necessary, as it is very difficult to reinsert it. Each key should sit squarely on the end of its operating rod, which should be flat and not rounded with wear. Check that the operating rod is not binding in the small hole in the top of the pallet beneath it.

The organ will play raggedly unless each key has the same amount of travel. Any keys which are out of line can be levelled with washers, which should be made from a hard, good quality paper; do not use a compressible material such as blotting-paper. First, make the holes in the middle with a darning needle, and then cut out the washers with a piece of tube of the right size, one end of which has been sharpened to a cutting edge. The washers must be small enough to pass through the guide holes in the bar which support the operating rods. Take a steel straightedge and lay this across the keys. Mark with chalk any keys in need of adjustment and deal with them one by one. Lift the key and remove the operating rod without bending it. Pack paper washers over the pin at the lower end of the rod until the key is level. As the job proceeds you may have to return to a key already dealt with for further adjustment. When the work is finished the tips of the keys must be in line, and parallel with the surface of the metal comb through which they pass. If they are not, one end of the key frame is going to respond at a different rate from the other.

The wooden board which covers the keys and supports the music can prevent the keys from rising properly if it is too close to their upper surfaces, especially at the end where the grooved roller is. The board may be warped, or the grooves which locate it may have collapsed or worn away. If you make a new board be quite sure that the profile of the underside allows the keys to rise correctly.

Transport Rollers

If the rubber coverings on the transport rollers are worn the local typewriter shop will probably be able to resurface them for you. If the gears on the rollers need renewing, get new ones made by a small engineering firm. The spring above the upper roller should be removed and cleaned, together with its adjusting screws. The bearings of these screws may be badly worn. As the thread is probably of an old continental pattern, it will probably be best to replace the screws with modern ones and retap the holes accordingly. When this part of the frame has been reassembled insert a music book in the frame and let it run through the rollers. Adjust the screws until the music runs correctly against the metal guide on the hinged side of the frame.

Key Frame Mute

If the key frame is muted by a manually operated system any defects in the mechanical linkage can easily be seen and rectified.

If the muting system incorporates a ventil which is operated from the music books it may need more attention. Figure 58 shows one such arrangement in simplified form. It is fixed to one end of the key frame, a little below the touch-boxes. Many of the faults found in the touch-boxes may also be found in the valve system of the ventil. The air channel which runs between

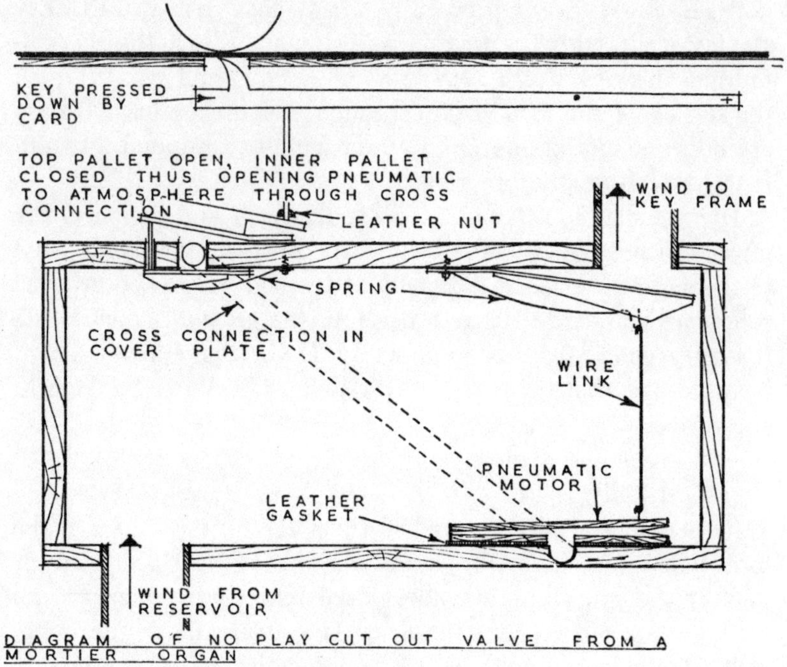

Fig 58. Key frame muting mechanism

the pallets at the top and the motor at the bottom should be examined. Although this is small, especially if it is worked into the side of the chest, it has to allow air to pass both to and from the motor. Ensure, also that any gaskets are sound. As usual, the leather will be blackened with dirt in the vicinity of any leak. The leather nut at the bottom end of the push-rod should be examined to see if it has become loose. If it has, the operation of the valves will be affected.

A wire link connects the main valve to the motor. The best

way to see if this is working properly is to remove the faceboard and replace it with an inspection panel made from Perspex. Make a rough copy of the existing gasket and sandwich this between the Perspex panel and the side of the chest, and then secure the Perspex panel with masking tape. Wear is not always obvious as it takes place on the insides of the screw eyes and the loops on the wire link. The motor must be tested. Re-cover it with thin pneumatic skiver if necessary, ensuring that the new motor has the same amount of movement as the old one. Renew the gasket on the underside of the motor at the same time, having cleaned away all the old glue. Glue the new gasket to the underside of the motor, and not to the surface of the chest. Make sure that the feed hole in the motor lines up with the hole in the bottom of the chest. Generally, there is enough dirt round the motor to enable it to be positioned accurately, but test as you go, before the glue sets. Do not apply lard to the gasket in this case.

The adjustment of the key frame muting system is critical and cannot be completed until the rest of the key frame and the main part of the organ are in order. Any work done on the key frame muting system affects the settings of the valves it operates. If these are incorrect, the amount of air passing into the touch-boxes will be restricted and the puffs on the main wind-chest will, in turn, be starved of air.

Adjusting the Grooved Roller

When the key frame has been repaired and put together the grooved roller should be adjusted. If the keys are pressed well down by the cardboard when the music is in the frame, the amount of movement they will have to make before releasing their air signals to the puffs will be large. If, on the other hand, the keys are set so that they operate their valves as soon as they move, or as soon after they move as is practicable, the action will respond promptly and the organ will play well.

Disconnect the key frame drive and depress all the keys by placing the cover of a music book in the frame. The organ should be silent. Lift the top pallet of the muting valve to its full extent and see if the organ 'howls'. If it does not, slacken the screws which hold the grooved roller down until it does. If this is not

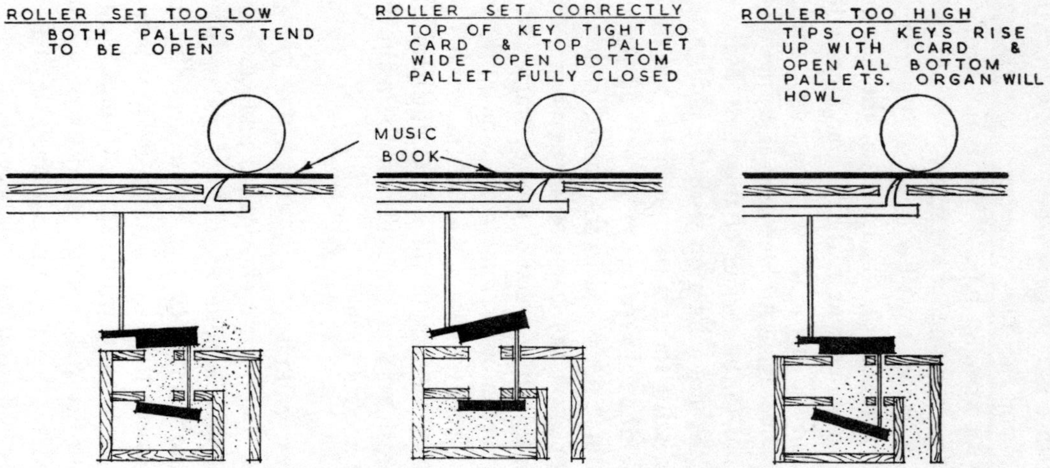

Fig 59. Effect of adjusting the height of the grooved roller

effective, check your work on the muting ventil until the desired effect is obtained. Work can now proceed again. With the top pallet of the muting valve still open slowly screw the roller down at the front end until the organ is silent. Then slacken off the screw about half a turn until it howls again. Now screw the rear screw down until the howl stops. Slacken the front screw slightly and when the howl starts again a very slight increase in pressure will suffice to stop it. The rear screw can then be slackened slightly until the howl starts, then increase the pressure until it stops. Reference to Figure 59 will help to make the method of adjustment clear.

The leather nut on the cut-out valve must now be adjusted until the valve stays in the position in which it has been held while the adjustments have been taking place. The work needs two pairs of hands to be done properly, but you can cope with the operation single-handed if you wedge the valve open with a piece of folded paper.

In time, due to the music going through the frame, the screws which hold the grooved roller down are apt to rotate slightly and become in need of adjustment. The setting of the cut-out mechanism can, however, be left alone. If the organ has been fairly well looked after you may find that you can adjust the setting of the grooved roller without disturbing the setting of the cut-out valve at all.

The adjustment of the key frame is now complete and it is ready to use. Obviously this is the last job to tackle as no test of its efficiency can be made until the rest of the instrument is in good order.

APPENDIX II

A Barrel Organ Score

So far as can be ascertained no fair organ music has yet been published in a form equivalent to that of an orchestral score. It has, however, been possible to arrange for one such score to appear as part of this appendix. The story behind it may be of interest.

The author is lucky to have Francis J. Buckley as a friend. He is a retired engineer and a keen amateur musician, and was and still is interested in all aspects of fairground life, especially mechanical organs. He married the daughter of a famous showman and had some four years' active participation in the business with rides and their organs under his direct supervision. He subsequently spent much of his leisure up to the present time assisting his wife's father, brothers, and their descendants. From his early boyhood he paid particular attention to the organ music and, either consciously or unconsciously, committed many of the musical arrangements to memory. Years later he put some of these down on paper. He does not claim to have total recall, but says that his scores 'are more than ninety-five per cent accurate'.

He has always been a great friend of Peter Varetto who, at the time of writing, is one of the few surviving members of this famous Manchester firm. During a fairly recent meeting Peter Varetto asked him if he remembered a certain march, which he (Peter) had transcribed from a pianola roll many years before for a large Gavioli organ owned by Francis Buckley's brother-in-law. Francis Buckley remembered the tune and hummed a few bars to his friend. When he returned home he prepared from memory a full score of this march and sent it, with his compliments, to Peter Varetto who, in acknowledgement praised the effort with particular reference to the accuracy of the individual parts and augmentations.

One of Francis Buckley's transcriptions is reproduced in Figures 60a–d. The organ for which this music was arranged, marked, and pegged, was an 87 key Gavioli organ which had been converted to barrel operation. It was owned by John

REINE DES COEURS—WALTZ EMIL WALDTEUFEL

Fig 60a. Score of musical arrangement for an 87 key barrel organ (converted *from* book operation)

Fig 60b. Score (continued)

Fig 60c. Score (*continued*)

Fig 60d. Score (*continued*)

Collins, and was at one time in his famous four-abreast jumping horses ride. This was a quiet-running ride and the organ was the centre of attraction. The organ, one of the original importations of the late 90s, was bought for its essentially sweet tone and voicing. The saxophones, in particular, were carefully regulated to subdue what many musicians regard as a coarse or pungent element in the tone of the original orchestral instrument. These particular pipes approached the orchestral bassoon in tone and it is interesting to note that the experts from Wright & Holmes, who maintained the organ, invariably referred to them as 'bassoons'.

Wright & Holmes were responsible for the organ from its inception and they supplied most of the original book music. Later, they converted the organ to barrel operation and supplied all the barrels for the remaining twenty-five years of its existence. James Holmes, the firm's specialist, marked and arranged all the more important music for the books and barrels.

The score which is reproduced is an arrangement of one of the quick French waltzes by Emil Waldteufel, the composer of 'The Grenadiers', 'Estudiantina', and the famous 'Skaters'. In this arrangement of 'Reine des Coeurs' James Holmes paid particular regard to the three essentials of light music—melodic value, picturesqueness, and clarity, the latter being of the greatest importance. He also exercised restraint with regard to the more customary embellishments, especially the piccolo passages. He selected four sections of the waltz, three of sixteen and one of twenty-four bars, with his own bridge passage of eight bars to make up the total of eighty and to restore the key to the opening one of F major. It had become more or less standard practice, on barrels of the size used in this particular type of organ, to peg the equivalent of either eighty bars of music in quick waltz time or sixty-four bars in slow waltz time.

In the first section of sixteen bars the melody is given out entirely by clarinet in octaves. Notes above high B natural and below F natural, ie, outside the clarinet compass, are borrowed from piccolos and saxophones respectively. Some indication of this is given in the score by the small notations and brackets. In the second section, also of sixteen bars (from point A), we see one of the composer's notable picturesque running passages, here in quavers and continuous intervals of a third; there is an adroit syncopation at the third and fourth bars. The piccolo has been added to highlight the melody line. The side-drum is also introduced at the beginning of this section with single first-beat taps, as a substitute for the bellringers, or 'clochettes'. These could, ideally, have been used here, had they still been operated from their own independent key. After a full close, the next sixteen bars (from point B) bring a transition to C major and the entry of the saxophones with an original counter melody. Then (at point C) follows the bridge passage of eight bars referred to above. Finally (at point D) come the last twenty-four bars. This is actually the opening section as the composer wrote it, but it now forms a grand *tutti* and grandiloquent climax.

The pause mark shown over the third-beat rest in each ultimate bar is not a misplacement of the conventional sign of finality but an indication of the gap between the end and beginning of the peggings to provide clearance for the keys when the barrel shifts longitudinally on changing tunes.

APPENDIX III

Making Organ Pipes from Bristol Board

SEVERAL mechanical organs have been built, with varying degrees of success, by enthusiasts in their spare time. Quite often, however, in the early stages the would-be amateur builder is put off either by the enormous amount of work involved in pipe-making or by the expense of having them made professionally. Even if he adopts the latter course he may not know exactly what he wants as far as dimensions and so on are concerned. This appendix, therefore, gives information as to the way in which flue pipes (open or stopped) can be made quickly, cheaply, and easily at home from Bristol board, with the minimum of tools and equipment. Pipes made in this manner can be used for experimental purposes and discarded or replaced by wood or metal pipes with no great loss of time or money.

A small mechanical hand-turned house organ with cardboard pipes has, in fact, been made by a young Swiss enthusiast, who has supplied the author with the system of construction which follows. The author has also experimented himself and is satisfied that satisfactory results can be obtained. Needless to say, paper pipes are not suitable for outdoor use.

As a matter of historical interest paper pipes were used by professional organ builders many years ago. They are a practical proposition and constructional details may be seen in *Organ Building for Amateurs*, by Mark Wicks, a rare Victorian book available at some libraries. There is, in the Victoria and Albert Museum (London), a sixteenth-century German table positive organ with paper pipes. This instrument is described, with an illustration, by Alan T. Kitley in his book *The Big Problem of Small Organs.* The organ is not, however, in playing condition, and it is difficult to determine exactly how the pipes were made.

Bristol board can be obtained in a number of thicknesses. Use a thinner board for the shorter pipes than for the longer ones. Note that it will bend more easily in one direction than the other and bear this in mind when marking out the shapes. A list of measurements, from which all others can be obtained, is given at the end of these notes. (Halve the length to raise the pitch by an octave. Double the length to lower the pitch by an octave. The diameter halves on every seventeenth note of the chromatic scale.)

The pattern for each part is given on the left-hand side of Figure 61. The following dimensions are critical:

A. *The body*: The length (*a*) is obtained from the list of measurements. The circumference (*b*) equals the diameter (also obtained from the list) multiplied by 3·14. The width of the mouth (*c*) is one quarter of the circumference (*b*). The height of the mouth (*d*)—or 'cut-up'—is obtained by dividing the width of the mouth (*c*) by four for an open pipe, and by three for a stopped pipe.

B. *The upper lip*: This is the same shape as the opening cut in the body of the pipe, less the space for the mouth.

C. *The foot*: The radius (*e*) of the curve is not critical but it regulates the size of the angle (*f*). This in turn regulates the distance (*g*), which must be the same as the circumference of the body, (*b*) above. This shape may be set out by trial and error, or by using the following formula, which gives the size of the angle (*f*) in degrees:

$$\text{Angle } (f) = \frac{\text{Diameter of pipe} \times 180}{\text{Radius } (e)}$$

The width (*h*) of the cut for the lower lip is the same as the width (*c*) of the upper lip. Use slightly thinner board for the foot than for the body as it has to be bent more sharply.

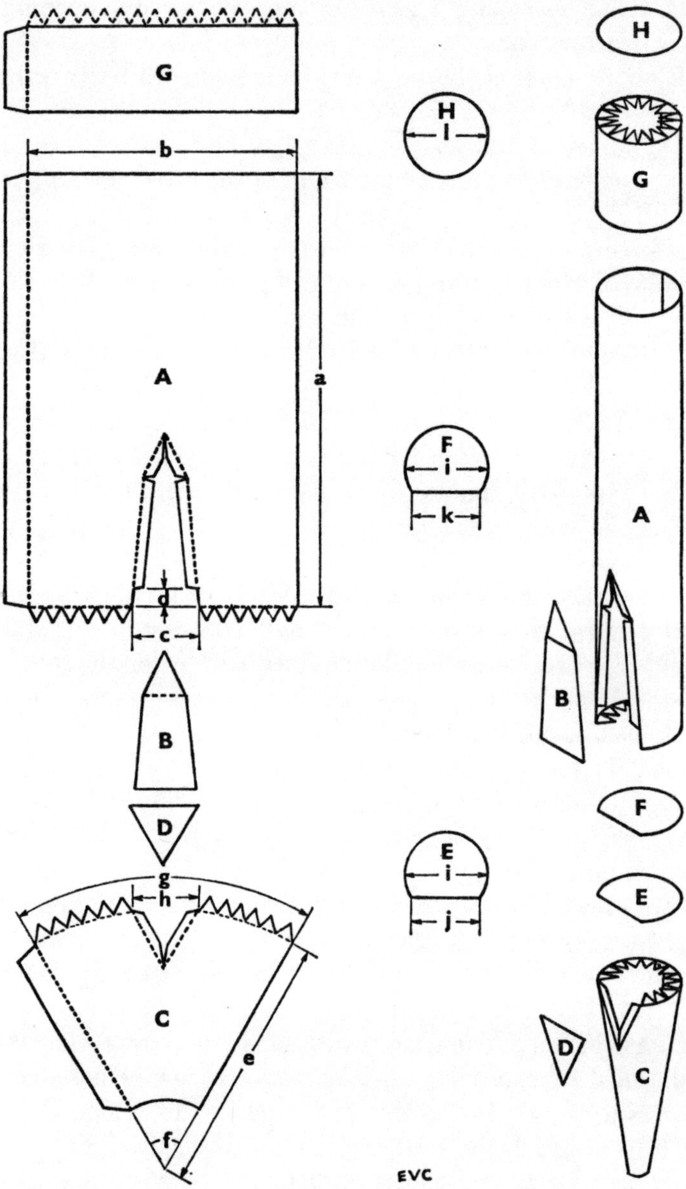

Fig 61. Method of making organ pipes from Bristol board

D. *The lower lip*: This is the same shape as the opening cut in the foot.

E. *The languid (lower part)*: This is shaped like a segment of a circle, the diameter (*i*) being equal to the outside diameter of the body of the pipe. Distance (*j*) is approximately the same as the width of the lower lip (*h*).

F. *The languid (upper part)*: A similar segment is used for this, except that distance (*k*) is slightly less than distance (*j*). The exact proportions call for some experiment.

G. *The tuning collar*: This must be a tight fit round the body. If a stopped pipe is being made glue tabs must be added as indicated by the zig-zag dotted lines.

H. *The cap*: This must be fixed to the tuning collar when making a stopped pipe. It is not required for an open pipe. Its diameter (*l*) should equal the outside diameter of the tuning collar.

When the component parts of a pipe have been drawn on the Bristol board they should be cut out. All glue tabs should be scored as indicated by the dotted lines, except for the long ones on the body, tuning collar and foot. The pipe may now be assembled as indicated on the right-hand side of the diagram, using UHU or a similar adhesive. First glue the body (A) to form a cylinder, then assemble the tuning collar (G) round the upper part of the body, making it fit as tightly as possible. If a stopped pipe is being made, attach the cap (H) to the top of the collar. Glue the upper lip (B) in place and then the upper part of the languid (F). Glue the foot (C) together to form a cone. Fix the lower part of the languid (E) in place and then the lower lip (D). Do this carefully, leaving a slight gap between them to form a windway. The exact width of the windway can best be established by experiment. Make it too narrow rather than too wide as it can always be enlarged with a razor blade.

The foot and body must now be glued together. Blow gently through the pipe and adjust the foot and body until a satisfactory note is obtained. This adjustment must, of course, be done before the adhesive sets. It is not an easy process and calls for some patience. The first one or two pipes will probably be failures, so be prepared for this. Various experiments can be carried out to see if the tone can be altered or improved. These include sealing the joints with shellac and coating the pipe with metallic paint. A rubber band positioned round the middle of a pipe's body may improve its tone.

LIST OF BASIC MEASUREMENTS

Length (a) in centimetres: C 32·9: C♯ 31·1: D 29·3: D♯ 27·6: E 26·1: F 24·6: F♯ 23·2: G 21·9: G♯ 20·7: A 19.5: A♯ 18·4: B 17·4: C 16·4.
Diameter in millimetres: C 32·6: C♯ 31·3: D 29·9: D♯ 28·7: E 27·4: F 26·3: F♯ 25·3: G 24·1: G♯ 23·1: A 22·1: A♯ 21·2: B 20·2: C 19·3: C♯ 18·6: D 17·8: D♯ 16·9: E 16·3 (to calculate the circumference (*b*) multiply by 3·14).

Acknowledgements

I make no apology for the length of this list, as many people have supplied me with information. I do apologise, however, for any omissions.

Thanks are due to the following, who have kindly allowed me to use their photographs: Colin Ball (page 108—above), Barrie Deamer (71—below), Harry Handley (125—above), William Keating (108—below, 125—below, and 143), Savages Ltd (18—below, and Figure 9), The Vestal Press (144) and Bill Walker (17—below). Bill Walker has also given plenty of other help. The remainder of the photographs are my own.

The drawings and much of the descriptive matter have been made possible by the organ owners who have supplied me with information and have allowed me to sketch various parts of their instruments. These include: William Barlow, Jack Boutwood (whose Hooghuys started me on the trail which led to this book), George Cushing, Herbert Epton, George Flynn, M. J. Gouweloos, Arthur Mason, Brian Oram, David Plumb, Ken and Ron Porter, Ken and Phyllis Redfern, and Teddy Reed. The following, who have built their own organs, also deserve thanks: Thomas Bader (the 'Swiss enthusiast'), Michael Bevis, and Peter Bish. Information has also been supplied by the following: Ted Bowman, Matthew Caulfield, Leonard Grymonprez, Clifton Hughes, Bob Penny, Arthur Prinsen, Alan Sefton, Tom Tilbury, Rodney Wakeman, and Norman Woodford.

The following deserve special mention. Francis Buckley is a mine of information on fairgrounds and organs, and has helped me enormously. He lent me the programme of the charity concert, and prepared the musical score for Appendix II and the sketch of the automatic change mechanism of the barrel organ. Dennis Chappell has entertained me for a number of weekends and given me access to his Gavioli and Mortier. Charles Hart has given me free access to his museum of mechanical musical instruments, and I have spent many happy hours there gathering material. Ronald Leach has kindly supplied the appendix on restoration, together with the drawings. He has learnt the hard way and the appendix is based on his own practical experience. Thanks go, also, to my wife Freda and elder son Stephen for the help they have given me.

Finally, I must include all those members of the Fair Organ Preservation Society whom I have not mentioned by name.

A Short Bibliography

A Guidebook of Automatic Musical Instruments
Q. David Bowers (The Vestal Press, New York)
Church and Chamber Barrel-Organs
Canon Noel Boston & Lyndesay G. Langwill
(Lyndesay G. Langwill, Edinburgh)
Collecting Musical Boxes and How To Repair Them
Arthur W. J. G. Ord-Hume
(George Allen & Unwin, London)
Fairground Architecture
David Braithwaite (Hugh Evelyn, London)
From Music Boxes to Street Organs
(Van Speeldoos tot Pierement)
R. de Waard (The Vestal Press, New York—in English)
Illustrated History of the Carousel
Frederick Fried (A. S. Barnes & Co, New York)
Piano Player Treasury
Harvey Roehl (The Vestal Press, New York)
Put Another Nickel In
Q. David Bowers (The Vestal Press, New York)
Savages Ltd—Engineers
Ronald H. Clarke (Savages Ltd, King's Lynn)
The World's Fair
(The Showman's Newspaper)
The Key Frame
(The Journal of the Fair Organ Preservation Society)
The Music Box
(The Journal of the Musical Box Society of Great Britain)

Index